The European Tour
Yearbook 1999

O F F I C I A L  P U B L I C A T I O N

Lennard
Queen Anne Press

HOW THE WINNERS TOLD EACH OTHER APART ON THE EUROPEAN TOUR

Tiger Woods
Johnnie Walker Classic

Thomas Björn
Heineken Classic,
Peugeot Open d'España

Ernie Els
South African Open

Tony Johnstone
Alfred Dunhill SA PGA

José Maria Olazábal
Dubai Desert Classic

Andrew Coltart
Qatar Masters

Stephen Leaney
Moroccan Open, Dutch Open

Thomas Levet
Cannes Open

Patrik Sjöland
Italian Open

Miguel Angel Jiménez
Turespaña Masters,
Trophée Lancôme

Darren Clarke
B&H International Open,
Volvo Masters

Colin Montgomerie
Volvo PGA, British Masters,
German Masters

Lee Westwood
Deutsche Bank-SAP Open, English Open,
Loch Lomond World Invitational, Belgacom Open

Mats Lanner
Madeira Island Open

Sam Torrance
Peugeot Open de France

Jesper Parnevik
Scandinavian Masters

Stephen Allan
German Open

Russell Claydon
BMW International

Sven Strüver
European Masters

#1 ball in golf

In 1998, no fewer than 19 different Titleist players between them won all but four of the 32 European Tour events. They included Colin Montgomerie - Order of Merit winner for a record sixth successive time - as well as his closest rivals Darren Clarke and Lee Westwood. In fact, 9 out of the final top 10 Pro's played Titleist. This feat illustrates their continuing trust in the consistency and performance of our advanced liquid-filled wound ball technology.

Globally, that faith equates to 154 Tour wins this year for the #1 ball in golf. That's well over four times more than our nearest competitor. At the game's highest level, it isn't so much which ball you play, as which Titleist. So perhaps it's no surprise that the world's best players add their marks of distinction to ours.

Titleist
#1 ball in golf.®
Titleist, St.Ives, Cambs PE17 4LS
www.titleist.com

* Source: Sports Marketing Surveys Ltd., (Europe), Darrell Survey (US). Figures correct as of 2nd November 1998.

Introduction from the European Tour

Executive Editor
Mitchell Platts

Editor
Chris Plumridge

Consultant Editor
Mark Wilson

Photographic Editor
David Cannon

Art Director
Rob Kelland

Production Controller
Denise Thurling

The European Tour Yearbook 1999
is published by
the PGA European Tour,
Wentworth Drive, Virginia Water,
Surrey GU25 4LX.

Distributed through Lennard Queen Anne Press.

Colour reproduction and printing by
The Manson Group.

© PGA European Tour.

ISBN 1 85291 592 7

This Yearbook, which vividly illustrates the breadth of competition in Europe, not only reviews another superb season in the history of the Tour but also looks forward to 1999 when we will see in European Tour terms the blueprint for the millennium.

Michael McDonnell has been recognised throughout his career as Golf Correspondent of the *Daily Mail* as one of the most perceptive writers of the sport. He points out in 'The Year in Retrospect' that the pioneering work the European Tour began by taking golf to other continents is now about to yield 'a massive dividend that promises as yet unseen benefits as the royal and ancient game moves into an established global structure.'

The European Tour, and indeed the game of golf, owes much to the equally perceptive and supremely persuasive skills of John Jacobs. As the first Tournament Director-General of the European Tour, John's inspirational direction determined that the Continent of Europe would play an increasingly important role in the development of the game. He laid the foundation for the growth of the European Tour and the globalisation of golf.

Now the new World Golf Championships, organised by the International Federation of PGA Tours and launched in 1999, will impact professional golf globally and fulfil the stated desire of many players to compete against each other more often with an orderly control.

All of which makes 1999 very exciting especially as Europe will be seeking, at The Country Club in Brookline, to win the Ryder Cup for a record third successive time and to keep possession of the prized trophy for the sixth time in the last eight Matches. Mark James has been appointed European Team Captain, and with Ben Crenshaw at the helm of the United States Team we can look forward to the 33rd Matches continuing the high values of sportsmanship and competitiveness which underline the tradition of this biennial encounter.

Looking back, Colin Montgomerie enjoyed another season-long encounter for number one honours. This time Lee Westwood and Darren Clarke emerged as contenders for the Volvo Ranking title, and it was not until the season-ending Volvo Masters that Montgomerie secured his place at number one for a record sixth time.

The drama of this wonderful contest as the year unfolded, is captured by the game's leading writers and photographers in this the 11th edition of the European Tour Yearbook, and we hope you enjoy the content in addition to witnessing first hand Tour competition at all our superb locations in 1999.

KENNETH D SCHOFIELD CBE
Executive Director • PGA European Tour

Contents

Blueprint for the world

The global impact of the European Tour

has provided maximum benefits for

both players and spectators

There is now clear evidence that the European Tour commands such high international reputation and respect that the world's most accomplished golfers eagerly seek to play on it whenever the opportunity permits.

It is a mutually beneficial process because their presence adds stature to the arena and in so doing inspires others to emulate their performance so that levels of achievement continue on an upward spiral.

The traditional attraction of the European Tour has always been its regionalised diversity and the adaptable skills it requires to cope with windswept links or lush parkland. But a new factor has entered the equation as the Tour stretches its influence far and wide around the world.

The pioneering work began by taking the sport to other continents is now about to yield a massive dividend that promises as yet unseen benefits as the royal and ancient game moves into an established global structure that had its origins and patterns

Global talent: Tiger Woods (above), Lee Westwood, Colin Montgomerie, Ernie Els and Mark O'Meara, (opposite, clockwise from top left).

in Europe. The fulfilment of the European dream is that geography no longer matters. Only the relevant tournament being played is of consequence to the contenders who have assembled because of

the prestige and rewards on offer. Even the nationality of individual characters is of secondary importance as they seek to be judged solely on sporting merit.

This then is the globalisation of the game and the reason why Europe has taken its rightful place along with its US counterpart at the core of the new order which brings breadth and dimension to the game and shapes its future into the next century.

The first genuine signs that this philosophy had taken a firm hold among the key players upon whose enthusiastic support the process depends was to be found in abundance on the 1998 European Tour in which five of the top ten players in the World Rankings emerged as winners.

The particular famous five in question were Tiger Woods, Mark O'Meara, Ernie Els together with Lee Westwood and Colin Montgomerie. The rest of the upper echelons of world golf assumed walk-on parts at various times throughout a glittering season that began in Thailand

6

in January and finished in Spain in late October after a pilgrimage that spanned thousands of miles and many countries.

For Europe, the confirmation of Lee Westwood as a player of truly world class was of major significance because it underlined an unbroken tradition of quality that began with Tony Jacklin and was handed on through each competitive generation by Severiano Ballesteros, Sandy Lyle, Nick Faldo, Bernhard Langer, Ian Woosnam, José Maria Olazábal and Colin Montgomerie.

It was evidence enough that the European Tour provides a steady supply of world beaters and more importantly that such talent can achieve obvious dominance while still operating from a home base. Westwood was unequivocal in his commitment to the European Tour while pulling off a remarkable victory in the Freeport McDermott Open in New Orleans. He then returned home for an immensely successful season in which he won the Deutsche Bank - SAP Open TPC of Europe and the National Car Rental English Open in successive weeks and later captured the Standard Life Loch Lomond and the Belgacom Open to set up a thrilling finale for top honours in the Volvo Ranking.

The other contender, inevitably, for much of the season was Colin Montgomerie who had dominated European golf for the last five seasons and gave clear warning he was still in commanding form when he started the

Darren Clarke keeps dry on the Giant's Causeway (above) and Miguel Angel Jiménez (below) takes to the water.

year by winning the Andersen Consulting World Championship of Golf in Arizona. That was the prelude to an astonishing run of form in which he gradually moved

towards the top of the money list by winning the Volvo PGA Championship at Wentworth followed by the One 2 One British Masters and the Linde German Masters to set up a neck-and-neck race with Westwood and Darren Clarke, winner of both the Benson and Hedges International Open and the Volvo Masters to finish second in the Volvo Ranking behind Montgomerie.

In terms of international achievement Andrew Coltart made his own impressive mark with a consistent run of form 'Down Under' that not only earned him the Australian PGA but later was good enough for him to capture top place in the country's Order of Merit coincidentally on the same day he scored his first European Tour win by taking the Qatar Masters.

It was a season in which several campaigners found their winning touch more than once and were able to peak at the right time to pull off various victories. Thomas Björn, a player who grows in stature with each season, began with the Heineken Classic in Australia and later took the Peugeot Open de España.

Miguel Angel Jiménez, the able second-in-command to Ballesteros in Europe's Ryder Cup triumph at Valderrama in 1997, proved he was still a very active and capable performer when he won the Turespana Masters Open Baleares early in the season then made a late charge against a world class field to take the Trophée Lancôme.

Australian Stephen Leaney passed two

milestones in that he not only became a first-time winner by taking the Moroccan Open but later bounced back again to capture the TNT Dutch Open.

Mark O'Meara, too, was a double winner because the genial American collected the Open Championship in positive style at Royal Birkdale then returned in late autumn to snap up the Cisco World Match-Play Championship title with a dramatic last green triumph over Tiger Woods, the world's top ranked player. By strict definition Woods himself became a first-time winner on the European Tour when he snatched the Johnnie Walker Classic in Thailand with a compelling last round of 65 to force a play-off with Ernie Els which he won at the second extra hole.

The former Masters Tournament champion headed an encouraging list of newcomers to the winners' circle that included French professional Thomas Levet (Cannes Open), Stephen Allan (Qatar Masters) David Carter (Murphy's Irish Open), Russell Claydon (BMW International Open) and the aforementioned Stephen Leaney.

Each first time success has its own imperishable memory for the winner but those of Carter and Claydon brought a warm glow to fans who had watched their careers and were well aware of the particular sagas that were involved. Claydon, a giant of a man had waited ten years for this moment

Top to bottom:
charity balls signed for auction
at Canon European Masters.
Ball catching Cactus at Qatar.
French Riviera comes inland
in Cannes. A vole-in-one at
Royal Birkdale.

but never doubted it would come while Carter, a genial young character, very nearly missed his moment of destiny when a year earlier he came close to death after collapsing in his hotel room during the Dubai Desert Classic, requiring brain surgery and extensive recuperation before he could play again. Indeed the footnote to this inspiring comeback was that he defeated the awesome Montgomerie in full flight to take the Irish title.

In terms of comebacks Sam Torrance's Peugeot Open de France win offered hope for all those who might have thought the glory days were past as the middle years approached. This long-serving campaigner admitted his pride had been hurt when he failed to earn a place in the 1997 Ryder Cup squad and was stung into action to put himself back into tip-top physical shape and subsequently earned his reward at Le Golf National in Paris.

The return of José Maria Olazábal as a winner again had a touch of true drama. A year earlier he had taken the first tentative steps back on Tour in the Dubai Desert Classic but in 1998 he returned in triumph to capture that title, amid the tears, in heroic style.

There was also a heart-

9

dable field and Jesper Parnevik made his mark by winning the Volvo Scandinavian Masters in front of his home crowd and later in the season making them even happier by rejoining the European Tour and in so doing being able to qualify for Ryder Cup points and the chance of a place in the 1999 squad which plays at The Country Club in Brookline, Boston.

A head count of the cast of players on the 1998 Tour reveals that players from 27 countries competed and the international strength of the European Tour was underscored by the fact that the winners came from Scotland, the United States, Denmark, South Africa, Zimbabwe, Spain, England, Australia, France, Sweden, Northern Ireland and Germany.

Player and caddie train in Qatar (above). José Maria Olazábal wants a quiet life (below left) while Lee Westwood (below right) agrees and goes fishing.

ening supply of wins from Tour regulars who invariably contend week-to-week then suddenly burst through when the wining chance present itself. Accordingly Peter Mitchell took the Portuguese Open, Mats Lanner captured the Madeira Island Open, Mathias Grönberg became Smurfit European Open champion and Tony Johnstone earned the Alfred Dunhill South African PGA title.

Sven Strüver successfully pursued the Canon European Masters against a formi-

Moreover, the Tour touched down in 16 countries – Thailand, Australia, South Africa, Dubai, Qatar, Portugal, France, Spain, Italy, England, Ireland, Scotland, Holland, Switzerland, Belgium and, counting the early Montgomerie win in Arizona, the United States too.

To cap a significant season of international golf, South Africa's Ernie Els, Retief Goosen and David Frost retained the Alfred Dunhill Cup at St. Andrews, when they beat Spain 3-0, and England won the World Cup of Golf.

Such global influences have made the European Tour the blueprint for others to follow and demonstrate that isolationist policies can only be self-defeating when compared to a European success story that simply goes from strength to strength and has shown beyond question the way the game must be played for maximum benefit to both players and their public. It is a European legacy for which all of golf should be grateful.

Michael McDonnell

The driving force in sport

Still the man to beat

Colin Montgomerie resisted the challenges
of Darren Clarke and Lee Westwood
for a sixth consecutive Volvo Ranking title

So, six seasons after he first lifted the European number one title Colin Stuart Montgomerie remains the man to beat. Viewed from any angle, analysed how you like, this record is phenomenal, an achievement so wonderfully unlikely it stands comparison with almost anything else witnessed in sport during the 20th Century.

To top the Volvo Ranking once would be a wonderful addition to any player's *curriculum vitae*, but to pull off this audacious trick six times on the bounce comes close to beggaring belief, especially if one then factors in the thought that success in golf can turn swiftly pear-shaped because of one wicked bounce of the ball, the intervention of a sprinkler head or the indiscriminate location of a divot mark.

Yet despite the peripheral dangers that thrive constantly in a sport that likes to feed so voraciously on the nerve-endings of its devotees, Montgomerie has remained impressively calm as well as relentlessly consistent since he first made it to the top of the pile in 1993.

Prior to this ascent his professional career had been on the sort of curve that knows only one way to go and that way is up. Since turning professional in 1987,

Montgomerie has embroidered the Volvo Ranking like no other player before him. Ten years ago he ended his first season in 52nd place, followed this with a move up to 25th, then 14th, fourth and third before securing the top spot.

To then maintain this position of pre-eminence despite the determined counter-attacks launched by both the emerging generation of players and the platoon of long-established stars suggests that Colin has discovered something the rest are still looking for.

In truth, however, Montgomerie has unearthed no great secret. He became Europe's top player, and remains so,

because of a talent so natural it must gall those who feel they have to spend their waking hours labouring away on the practice ground and because of an instinctive self-belief that encouraged him to suspect he was the best long before his achievements confirmed it. And yet the irony is that when he considered his targets for the 1998 season he never thought about a sixth Volvo Ranking title. As late as September and the One 2 One British Masters at Marriott's much improved Forest of Arden course he was insisting that pole position at the end of the year was not on his shopping list. This was understandable. After a record five succes-

13

COLIN MONTGOMERIE 1998 TOURNAMENT RECORD

Tournament	Pos		R1	R2	R3	R4	AGG	PAR	Winnings £	Cumulative £
Dubai Desert Classic	10	T	70	69	70	69	278	-10	14226	14226
Benson & Hedges Int. Open	5	T	69	68	69	72	278	-10	29010	43236
Volvo PGA Championship	1		70	70	65	69	274	-14	200000	243236
Deutsche Bank SAP Open	10	T	67	67	72	67	273	-15	20370	263606
National Car Rental English Open	4		64	72	69	69	274	-14	32500	296106
Peugeot Open de France	23	T	74	68	73	68	283	-5	5175	301281
Murphy's Irish Open	2		65	74	71	68	278	-6	106631	407913
Standard Life Loch Lomond	7	T	72	71	68	70	281	-3	23375	431288
127th Open Golf Championship	79	T	73	74			147	+7	1000	432288
Volvo Scandinavian Masters	16	T	70	74	69	69	282	-2	9768	442057
Smurfit European Open	91	T	73	79			152	+8		442057
BMW International Open	116	T	72	75			147	+3		442057
Canon European Masters	1	2T	70	66	69	67	272	-12	12960	455017
One 2 One British Masters	1		70	72	70	69	281	-7	125000	580017
Trophée Lancôme	11	T	69	68	69	73	279	-5	13400	593417
Linde German Masters	1		65	68	66	67	266	-22	166660	760077
Volvo Masters	3		70	67	69	68	274	-14	63000	823077
*Volvo Bonus Pool	1		–	–	–	–	–	–	170000	993077

Rounds: 62 – Strokes: 4319 – Stroke Average: 69.66 – Total Par: -121

sive Volvo Ranking titles Monty not only had the accolades, he had the T-shirts in several different sizes and colours.

Actually, prior to his One 2 One British Masters win, few felt that he had a genuine chance of catching up, never mind passing, Darren Clarke and Lee Westwood who seemed to have settled emphatically into a private duel for the top berth. Following two successive missed cuts in Europe and a desultory showing in the US PGA Montgomerie appeared to be stuck in reverse. Suddenly the dependable swing that had made his fortune deserted him and for the first time in his career he looked startled. Briefly. Having broken down on the side of the fairway he rang for help, re-establishing contact with Bill Ferguson, the coach first charged with teaching him how to play 30 years ago.

Their relationship had been terminated 18 months earlier by Montgomerie who felt that a change of advice just might nudge him in the direction of the major title he has craved so much for the last several years. It seemed like a good move when he secured a best-to-date share of eighth place at the US Masters but he never figured in the US or British Opens or the USPGA and so he made his call to Harrogate Golf Club and the club pro who had helped create him.

'Colin had a different swing when he came back to me.' Ferguson subsequently told The Times. 'It was more rounded than the one I had taught him. People had been telling him that he would not win the Masters unless he could hook the ball. I do not believe that. I believe that if you can hit it straight then you can win any event. Anyway, I have taken him back to up and under so that he can fade the ball again. This rounded swing was wrong for him.'

Armed with the old technique once again, Montgomerie finished his season as he had started it. In January he had won a million dollars at the Andersen Consulting World Championship in Arizona and followed this up with victory at Wentworth in the Volvo PGA Championship. Now, with Ferguson once more at his side, he won the One 2 One British Masters, finished 11th in the Trophée Lancôme, won the Linde German Masters and, of course, finished third in the Volvo Masters.

This is an awful lot of Masters and even if the one he would really, really like is not amongst them, at least Ferguson can say with justifiable pride 'I told you so.'

Montgomerie, meanwhile, can look back on another outstanding season. That major win might still remain frustatingly just outside his reach but he can console himself with the thought that he has just set a benchmark in European golf that few of us expect to see surpassed in our lifetime. Unless, of course, the man himself goes out and does it again in 1999.

Bill Elliott

ROLL OF HONOUR

	1993	1994	1995	1996	1997	1998
Volvo Ranking Position	1	1	1	1	1	1
Volvo Ranking Money	£613,682	£762,719	£835,051	£875,146	£798,948	£993,077
Tournaments	24	21	20	18	19	17
Wins	2	3	2	3	2	3
Top Tens	9	13	14	8	11	10
To Par	-65	-160	-146	-87	-177	-121
Stroke Average	70.81	69.60	69.70	70.26	69.37	69.66
Total Money	£798,145	£920,647	£1,038,708	£1,035,337	£1,705,773	£1,222,485

Colin Montgomerie acknowledges his record at the Volvo Masters.

You'll find a lot of things in his bag.
Fear is not one of them.

José Maria Olazabal *plays Tourney® Forged Personals and progressive Musclebacks.*

The benefits continue

The benefits of European Tour Training School
continued under the MacGregor banner

The 1998 European Tour Training School was the first under the MacGregor banner and once again the week provided invaluable advice and tuition for players on the threshold of launching their careers at the highest level.

The 20 graduates from the European Challenge Tour and Qualifying School, representing seven countries on the European Tour, received expert tuition on all aspects of the game from coaches, psychologists, physiologists and nutritionists. While most were embarking on their first season on the Tour, established players were also a San Roque on the Costa del Sol to both offer and receive advice.

Distinguished guest José Maria Olazábal emphasised the importance of the week for all players on the Tour. He said: 'MacGregor Week is a great idea, not just for new players who want to dedicate their lives to the professional game but also for established players like myself. It's a nice week to be able to check your swing, short game, to have help with the psychological side of the game, in fact with everything. It also helps the young players to meet the media and find out what is going on.'

Padraig Harrington, a graduate from the Class of 1996, one of the most success-

MacGregor Week guest of honour, José Maria Olazábal.

ful in recent seasons, was among those invited back to offer advice. He explained: 'Coming back to this week for me is like a refresher course. I learned so much when I came here the first time and each time I return I learn a little bit more. You are always learning, you always go away from this week with something new so it's very important to me to come back each year. When I do come back I hope some of the rookies can learn from me, which for me is also very important. Golf is an individual game, but it is good to help each other.'

The success of the training week was

highlighted by Andy Taylor, Managing Director of Apollo, the golf shaft manufacturing company which sponsored the week from its inception in 1989, when he pointed out that more than 150 players have attended in the past ten years. They have amassed more than £32 million in prize money, claimed 52 tournament victories and five have graduated to Ryder Cup status.

The object of the week has always been to give the players knowledge and advice. Former Ryder Cup player and three times winner of the European Seniors Tour Money List, Tommy Horton was among the team of coaches that included John Jacobs, the former Ryder Cup captain and first Director General of the European Tour and now recognised as one of the finest teachers in the game; Denis Pugh, principal tutor at the Warren Golf Academy; putting expert Harold Swash; consultant on the psychological parts of the game, Alan Fine; and the head of the European Tour physiotherapy unit, Guy Delacave.

Following the MacGregor Challenge at Valderrama, won by former Spanish International Ivo Giner, the players were given a taste of facing the media withPress room interviews conducted by Dave Hamilton, radio interviews by Tony

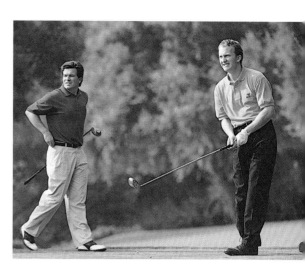

BBC Radio's Tony Adamson interviews Sweden's Ola Eliasson (left),
Cameron Clark is congratulated by George O'Grady (centre) and Miles
Tunnicliffe and Carl Watts in action on the course (right).

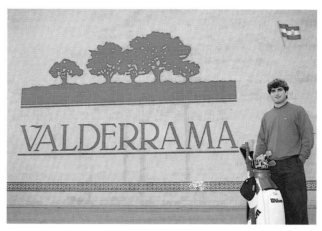

MacGregor Challenge winner, Ivo Giner (top). Coach trip by
Tommy Horton, John Jacobs, Harold Swash and Denis Pugh (above).

Adamson and James Porter from Radio Five Live, and Sky Sports's Steve Beddow interviewed each player in front of the camera.

Life on the Tour involves a great deal more than simply playing golf and a series of lectures addressed other aspects of tournament golf. John Paramor, the European Tour Chief Referee, and David Garland, the European Tour Director of Operations, covered all aspects of the rules. Garland also gave a talk entitled 'Inside the PGA European Tour' detailing how the Tour functions.

John Ennis, MacGregor's Vice-President Europe and Africa, explained everything about MacGregor Golf, and from Apollo, Graeme Horwood and Mike Perry held a seminar on 'The Role of the Golf Shaft'. Another former Ryder Cup player, John O'Leary was on hand to give advice on course management, while Scott Kelly and Doug Billman handled 'Sponsorship and Television on the European Tour.'

More help came from the International Management Group with Guy Kinnings, Colin Montgomerie's manager heading a seminar on 'Management and Sponsorship' along with John Ennis and 'Financial planning' was handled by Jonathan Dudman, also of IMG.

Midlander Cameron Clark, voted graduate of the week by all the coaches, summed up the importance of the training. He said: 'This week has opened my eyes about the whole running of the Tour and how much harder I have got to work on my own game. It's not a week to just come and hit balls all day, you've got to take the knowledge away and work on it.'

George O'Grady, Deputy Executive Director of the PGA European Tour and one of the founders of Apollo Week, said at the farewell dinner that 1997 had been another highly successful season on the European Tour and he welcomed all the new graduates to the 1998 European Tour.

'We think this week is unique,' O'Grady said. 'Senior professionals give their time to help the younger pros and long may it continue. We firmly believe that every professional who attends the European Tour Training Week benefits from the advice that is offered, and we congratulate MacGregor for their foresight in supporting the Tour.'

Roddy Williams

17

Montgomerie is $1 million man

With a stunning second shot to the final green Colin Montgomerie clinched his biggest prize

The year could not have started much brighter for Colin Montgomerie as he further enhanced his reputation as one of the game's finest match-play exponents by winning the final of the Andersen Consulting World Championship of Golf and the $1 million first prize.

Two superb shots to the last green at the Grayhawk Club in Scottsdale, Arizona, finally set up his victory over 1997 US PGA champion Davis Love III, who had battled back from four down with four to play to take the match to the 36th hole.

Montgomerie appeared to be coasting to victory after a burst of three birdies in four holes sent him four ahead with as many holes to play, but Love recovered with two birdies and then won the 35th when Montgomerie three-putted.

But Europe's number one golfer for a record five successive years closed out his rival in stunning style. The three iron he hit to within ten feet of the pin from 223 yards over the intervening water was one of the finest shots he has ever struck. When Love failed in his all-or nothing 40 feet eagle putt, the match was conceded and Montgomerie became $1 million richer.

Love said: 'I thought I was buried but then I suddenly had a chance. But I've got to give Monty a lot of credit for the way he played at the last hole, those were two real pressure shots and he executed them perfectly.'

On his way to securing his second win on US soil, the first being the individual title in the World Cup of Golf at Kiawah Island six weeks earlier, Montgomerie beat two of the reigning major champions – Love and US Open champion Ernie Els. He said: 'This was a very important victory for me. I beat Ernie Els and Davis Love, both current major champions. They are also above me in the Official World Ranking so it was a big boost at the start of a new year.'

The 36-hole final, featuring two of the world's best golfers, provided moments of high drama especially over the closing stretch. Montgomerie lunched at one up, after a 69 to Love's 71, but over the first two holes in the afternoon he failed to build on his lead, missing a birdie chance on the first and then driving into the

The Grayhawk club in Scottsdale, Arizona (above), Ernie Els (right) bowed out to Colin Montgomerie in the semi-finals.

bunker on the second and dropping back to all-square.

The match ebbed and flowed in the afternoon although Montgomerie maintained the upper hand and then moved to two up. At the 13th he made his decisive move. A towering second shot, covering the pin all the way left him with a putt of only a foot that was conceded by Love. Love missed with his attempt to chip-in and Montgomerie was three up with five to play. Next the 34-year-old

Japan's Hajime Meshiai (left) was in trouble against Davis Love in the semi-finals (above right).
Colin Montgomerie victorious (below).

Scot hit a controlled shot into the 14th. He pitched the ball and it rolled to within three feet of the hole. The pressure was on Love who missed the green and failed to get up and down.

At four up with four to play, Montgomerie looked set to finish the match but an indifferent approach at the par five 15th opened the door to Love to claim one hole back with a birdie. A 24-feet putt for his second consecutive birdie at the par three 16th reduced the deficit to two and Love's par at the 17th was good enough to take the match to the last.

As in the Ryder Cup by Johnnie Walker at Valderrama a few months earlier Montgomerie rose to the occasion, hitting the perfect drive and then the brilliant second shot to the green. It was a pivotal moment in his outstanding career, providing further evidence of his ability to beat the best on American soil.

On his way to the $1 million first

prize Montgomerie had defeated José Maria Olazábal, Sam Torrance and Costantino Rocca in the regional matches

at the excellent Buckinghamshire Club to progress to the semi-finals in which he faced South African, Ernie Els, at Grayhawk.

Twice Els had denied Montgomerie his first major, the first when Els won a play-off for the US Open in 1994 and then in 1997 when Els claimed his second US Open crown by a shot, but there was no denying Montgomerie on this occasion. With six birdies in a bogey-free performance he was never behind and secured victory with a 25-feet putt on the 16th green to bring to an end a match enriched not only by the quality of golf but also the spirit in which it was played.

The third place play-off was won by Els, leading all the way against Japan's Hajime Meshiai to win 4 and 3, but for Colin Montgomerie 1998 had begun in the best possible vein. The Scot was on top of the world.

Roddy Williams.

Tiger earns his stripes

Tiger Woods came from eight shots behind in the final round to win for the first time on the European Tour

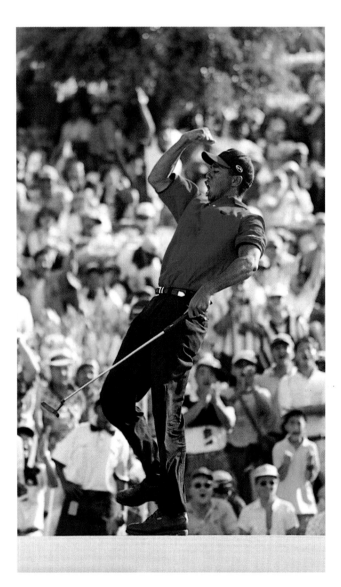

For Tiger Woods a first win in the prestigious Johnnie Walker Classic, the jewel in an increasingly impressive list of top quality events staged in Asia, was particularly gratifying. His come-from-behind victory at the Blue Canyon Golf and Country Club in the Thai resort of Phuket over such golfing luminaries as double US Open champion Ernie Els and six-time major winner Nick Faldo made him especially proud.

Eleven shots behind pace-setter Els at the halfway stage, and still eight behind with a round to go, 22-year-old Tiger was clearly frustrated at not being able to produce the same brand of golf which had earned him top money spot on the US Tour in 1997 and eased him past Greg Norman to the top of the Official World Ranking. What made it even more embarrassing for him was that his father and Thai-born mother, Kultilda Woods were daily in the gallery. Although he had once come from nine behind to win an amateur event, his chance of victory seemed unlikely even for this golfing phenomenon, but then things happen when Tiger is around.

At the end of a dramatic final day in which all the other favoured title-challengers would drop out like green bottles fall off the proverbial wall, Tiger emerged victorious over Els at the second hole of the play-off that should never have happened. Although he shot eight birdies in his last 16 holes for a closing 65, the best round of the week, even Tiger would have to admit that this was the tournament half-a-dozen others threw away.

When Woods, wearing, as he has since his junior golf days, his traditional last day red shirt representing power, finally holed the eight feet birdie putt that saw off Els on Phuket's 18th green below the magnificent clubhouse, he could reflect that he had never done anything quite like it in his short professional career. Although the incredible 22-year-old had won the 1997 Masters at Augusta by 12 shots, setting a new low record winning aggregate in the process, he still considered his Johnnie Walker victory 'right

THE COURSE

Built on the site of an old tin mine, the original Blue Canyon course was designed with considerable ingenuity by Japanese architect Yoshikazu Kato who has achieved the difficult task of providing a test that can be both enjoyable off the less challenging tees for those amateurs visiting the resort, yet be a real test for professionals off the back tees even if some of the par fives are very reachable in two by the longer hitters. The finish, however, is dramatically testing – the tricky 360-yard dog-leg par four 16th where Lee Westwood twice came a cropper, the challenging 221-yard 17th played over the corner of one of Phuket's huge lakes, and the 413-yard par four last where a pushed drive, like Peter O'Malley's on the last day, can end up in the water. Designer Kato moved only 250,000 cubic metres of earth, a fraction of what is usual these days, to produce his spectacularly interesting layout.

up there with all my other achievements in golf.' Amazingly, on the final day he leap-frogged 17 other players to land the £133,330 first price and get the 1998 European Tour season off to a dramatic start.

After the first day, Els had commented: 'When Tiger is on the leaderboard you know you have hard work ahead of you, especially if he is up there with a round to go.' After Phuket he might consider changing his mind. Even if Tiger is not on the leader board after 54 holes nobody is safe. Yet Tiger's positive

Tiger Woods and Ernie Els (right) went head-to-head. Alexander Cejka (opposite) makes a splash.

Former champion Ian
Woosnam missed the cut.

Although Padraig Harrington holed for an ace at the second and Peter Hedblom did the same at the tough 17th, graveyard for so many title challengers on the final day, pride of place on the week must go to one of Tiger Woods' last day gems, one of those shots that underline his undoubted class. His long hitting is legendary but after driving into a greenside bunker at the 394 yard 13th across the corner of the old quarry around which the course has been built, he played an exquisite sand wedge to two feet for the sixth of his eight last-day birdies. That shot maintained the momentum which swept him to eventual victory.

Third place for Retief Goosen.

attitude was apparent even when he trailed in the leaders by a distance. Asked at the halfway stage whom he thought might win the title Tiger had a succinct answer for the group of experienced international reporters attending the event. He told them 'Put your money on me.' But few did, putting Tiger's answer down to youthful arrogance.

Credit for Tiger's victory must go in some measure to his father who spotted a minor technical fault which was preventing his son hole the usual number of putts. Tiger's putter was ice-cold for opening rounds of 72, 71 and 71 – decidely lacklustre scoring by his high standards, but Earl Woods had been on the case and finally solved the problem. His son's hands were too low at address. A quick adjustment before the final round proved a winning move. On the back nine on Sunday he admitted he was 'really clicking' to the extent that he was just a little disappointed not to have set a new course record 62.

So what happened on that final day in the warm Thai sunshine? Els, who reckoned he really lost the title with a scrappy back nine on the third day when he had a

chance to open up a substantial lead on the field, again stumbled on the inward stretch on Sunday. Nick Faldo never quite got going, having trouble, too, with the putter and those others who were in contention could not finish the job off. Retief Goosen of South Africa had a chance but bogeyed the last, Scot Andrew Coltart, England's Lee Westwood, Alexander Cejka of Germany, Irishman Padraig Harrington, Thailand's talented Prayed Marksaeng and Australian Stephen Leaney all threatened at one point to take the title but no challenger was more disappointed than Sydneysider Peter O'Malley who led the field by a shot with two to play and would have won with a par, par finish. Sadly he went double-bogey, bogey holing from 35 feet on the par four last for his five.

As Woods stormed home it looked at one point as if he might win without a

play-off, but Els holed from 12 feet at the last for the birdie to force the event into extra holes. Although the South African had a chance to win on the first extra hole where he missed from 12 feet, it was Woods who triumphed a hole later when he holed from fifteen feet after a gloriously precise approach shot to a difficult pin. Among the first to congratulate him was mum Kultilda, proud her son had added the Johnnie Walker title to the Honda Classic first prize he had won in Thailand a year earlier. Then his victory was by ten shots. This time it had been much more difficult, but just days before the start of the Chinese Year of the Tiger he had encapsulated everything a Tiger Year stands for – years in which the daring, the audacious and those with nerves of steel enjoy the thrill of living dangerously, a year associated with dramatic, intriguing, passionate and momentous events.

Perhaps Ernie Els, philosophical in defeat and ready to turn the tables on him when they are next together in an event, summed it all up best: 'What Tiger did this week was really amazing.' Nobody could deny that.

Renton Laidlaw

BLUE CANYON CC, PHUKET, THAILAND, JANUARY 22-25, 1998 · YARDAGE 7099 · PAR 71

Pos	Name	Country	Rnd 1	Rnd 2	Rnd 3	Rnd 4	Total	Prize Money £
1	Tiger WOODS	(USA)	72	71	71	65	279	133330
2	Ernie ELS	(SA)	67	65	74	73	279	88880
3	Retief GOOSEN	(SA)	71	71	69	69	280	50070
4	Andrew COLTART	(Scot)	71	68	72	70	281	31470
	Lee WESTWOOD	(Eng)	71	66	73	71	281	31470
	Alex CEJKA	(Ger)	67	68	74	72	281	31470
	Peter O'MALLEY	(Aus)	69	68	72	72	281	31470
8	Stephen LEANEY	(Aus)	70	68	72	72	282	17140
	Padraig HARRINGTON	(Ire)	69	67	73	73	282	17140
	Prayad MARKSAENG	(Thai)	67	72	69	74	282	17140
	Nick FALDO	(Eng)	71	67	69	75	282	17140
12	Peter LONARD	(Aus)	70	71	71	71	283	13320
	Robert ALLENBY	(Aus)	75	70	66	72	283	13320
14	Michael LONG	(NZ)	76	71	67	71	285	12000
	Peter BAKER	(Eng)	73	69	68	75	285	12000
16	Steve ALKER	(NZ)	68	71	72	75	286	10384
	Bradley KING	(Aus)	71	72	68	75	286	10384
	José Maria OLAZABAL	(Sp)	72	72	70	72	286	10384
	Phillip PRICE	(Wal)	69	72	71	74	286	10384
	Rodney PAMPLING	(Aus)	73	72	73	68	286	10384
21	Shane TAIT	(Aus)	69	75	70	73	287	9240
	Paul MCGINLEY	(Ire)	69	71	76	71	287	9240
23	Frankie MINOZA	(Phil)	73	70	74	71	288	8760
	Hajime MESHIAI	(Jap)	73	71	71	73	288	8760
25	Sven STRÜVER	(Ger)	73	70	75	71	289	7920
	Felix CASAS	(Phil)	72	72	76	69	289	7920
	Arjun ATWAL	(Ind)	70	71	73	75	289	7920
	Greg TURNER	(NZ)	73	71	73	72	289	7920
	Ian GARBUTT	(Eng)	74	73	68	74	289	7920
30	Wayne SMITH	(Aus)	69	75	75	71	290	6594
	Lian-Wei ZHANG	(Chi)	70	72	74	74	290	6594
	Jim PAYNE	(Eng)	75	72	74	69	290	6594
	Lucas PARSONS	(Aus)	68	75	76	71	290	6594
	Greg CHALMERS	(Aus)	72	68	76	74	290	6594
	Fabrice TARNAUD	(Fr)	73	69	77	71	290	6594
	Rick GIBSON	(Can)	72	74	69	75	290	6594
37	Patrik SJÖLAND	(Swe)	71	75	74	71	291	5760
	Darren COLE	(Aus)	70	75	71	75	291	5760
	Anthony GILLIGAN	(Aus)	73	73	73	72	291	5760
40	Tse-Peng CHANG	(Tai)	73	72	78	69	292	5360
	Thammanoon SRIROJ	(Thai)	70	75	74	73	292	5360
42	Zaw MOE	(Myr)	72	75	72	74	293	4960
	No-Seok PARK	(Kor)	72	72	76	73	293	4960
	Justin COOPER	(Aus)	71	70	71	81	293	4960
45	Marcus WHEELHOUSE	(NZ)	72	74	72	76	294	4160
	Jonathan LOMAS	(Eng)	72	74	75	73	294	4160
	Mike HARWOOD	(Aus)	73	72	73	76	294	4160
	Scott LAYCOCK	(Aus)	76	69	77	72	294	4160
	Van PHILLIPS	(Eng)	78	69	73	74	294	4160
	Roger CHAPMAN	(Eng)	77	70	74	73	294	4160
	Craig JONES	(Aus)	72	75	73	74	294	4160
52	Daniel CHOPRA	(Swe)	68	73	76	78	295	3440
	Stephen ALLAN	(Aus)	76	69	76	74	295	3440
54	Chris VAN DER VELDE	(Hol)	75	72	78	71	296	3120
	Per HAUGSRUD	(Nor)	74	73	74	75	296	3120
56	Nam-Sin PARK	(Kor)	73	72	74	78	297	2608
	David HOWELL	(Eng)	74	72	72	79	297	2608
	Mark ALLEN	(Aus)	68	75	82	72	297	2608
	Gary ORR	(Scot)	73	74	77	73	297	2608
	Jean Louis GUEPY	(Fr)	74	71	76	76	297	2608
61	Matthew ECOB	(Aus)	75	68	76	79	298	2280
	Don FARDON	(Aus)	73	73	76	76	298	2280
63	David ECOB	(Aus)	73	74	77	75	299	2080
	Paul LAWRIE	(Scot)	71	75	76	77	299	2080
	Jack O'KEEFE	(USA)	76	70	73	80	299	2080
66	Leith WASTLE	(Aus)	71	75	77	77	300	1198
	Elliot BOULT	(NZ)	71	76	76	77	300	1198
	Gary EVANS	(Eng)	73	73	75	79	300	1198
69	John SENDEN	(Aus)	75	72	77	78	302	1194
70	Martin GATES	(Eng)	75	72	74	84	305	1192

**Sad finish for
Peter O'Malley.**

Björn triumphs in the wind

Thomas Björn remained composed
on a blustery final day to capture his
second European Tour title

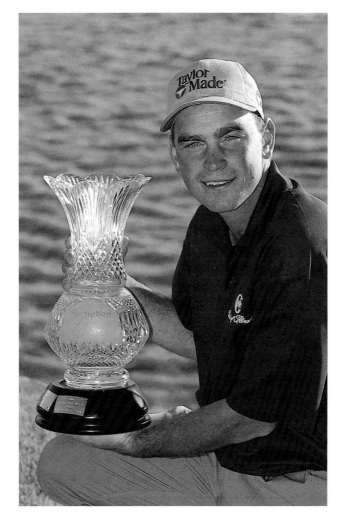

Since the Heineken Classic, played annually at The Vines Resort, has become a highly respected joint venture between the European Tour and the Australasian circuit, no Australian golfer has triumphed. Welshman Ian Woosnam in 1996 and Spaniard Miguel Angel Martin, who did not defend his 1997 title win, had previously taken first prize and this year Danish Ryder Cup star Thomas Björn ensured that that record was maintained.

For Björn victory had an extra special significance. Only he of the 24 players involved in the dramatic Johnnie Walker Ryder Cup match at Valderrama in 1997 had failed to earn an invitation to play in the first major of the year – the Masters at Augusta. Björn, apparently omitted because he was not a tournament winner in Europe in 1997, had cause for disappointment. All 12 members of the American side were given Masters' invitations, including three who had failed to win titles in 1997. Björn was sensibly philosophical, however, when tackled about the matter in Perth. He was

sure he would make it another year.

Björn won at The Vines after a dramatic last day battle with former winner Woosnam, leader after the first and third rounds, who came within a centimetre or two of forcing a play-off when his marginally over-borrowed putt for a closing eagle three on Sunday edged past the hole on the massive undulating home green. So

close was it at the end that no fewer than four players shared third spot – José Maria Olazábal from Spain, playing his first event in Australia, Ernie Els, Peter Baker and the late charging Padraig Harrington, who had to be brought back from the airport just in case he might be involved in a play-off after shooting a last round best-of-the-day 66. He had only just made the halfway cut.

Harrington had permission from the sponsors to leave for the late afternoon plane to London, but as the leaders, finding it tough to hole putts on the ever-quickening greens, began dropping shots a quick phone-call stopped him and new wife Caroline from boarding the British Airways jumbo jet. The Irishman, whisked back by courtesy car, returned only to join in the prize-giving ceremony. This time his luck had run out as Björn achieved what he had set out to do at the start of the week.

It was a remarkable change of fortune for the two main challengers on that final day. A week earlier at Phuket where he

Former English Amateur champion Ian Garbutt splashed out 10,000 Australian dollars (nearly £5000) to play the early season events on the European Tour and was richly rewarded when he aced his six iron tee shot at the 196-yard 16th on Saturday. The ace, the fifth of the 25-year-old Doncaster golfer's career, earned him $Aus100,000 worth of chips from one of the tournament's top sponsors – the local Burswood Casino. Earlier in the week Garbutt had had a flutter and lost $Aus100 but even after a third of his hole-in-one prize had been taken by the Australian taxman, the Englishman had a sizeable amount to invest on the new house he planned to buy.

Final round 66 boosted
Padraig Harrington

had nearly won the Johnnie Walker Classic in 1994, Woosnam, troubled by a pinched nerve, had missed the halfway cut and so, too, had Bjorn, who having shared the first round lead on 67, had fallen victim to a stomach bug, and struggled to a second round 81 for a 36-hole aggregate which was one too many to make the weekend. That disappointment was forgotten in the sometimes searing heat of Perth where Australian Craig Parry, winner at the end of 1997 of the Japanese and Indonesian Opens, Olazábal and Bernhard Langer, using his new Ping clubs, were also strong title challengers for a time.

Langer, after rounds of 69 and 66 had led at halfway, but a third round 76 ended his chance of taking the title. Olazábal's threat disappeared effectively when he tumbled to five over par for the first five holes of the final round. Parry's fall from grace came on the final nine as he stumbled home in an uncharacteristic 41. After Parry faltered the real battle on the final afternoon developed into a duel between

the experienced campaigner Woosnam, whose Phuket injury, caused during the winter by swinging a very heavy club, had been sorted out by Australasian Tour physiotherapist, Dale Richardson, and Björn, playing with the same determination that showed in the Ryder Cup at Valderrama when he came from four down after four to halve his game with Open champion Justin Leonard.

Woosnam led by one

Refreshing play from Ernie Els (above).
Bernhard Langer (below) faded in the last two rounds.

after the eighth but then dropped shots as the next four holes to let Björn once again snatch a lead he never relinquished. The final hole is a testing par five with a bunker in driving range on the right and water lying menacinngly for a hooked tee shot. Woosnam, one behind but with the honour after making a birdie at the 17th, hit a magnificent drive but Björn was equal to the task. Both hit solid second shots with Woosnam doing

31

THE COURSE

Former European Tour player Graham Marsh, now doing well on the US Senior Tour, designed The Vines course which reflects the way he himself played golf. Never noted as one of golf's big hitters, Marsh built a tight course which puts a premium on accuracy through the green. Indeed the course is so well bunkered that there are times when, although you could use the driver, it would be foolish to do so unless you could hit it long and straight. Yet even using a three wood off the tee does not eliminate the danger. The course, home to many kangaroos, is a favourite with most players because of the questions it asks through the greens and the problems then posed by the devilishly undulating greens.

Ian Woosnam just missed a play-off.

rather better than his younger opponent. As the tension mounted Björn missed his eagle putt from 15 feet but then Woosnam missed for eagle from eight feet and an engrossing closing day ended with the Dane the winner by a shot

If there was any disappointment during the week it was only that 62-year-old Gary Player failed in his bid to make the halfway cut despite a second round 75. There never was a chance that Player could win but his enthusiastic participation on the course for two days and his involvement in commentary for Channel Seven at the weekend added considerably to the ever-improving international reputation of the masterfully-staged Heineken event. Winner of 162 titles worldwide, the irrepressible South African was happy to be back competing again in the country where he won seven Australian Opens in the 1960s.

In the end, however, it was Björn who achieved his goal. He sent his message of disappointment halfway across the world to Augusta. He had let his clubs do the talking and proved a gracious winner.

Renton Laidlaw

Pos	Name	Country	Rnd 1	Rnd 2	Rnd 3	Rnd 4	Total	Prize Money £
1	Thomas BJORN	(Den)	70	68	68	74	280	108935
2	Ian WOOSNAM	(Wal)	66	69	70	76	281	61732
3	Ernie ELS	(SA)	70	71	70	71	282	28975
	José Maria OLAZABAL	(Sp)	67	72	68	75	282	28975
	Padraig HARRINGTON	(Ire)	74	71	71	66	282	28975
	Peter BAKER	(Eng)	73	71	67	71	282	28975
7	Thomas GÖGELE	(Ger)	68	73	70	72	283	19364
8	David HOWELL	(Eng)	72	68	69	75	284	16341
	Greg CHALMERS	(Aus)	73	72	70	69	284	16341
	Jarmo SANDELIN	(Swe)	77	68	67	72	284	16341
11	Paul BROADHURST	(Eng)	71	70	71	73	285	11651
	Scott LAYCOCK	(Aus)	69	72	70	74	285	11651
	Grant DODD	(Aus)	70	71	72	72	285	11651
	Bernhard LANGER	(Ger)	69	66	76	74	285	11651
15	Terry PRICE	(Aus)	69	71	72	74	286	8066
	Jay TOWNSEND	(USA)	73	69	77	67	286	8066
	Andrew BEAL	(Eng)	70	70	73	73	286	8066
	Andrew COLTART	(Scot)	68	70	71	77	286	8066
	Jeev Milkha SINGH	(Ind)	69	70	75	72	286	8066
20	Paul MCGINLEY	(Ire)	69	70	74	74	287	6174
	Robert KARLSSON	(Swe)	70	74	72	71	287	6174
	Craig PARRY	(Aus)	71	67	70	79	287	6174
	Peter MCWHINNEY	(Aus)	74	70	75	68	287	6174
	Glenn JOYNER	(Aus)	71	71	72	73	287	6174
25	Gavin COLES	(Aus)	70	74	71	73	288	4590
	Robert ALLENBY	(Aus)	68	71	75	74	288	4590
	Alex CEJKA	(Ger)	71	73	70	74	288	4590
	Elliot BOULT	(NZ)	74	71	71	72	288	4590
	David SMAIL	(NZ)	74	71	71	72	288	4590
	Kenny DRUCE	(Aus)	70	74	71	73	288	4590
	Peter LONARD	(Aus)	73	68	75	72	288	4590
32	Richard GREEN	(Aus)	72	72	68	77	289	3633
	Ian GARBUTT	(Eng)	72	70	71	76	289	3633
	Peter O'MALLEY	(Aus)	72	68	73	76	289	3633
35	Martin GATES	(Eng)	68	75	72	75	290	3146
	Greg TURNER	(NZ)	71	74	69	76	290	3146
	Stephen SCAHILL	(NZ)	70	69	75	76	290	3146
	Jim PAYNE	(Eng)	73	68	73	76	290	3146
	Daniel CHOPRA	(Swe)	71	73	73	73	290	3146
40	Gary EVANS	(Eng)	73	72	70	76	291	2480
	Michael LONG	(NZ)	70	71	77	73	291	2480
	Nicholas O'HERN	(Aus)	71	71	72	77	291	2480
	Robert WILLIS	(Aus)	72	73	74	72	291	2480
	Jon ROBSON	(Eng)	70	71	77	73	291	2480
	Raphaël JACQUELIN	(Fr)	74	71	72	74	291	2480
46	Paul EALES	(Eng)	72	72	71	77	292	1710
	Peter SENIOR	(Aus)	69	73	74	76	292	1710
	Rolf MUNTZ	(Hol)	70	72	80	70	292	1710
	David CARTER	(Eng)	73	72	72	75	292	1710
	Rodney PAMPLING	(Aus)	71	71	72	78	292	1710
	Robin BYRD	(USA)	73	69	72	78	292	1710
	Steve CONRAN	(Aus)	74	69	76	73	292	1710
53	Rodger DAVIS	(Aus)	71	70	77	75	293	1348
	J. J. WEST	(USA)	69	75	77	72	293	1348
55	Craig JONES	(Aus)	69	76	71	78	294	1288
	Leith WASTLE	(Aus)	71	74	73	76	294	1288
	Gary ORR	(Scot)	71	73	70	80	294	1288
	Lucas PARSONS	(Aus)	73	72	73	76	294	1288
	Sven STRÜVER	(Ger)	76	68	75	75	294	1288
	Philip WALTON	(Ire)	72	73	74	75	294	1288
61	Phillip PRICE	(Wal)	72	73	74	76	295	1247
62	Brian DAVIS	(Eng)	71	71	73	81	296	1224
	Jack O'KEEFE	(USA)	71	73	74	78	296	1224
	Doug DUNAKEY	(USA)	74	71	77	74	296	1224
65	Jeff WAGNER	(Aus)	72	72	71	82	297	1195
66	Marcus WHEELHOUSE	(NZ)	72	73	80	76	301	1184

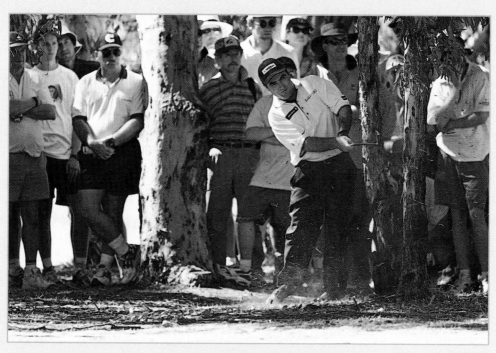

No thrust from Craig Parry in the final round.

Third Open title for Els

Ernie Els took his third

South African Open title with a

commanding performance in Durban

*E*rnie Els is not a super-stitious man. He likes the number 13. That is the figure he had in mind when he clinched his third home Open title at a sweltering Durban Country Club to end a run of disappointments at the start of his 1998 season.

Gary Player has won the South African Open 13 times, Els, thus has a target for the next 20 years or so – on average, to win every other year.

'Three's not bad at 28 but I've got a lot of catching up to do,' said Els after freezing out the only player who had any realistic chance of catching him on the final day, fellow-countryman and fellow Alfred Dunhill Cup team member, David Frost.

'But I don't know whether 13 is possible. Maybe I could get close to nine like Bobby Locke. But it's a lot tougher competition nowa-days than they had.'

Certainly, Els had a strong field matched against him in Durban at a course toughened up, in places, close to US Open specification, which had

not always been very kind to him. For instance, as a young-ster in the 1986 Natal Stroke-play at the Country Club, he had been leading by a stroke in the morning and then shot 88 in the afternoon.

Indeed, despite also win-ning the Wednesday pro-am, elegant Els warned: 'They've really brought the rough in and the course is much tougher. There may be a few basket cases out there this week – and I might be one of them.'

Not so for Els in the opening round. An imperi-ous eight under par 64 left his playing companion Ignacio Garrido gasping in admira-tion. And the young Spanish Ryder Cup player shot 66 to share second place with Mark McNulty, Greg Chalmers and Mats Hallberg.

'I had to work and work for my score,' said Garrido, after birdieing the last three holes to keep in the hunt, 'but Ernie could have shot any-thing, even less than his 64. He scored it easily. He made me look like an amateur.'

SHOT OF THE WEEK

Vital shots are nearly always the ones played on the final day when push comes to shove, and Ernie Els racked up several on the greens as he holed a succession of huge putts to fend off David Frost. But Els's blind wedge from the left semi-rough down in the hollow under the 17th in the third round which shaved the hole for eagle and finished four feet away for his birdie, was the shot that took him back in front, from where he was never headed.

Then in the second round, just as he had done when eventually capitulating to Tiger Woods a fortnight before, Els's momentum stalled.

Suddenly, he did start visiting that worrying rough. Rough that Eamonn Darcy had sworn 'if you get into it you're going nowhere fast' before running up the biggest score he could remember as a professional, an 82 in the opening round, and proving it.

His composure rattled, Els slid off the top of the leaderboard to hand the second day's advantage to Frost, who posted a 66 to move ten under par and lead his younger compatriot by two, with Chalmers a further stroke back.

Els was not exactly a basket-case, but he knew then he had a fight on his hands. There were those who could have been

David Frost (left) challenged,
Mark McNulty (above right) struggled
and Ignacio Garrido (below) was consistent.

labelled so, though. Mark McNulty might have needed the straight-jacket if he hadn't birdied the last for a 79, and like Darcy the previous day, shaking his head and muttering about never remembering a round like it.

The player who surely did start thinking about checking into a padded cell was

the young Australian left-hander, Chalmers.

Starting at the tenth, the Australian TPC champion had captured the lead just after the turn. He faltered by dropping a stroke on the second, but he could never have prepared himself for what came next.

After tweaking his drive into trees and chipping out he found the cloying, six-inch high rough that had been allowed to flourish close to the greens. Chalmers was only 30 yards from the green but the clinging rough was not going to allow him his freedom easily. A poor chip made up only half his ground, still leaving him buried 15 yards from the haven of the green.

Three virtual 'air-shots' later, a disbelieving Chalmers was still a prisoner. When he finally broke free and missed his

Five years before the latest South African Open at Durban, John Bland set the course record of 62, and the tournament agronomists decided to try to protect the 6,667 yard par 72, seaside layout by using a few ploys of which the USGA would have been proud. In came the rough to squeeze the fairways – Ernie Els measured one of them at only 16 yards across, about ten of his strides, and provide the several dog-leg holes with a treacherous route to the greens.

first putt, the dazed Australian marked a ten on the card.

Not with anger, though. 'A ten is beyond the point of upset or anger,' said the 24-year-old. 'It's ridiculous!'

Saturday proved to be a see-saw day at the course near to the Durban seaside funfairs. What Els lost on the round-abouts, he gained on the swings.

Three two-shot swings during the afternoon brought him back in contention. Every time his chief opponent for the £71,465 first prize, Frost, made a mistake, Els capitalised and three birdies in the last four holes for the reigning US Open champion, took him back to the top of the leaderboard.

After going in on 12 under par, one shot ahead of Frost, caution was again the byword for Els. Even though he and

Frost, whose closest rivals were five strokes away, had distanced themselves from the field, they refused to envisage a match-play finale.

That was because the South African Open defending champion, Vijay Singh, who had beaten him in the Toyota World Match-Play a few months before, would play alongside the home favourites as one of the third-placed men. And Bernhard Langer was another on six-under.

His caution, however, was unnecessary. Despite both top men bogeying the first, the final round was a two-horse race.

And when Frost, who had grabbed a share of the lead again at the third, inexplicably launched a seven iron second shot into the trees on the seventh to double-bogey, it became a one-horse race.

Putting brilliantly to firstly save pars

and then pick up the shots to leave Frost trailing in his wake, Els grabbed the tournament by the scruff of the neck with three birdies in four holes after the turn.

Victory came at a canter as he carded 69 for a total 15 under par, three strokes better than Frost, the distance flattered by a late three-putt from Els and a chip-in by the second placed man on the 17th. The Durban rough took several prisoners and left more than one casualty among the finishers, but that did not include Patrik Sjöland, the Swede coming up on the rails to take third place.

'At last I won a tournament,' said a relieved Els after putting behind him his earlier 1998 disappointments. 'Another South African Open. Three down, ten to go.'

Norman Dubell

DURBAN COUNTRY CLUB, FEBRUARY 5-8, 1998 · YARDAGE 6667 · PAR 72

Pos	Name	Country	Rnd 1	Rnd 2	Rnd 3	Rnd 4	Total	Prize Money £
1	Ernie ELS	(SA)	64	72	68	69	273	71465
2	David FROST	(SA)	68	66	71	71	276	52015
3	Patrik SJÖLAND	(Swe)	69	74	68	69	280	31300
4	Nic HENNING	(SA)	69	71	70	71	281	18966
	Marco GORTANA	(It)	70	71	70	70	281	18966
	Bernhard LANGER	(Ger)	71	68	71	71	281	18966
7	Ignacio GARRIDO	(Sp)	66	72	72	72	282	12235
	Mark MCNULTY	(Zim)	66	79	67	70	282	12235
9	Richard KAPLAN	(SA)	69	73	72	69	283	7581
	Brett LIDDLE	(SA)	71	71	71	70	283	7581
	James KINGSTON	(SA)	74	70	70	69	283	7581
	Alex CEJKA	(Ger)	73	72	70	68	283	7581
	Vijay SINGH	(Fij)	71	72	67	73	283	7581
	David HOWELL	(Eng)	72	72	70	69	283	7581
	Massimo FLORIOLI	(It)	72	72	68	71	283	7581
	Thomas GÖGELE	(Ger)	69	69	73	72	283	7581
17	Chris WILLIAMS	(Eng)	70	69	71	74	284	5744
	Greg CHALMERS	(Aus)	66	71	74	73	284	5744
	Anthony WALL	(Eng)	73	72	71	68	284	5744
20	Gary ORR	(Scot)	71	71	76	67	285	5246
	Steve WEBSTER	(Eng)	69	76	68	72	285	5246
22	Mark MOULAND	(Wal)	72	75	67	72	286	4681
	Heinz P THÜL	(Ger)	70	74	72	70	286	4681
	Roger WESSELS	(SA)	73	71	74	68	286	4681
	Jeff REMESY	(Fr)	68	73	73	72	286	4681
	André CRUSE	(SA)	69	71	74	72	286	4681
	Knud STORGAARD	(Den)	72	71	73	70	286	4681
28	Jean VAN DE VELDE	(Fr)	70	68	73	76	287	3912
	Scott DUNLAP	(USA)	73	74	67	73	287	3912
	Adam HUNTER	(Scot)	69	73	74	71	287	3912
	Adilson DA SILVA	(Bra)	70	73	69	75	287	3912
	Craig KAMPS	(SA)	72	69	70	76	287	3912
	Dean VAN STADEN	(SA)	74	72	67	74	287	3912
34	Deane PAPPAS	(SA)	70	75	74	69	288	3437
	Chris DAVISON	(SA)	69	72	75	72	288	3437
	Jonathan LOMAS	(Eng)	74	68	71	75	288	3437
	Andrew MCLARDY	(SA)	69	75	74	70	288	3437
38	Tony JOHNSTONE	(Zim)	70	73	71	75	289	3120
	Jamie SPENCE	(Eng)	72	75	73	69	289	3120
	Bruce VAUGHAN	(USA)	73	74	71	71	289	3120
	Trevor IMMELMAN (AM)	(SA)	73	70	70	76	289	
41	Jeff HAWKES	(SA)	70	72	73	75	290	2759
	Frank NOBILO	(NZ)	70	73	72	75	290	2759
	Rolf MUNTZ	(Hol)	73	74	71	72	290	2759
	Paul AFFLECK	(Wal)	69	75	75	71	290	2759
	Michael ARCHER	(Eng)	72	71	75	72	290	2759
46	Sven STRÜVER	(Ger)	72	75	70	74	291	2442
	Phillip PRICE	(Wal)	70	69	75	77	291	2442
48	Desvonde BOTES	(SA)	72	73	70	77	292	2171
	David LYNN	(Eng)	71	76	74	71	292	2171
	Wayne BRADLEY	(SA)	72	73	77	70	292	2171
	Andrew PITTS	(USA)	74	72	72	74	292	2171
52	Paul BLAIKIE	(SA)	72	74	75	72	293	1718
	Andrew SANDYWELL	(Eng)	73	72	72	76	293	1718
	Kevin STONE	(SA)	73	74	76	70	293	1718
	Tjaart VAN DER WALT	(SA)	67	75	73	78	293	1718
	Mats HALLBERG	(Swe)	66	72	75	80	293	1718
	Van PHILLIPS	(Eng)	73	74	70	76	293	1718
	Ulrich VAN DEN BERG (A	(SA)	70	72	77	74	293	
58	Warren ABERY	(SA)	73	71	78	72	294	1379
	Michael SCHOLZ	(SA)	72	74	68	80	294	1379
	Ian PALMER	(SA)	69	72	75	78	294	1379
	Søren KJELDSEN	(Den)	72	74	73	75	294	1379
62	Steve VAN VUUREN	(SA)	74	72	72	77	295	1221
	Pelop PANAGOPOULOS	(SA)	74	70	77	74	295	1221
	Fredrik JACOBSON	(Swe)	76	70	72	77	295	1221
65	Gary EVANS	(Eng)	70	73	73	80	296	1108
	Costantino ROCCA	(It)	76	71	71	78	296	1108
	Steven SHEARER (AM)	(SA)	74	73	77	72	296	
67	Malcolm MACKENZIE	(Eng)	77	70	70	80	297	1017
	Wayne RILEY	(Aus)	76	68	74	79	297	1017
69	Anders FORSBRAND	(Swe)	74	72	75	77	298	949
70	Carl WATTS	(Eng)	75	70	78	76	299	904
71	Warren SCHUTTE	(SA)	73	71	79	77	300	904
72	Anssi KANKKONEN	(Fin)	71	76	79	75	301	904
	Hugh INGGS	(SA)	74	73	78	76	301	904
74	Hendrik BUHRMANN	(SA)	74	73	81	77	305	904

Bernhard Langer.

Johnstone sees the way

A visit to an eye specialist
brought a long-awaited victory
into view for Tony Johnstone

*T*he myopic Tony Johnstone was so worried about his failure to spot a line on a green, or sometimes even an uphill or downhill putt, that he had, long before the second event of the South African-European Tour double, been ready to look for another day job.

But, with his confidence brimming to overflow after visits to two experts, the 41-year-old Zimbabwean added another PGA title to his record when he won the Alfred Dunhill South African version for the second time, just under six years after

his triumph in the Volvo PGA Championship at Wentworth.

To win his Volvo PGA Championship the Bulawayo-born veteran kept an illustrious field at bay over the Burma Road in 1992. At the Houghton course, once more rocked and then rolled over to Monday by electrical storms, there was the formidable Els to keep out.

Despite rising several times at the crack of dawn – indeed, before it cracked on one occasion – and once having to undergo a severe test of that legendary

poor eyesight, Johnstone produced a famous and determined victory.

There was certainly nothing short-sighted about it. Ten birdies in a round of 64 to stun the field on a Friday in which he played 33 holes, at one time seven strokes clear of everyone, then eventually shrugging off the lurking Els, who was looking for back-to-back South African victories, Johnstone won in style.

He won and then modestly handed much of the credit to his coach, who transformed his swing only days before, when it seemed his play off the tee especially, was leading him nowhere fast. And he also paid tribute to an eye specialist who had diagnosed the astigmatism that played havoc with his green-reading, a man who had, in a few short hours, taught him how to combat his sight problem enough for Johnstone to change his mind and come to Houghton instead of taking the week off.

Els was always going to be the danger man but his game never really came alight until the third round. When it did it put

THE COURSE

Unlike the previous week, Houghton's kikuyu fairways were made generous in width and the 7,035 yard, par-72 parkland course protected itself by way of its water on nine holes and myriad trees. Early slick greens slowed down after Thursday afternoon's rain.

the squeeze on a front-runner who had not experienced such heights for many a tournament, certainly not a year before, when Johnstone's golf deteriorated so badly he was all for giving up tournament play.

But the player affectionately called 'Ovies' by all the longstanding members at Houghton, was up to it. Johnstone was awarded his nickname when he enquired, after hitting a tee shot into oblivion in one of his first friendly pro events, 'are there any ovies?' a Zimbabwean equivalent to a 'Mulligan'.

There was many a professional wishing that ovies were in on a Thursday morning in which several top names failed

to trouble the leaderboard scorers. This was so of a subdued Greg Norman, arriving at Houghton on the back of winning his own Holden International the week before, only level par. It was true of Nick Price, the defending champion, who had to hew his 71 from stone. It was certainly so of an off-colour David Frost, who had lost a play-off to Price in 1997 for the South African PGA title, producing nothing like his previous week's form.

The slimline Welshman, Paul Affleck, admitting he was working out in the gym and aiming to put on weight to try to muscle up his driving to get within 50 yards of Tiger Woods, proved the morning heavyweight before an electrical storm

at midday cost a whole afternoon's play. Affleck's 67 eventually earned him a one-stroke lead.

However, it was not until the next day that that materialised and it was Johnstone who proved to be one of Affleck's four nearest challengers, going back at first light but unable to tee-off again until 9am.

When Johnstone repeated his ten-birdie feat of 1990 at Fulford in the Murphy's Cup, though, giving himself indigestion through gobbling down a plate of shepherd's pie in under ten minutes' turnaround after shooting his 68, the field was scattered, if not the sheep.

Scott Dunlap regretted being a stroke adrift of a Dunlap 65 but the American

42

Nick Price (left) Greg Norman (centre) and Anders Forsbrand (right).

hauled himself to within three shots of the lead in second place by Friday night when Johnstone went to bed on 12 under par.

There was never any chance of the third round completing on a Saturday in which Johnstone re-established his domination, seven shots ahead on 17 under par after another devastating attack on the course in the middle of his 13 holes.

Despite a sudden double-bogey on the short 17th in the morning, birdies before and after ensured he took a five-stroke lead over the awakening Els, who, at last, hit blistering putting form with a 66, into the final round. A round which took over four hours to get started after another lightning break.

Inevitably, the protracted day ended with the leaders again playing in near darkness, much to short-sighted John-stone's disadvantage. Birdies on the seventh and eighth by his playing companion Els, too, left Johnstone with plenty to think about before rising early again now holding only a three-shot advantage over the player who would loom large physi-cally, too, over him for the denoument on

SHOT OF THE WEEK

Tony Johnstone's magnificent seven iron to just four feet on the 17th for a birdie put him one ahead and left Ernie Els needing to hit a big drive to try to pick up a shot himself on the last on Monday morning to try to force a playoff. It was the shot which finally left Els too much to do.

Monday morning.

As Johnstone put it himself 'Ernie's long and strong. I was born a runt and I'll always be a runt. But I'm a determined runt.'

Twice Els caught him over the remaining ten holes, but Johnstone would not be denied. His towering finish with a shot in to just four feet for birdie on that same 17th that had shaken him the morn-ing before, left Els having to go for broke on the last – and bankrupting his victory chance by driving into the rough.

Thus Johnstone's 72 for a 17 under par total left him two better than Els and four better than Retief Goosen, who had charged through the field the evening before, and Nick Price, who paid for an enigmatic week. The dogged Dunlap was a further stroke back.

The jubilant winner could have had plenty to crow about but just promised himself an early night after all his early starts, while hoping victory meant a new dawn on his revived career. 'I just hope if I come back in the next life,' said John-stone, 'it's not as a cockerel.'

Norman Dabell   43

Houghton GC, Johannesburg, February 12-16, 1998 • Yardage 7035 • Par 72

Pos	Name	Country	Rnd 1	Rnd 2	Rnd 3		Total	Prize Money £
1	Tony JOHNSTONE	(Zim)	68	64	67	72	271	64130
2	Ernie ELS	(SA)	69	69	66	69	273	46698
3	Retief GOOSEN	(SA)	71	70	69	65	275	24018
	Nick PRICE	(Zim)	71	67	69	68	275	24018
5	Scott DUNLAP	(USA)	69	66	71	70	276	16782
6	Phillip PRICE	(Wal)	69	71	66	71	277	14390
7	Anthony WALL	(Eng)	71	72	67	69	279	11999
8	Anders FORSBRAND	(Swe)	68	70	72	71	281	10012
9	Mathias GRÖNBERG	(Swe)	73	68	71	70	282	8796
10	Bruce VAUGHAN	(USA)	75	68	71	69	283	6722
	Andrew MCLARDY	(SA)	72	71	70	70	283	6722
	Mark MCNULTY	(Zim)	71	74	70	68	283	6722
	Steve VAN VUUREN	(SA)	70	72	67	74	283	6722
	Rolf MUNTZ	(Hol)	72	67	72	72	283	6722
	Tom GILLIS	(USA)	69	69	73	72	283	6722
16	Greg CHALMERS	(Aus)	74	70	69	71	284	5090
	Nic HENNING	(SA)	72	72	68	72	284	5090
	Don GAMMON	(SA)	71	72	72	69	284	5090
	André CRUSE	(SA)	70	72	69	73	284	5090
	Paolo QUIRICI	(Swi)	70	72	70	72	284	5090
	Malcolm MACKENZIE	(Eng)	74	68	70	72	284	5090
	Bradley DREDGE	(Wal)	69	72	72	71	284	5090
23	Craig KAMPS	(SA)	74	69	70	72	285	3972
	Andrew CLAPP	(Eng)	74	69	72	70	285	3972
	Greg OWEN	(Eng)	70	73	70	72	285	3972
	Greg PETERSEN	(USA)	71	71	71	72	285	3972
	Roger WESSELS	(SA)	68	74	70	73	285	3972
	Brett LIDDLE	(SA)	71	71	70	73	285	3972
	Raphaël JACQUELIN	(Fr)	72	68	73	72	285	3972
	Mark WILSHIRE	(SA)	69	70	72	74	285	3972
	Sven STRÜVER	(Ger)	69	70	76	70	285	3972
32	James KINGSTON	(SA)	69	74	69	74	286	3324
	Marco GORTANA	(It)	73	72	70	71	286	3324
	John HAWKSWORTH	(Eng)	71	71	76	68	286	3324
	Steve WEBSTER	(Eng)	71	69	73	73	286	3324
36	Greig HUTCHEON	(Scot)	70	73	72	72	287	2878
	Jeev Milkha SINGH	(Ind)	69	75	71	72	287	2878
	Costantino ROCCA	(It)	68	76	73	70	287	2878
	Ashley ROESTOFF	(SA)	71	74	74	68	287	2878
	Wayne BRADLEY	(SA)	71	74	75	67	287	2878
	Michael ARCHER	(Eng)	71	74	75	67	287	2878
	Ian HUTCHINGS	(Eng)	71	69	69	78	287	2878
43	Mark MOULAND	(Wal)	70	73	69	76	288	2391
	Heinz P THÜL	(Ger)	71	73	73	71	288	2391
	Carl WATTS	(Eng)	72	73	74	69	288	2391
	Clinton WHITELAW	(SA)	71	72	72	73	288	2391
	Nico VAN RENSBURG	(SA)	74	68	73	73	288	2391
48	Paul AFFLECK	(Wal)	67	76	70	76	289	1905
	Michele REALE	(It)	70	73	76	70	289	1905
	Jeff REMESY	(Fr)	72	73	72	72	289	1905
	Gavin LEVENSON	(SA)	72	73	70	74	289	1905
	Alex CEJKA	(Ger)	74	69	73	73	289	1905
	Bobby LINCOLN	(SA)	74	68	74	73	289	1905
	Jarmo SANDELIN	(Swe)	71	68	80	70	289	1905
55	Deane PAPPAS	(SA)	73	70	73	74	290	1426
	Massimo FLORIOLI	(It)	73	71	72	74	290	1426
	Lian-Wei ZHANG	(Chi)	72	73	75	70	290	1426
	Olivier EDMOND	(Fr)	69	73	78	70	290	1426
	Chris DAVISON	(SA)	72	69	75	74	290	1426
60	Warrick DRUIAN	(SA)	72	73	72	74	291	1195
	Mark MURLESS	(SA)	74	71	72	74	291	1195
	John MASHEGO	(SA)	74	69	74	74	291	1195
	Bobby COLLINS	(USA)	73	69	71	78	291	1195
64	Adilson DA SILVA	(Bra)	70	74	76	72	292	738
	Hendrik BUHRMANN	(SA)	75	69	74	74	292	738
	Fran QUINN	(USA)	72	72	72	76	292	738
	Ivo GINER	(Sp)	72	73	74	73	292	738
	Mats HALLBERG	(Swe)	78	67	78	69	292	738
	Tjaart VAN DER WALT	(SA)	70	75	75	72	292	738
	Raymond BURNS	(N.Ire)	74	68	73	77	292	738
71	Dennis EDLUND	(Swe)	76	68	74	75	293	597
	Jean VAN DE VELDE	(Fr)	73	70	73	77	293	597
73	Alan MCLEAN	(Scot)	69	74	75	76	294	593
	Søren KJELDSEN	(Den)	71	72	75	76	294	593
75	Phil GOLDING	(Eng)	73	70	75	77	295	590
76	Eamonn DARCY	(Ire)	77	68	74	80	299	588
77	Maarten LAFEBER	(Hol)	72	73	77	78	300	586
78	Greg NORMAN	(Aus)	72	70	68	DISQ	210	

The Alfred Dunhill SA PGA Championship trophy.

The difference is evident

cotts products are chosen by professionals looking for the very best results: the PGA European Tour recommend Greenmaster turfcare products such as those used the Wentworth Club. The All England lawn Tennis and Croquet Club, Vimbledon, also uses Scotts products on its famous courts. Scotts is dedicated producing the best for the gardener too, with leading brands such as

Scotts

The Scotts Difference®

Levington compost, Evergreen lawncare products, Miracle-Gro and Tomorite plant foods and Weedol and Pathclear weedkillers. We are so confident of their performance that we will offer you your money back if you use our products as recommended and are not completely satisfied. And if you want help or advice about any of our products just phone our Freecall garden advice line on 0500 888558.

Salisbury House, Weyside Park, Catteshall Lane, Godalming, Surrey, GU7 1XE. Tel: (0) 1483 410210 Fax: (0) 1483 410220

The Scotts Company is the leader in research, manufacturing and marketing of products for domestic lawn care and gardening, professional turf care, ornamental horticulture and field and vegetable production. From bases in the U.S.A. and Europe, Scotts sells its products in more than 50 countries worldwide."

Beware the sick golfer

A severe throat infection did not stop

José Maria Olazábal from

storming home in the desert

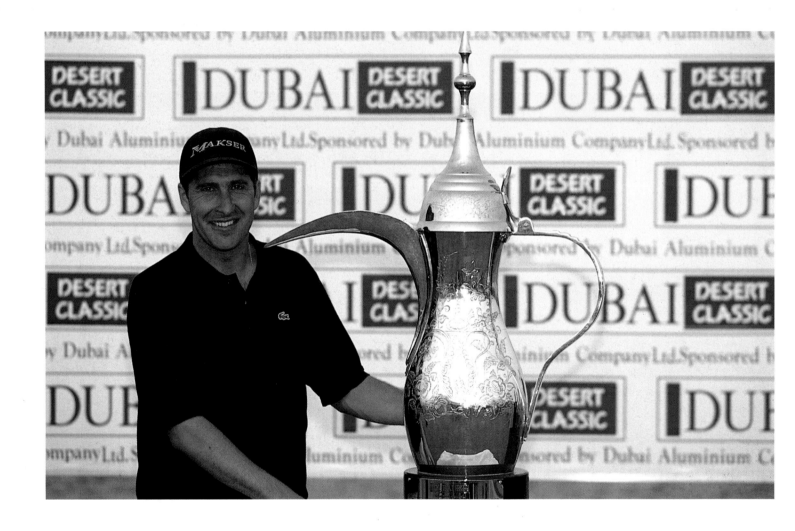

In February, 1997, the Emirates Golf Club in Dubai was the scene of José Maria Olazábal's return to action from nearly 18 months out battling the crippling foot injury which threatened his career.

Colin Montgomerie reckoned that after such a long absence it would take a monumental effort from the Spaniard just to survive the halfway cut. But he did it, shot 65 in the third round and 24 hours later finished 12th. Two tournaments later he was a winner again. Tears flowed then and more followed after he had regained his Johnnie Walker Ryder Cup place and played his part in the defeat of the Americans at Valderrama. Having feared his future might be in a wheelchair, Olazábal's

comeback was perhaps the most heartwarming story in the whole of sport during the year.

On his arrival back in the Gulf for the ninth staging of the Dubai Desert Classic the 32-year-old was still in upbeat mood. He had just finished third in the Heineken Classic in Perth and second in the Greg Norman Holden International in Sydney.

He was coming not purely to compete this time, but to try to win. That was until the eve of the £770,000 tournament – boasting three of the four top-ranked players in the world in Norman, Ernie Els and Montgomerie – when a throat infection sent his temperature soaring to 102 degrees. A doctor told Olazábal he had acute pharyngitis and was too sick to play. Five minutes before his tee-off time they were still debating the issue. 'His decision or mine?' Olazábal somewhat painfully asked Tournament Director Mike Stewart. 'Yours,' replied Stewart. 'Right, I play.'

He felt awful and thoughts of winning went out of his mind. 'Every muscle ached, every step was hard to take and I couldn't swallow a thing.' Yet, remarkable golfer that he is, he posted a 69 and was only three behind leader Robert Karlsson.

The Swede was to stay top the following day, stretching his advantage over the field from one to three with a fine 65 that contained eagles on the tenth and 13th, both the result of superb long-iron shots. Olazábal, still looking and sounding like death warmed-up, scored 67.

Round of the day, though, was unquestionably played by Els. Back on the scene of one of his most memorable performances, a 61 that put him on the road to a six-shot victory in 1994, the Volvo Ranking leader covered the back nine first in a five under 32 – even with two par fives on his card –

 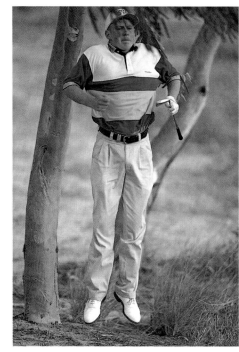 

Tree trouble for Ernie Els (left), Stephen Allan (centre), and Ian Woosnam (right).

and had four more birdies in the next six holes. A repeat of his course record was a possibility, but in the end if was 'only' a 64, eight better than his first round effort. 'I'll take that any day,' he said. And who wouldn't?

Karlsson, rating his current form the best of his life, knew that playing with the double US Open champion the following day was going to be a test for him. He came through it with flying colours, both firing 67s. But there was still one more

day to go and he didn't just have Els to worry about.

Ignacio Garrido's 66, following as it did two 67s, put him second, two behind Karlsson; Olazábal, continuing to improve only slowly health-wise, was still in fine shape golf-wise and a 65 brought him alongside Els. With Ian Woosnam fifth, Norman sixth and a resurgent Severiano Ballesteros only two strokes further back a final day shoot-out of the stars was assured.

An extra ingredient was added as they gathered for the conclusion of the event. The 'shamal' wind blew in from the desert so strongly that it produced a sandstorm. They say that when the going gets tough the tough get going and it was only now that Montgomerie, back after a seven-week break, made his considerable presence felt, a 69 setting the clubhouse target at 278, ten under par.

Karlsson, though, had already reached 18 under after 54 holes and it was going to

THE COURSE

The lavish Emirates course is one of the wonders of the golfing world. The clubhouse has been called the sport's equivalent of the Sydney Opera House, comprising seven inter-connecting concrete, steel and glass bedouin tents. The 18 holes are a masterpiece of design too, with water coming into play on ten of them and large areas of sandy wasteland a reminder that this was no ordinary plot of land.

take more than a wind to bring him and the chasing pack back as far as Montgomerie. The overnight leader resumed with eight straight pars and even when he bogeyed the difficult ninth and Els spectacularly birdied it – see 'Shot of the Week' – Karlsson still led by one.

Olazábal, meanwhile, had gone to the turn in a level par 35. A six feet birdie putt on the short 11th brought him only one behind and two holes later he leapfrogged over Karlsson in dramatic fashion with a 77-yard pitch shot into the cup for an eagle three. Now it was the Spaniard looking over his shoulder and racing into view came young Australian Stephen Allan with an inspired run of five back-

nine birdies, including one off the rocks at the 13th, another from a fairway bunker at the next and finally a chip-in on the 17th.

With Olazábal three-putting the 16th they were level, but Allan reckoned he needed to pick up one more shot at the 547-yard last. When his drive was pulled onto sand he still considered the lie good enough to attempt a three wood through the trees and over the lake. It didn't come off and he bogeyed, but even a four might not have been enough.

Olazábal, realising the possibilities of a truly astonishing victory, holed from 15 feet on the 17th to put himself two ahead and added the *coup de grâce* with a putt from 12 feet on the last.

There are shots that win tournaments and there are shots that just make you go 'Wow'. José Maria Olazábal's 77-yard pitch into the hole for an eagle three at the 13th was the single most important moment in his winning of the title, but the 'Wow' moment came four holes earlier from his playing companion Ernie Els. The wind was hard left-to-right on the 440-yard ninth and the flag was in the front left corner only a few paces from the lake. Els drew his 168-yard six-iron out over the water and then allowed the wind to drift it back onto dry land – a foot from the hole. Watching television commentator Ken Brown said: 'It was fantastic shot. I don't think anybody else would have attempted it and certainly not executed it as well as Ernie.'

Seve Ballesteros (top) and Ignacio Garrido (left), both in recovery mode.

He nearly didn't play, and ended up a three-stroke winner, with a 19 under par total of 269 that was only one outside the tournament record. 'I've eaten nothing solid since Wednesday,' he stated. 'If somebody had said I was going to win I would have slapped him in the face and said 'Wake up – you're crazy.' It's incredible.'

Mark Garrod   49

Emirates GC, February 26-March 1, 1998 · Yardage 7079 · Par 72

Pos	Name	Country	Rnd 1	Rnd 2	Rnd 3	Rnd 4	Total	Prize Money £
1	José Maria OLAZÁBAL	(Sp)	69	67	65	68	269	130000
2	Stephen ALLAN	(Aus)	67	70	67	68	272	85000
3	Robert KARLSSON	(Swe)	66	65	67	75	273	43500
	Ernie ELS	(SA)	71	63	67	72	273	43500
5	Ian WOOSNAM	(Wal)	68	69	65	73	275	33000
6	Ignacio GARRIDO	(Sp)	67	67	66	76	276	23000
	Lee WESTWOOD	(Eng)	69	69	68	70	276	23000
	Greg NORMAN	(Aus)	67	68	68	73	276	23000
9	Alex CEJKA	(Ger)	75	67	66	69	277	17000
10	Andrew OLDCORN	(Scot)	71	66	68	73	278	14226
	Seve BALLESTEROS	(Sp)	68	68	69	73	278	14226
	Colin MONTGOMERIE	(Scot)	70	69	69	69	278	14226
13	David CARTER	(Eng)	72	70	67	70	279	11550
	Darren CLARKE	(N.Ire)	68	68	70	73	279	11550
	Mats HALLBERG	(Swe)	71	69	69	70	279	11550
	José COCERES	(Arg)	71	67	67	74	279	11550
17	Roger WESSELS	(SA)	68	69	70	73	280	10050
	David GILFORD	(Eng)	72	71	73	64	280	10050
	Clinton WHITELAW	(SA)	70	71	67	72	280	10050
20	Paul AFFLECK	(Wal)	72	68	70	71	281	8383
	Phillip PRICE	(Wal)	68	71	73	69	281	8383
	Mark JAMES	(Eng)	71	70	72	68	281	8383
	Peter BAKER	(Eng)	69	70	72	70	281	8383
	Bob MAY	(USA)	73	68	67	73	281	8383
	Andrew COLTART	(Scot)	67	75	69	70	281	8383
	Robert COLES	(Eng)	73	70	65	73	281	8383
	Gary ORR	(Scot)	71	71	66	73	281	8383
	Fredrik JACOBSON	(Swe)	71	69	67	74	281	8383
29	Eduardo ROMERO	(Arg)	72	67	73	70	282	6950
	Gary EVANS	(Eng)	72	66	72	72	282	6950
	Per-Ulrik JOHANSSON	(Swe)	69	67	71	75	282	6950
	Jim PAYNE	(Eng)	73	70	68	71	282	6950.
33	Des SMYTH	(Ire)	71	71	68	73	283	5850
	Paul MCGINLEY	(Ire)	72	68	64	79	283	5850
	Jarmo SANDELIN	(Swe)	73	68	66	76	283	5850
	Jonathan LOMAS	(Eng)	72	70	68	73	283	5850
	Michael JONZON	(Swe)	71	71	70	71	283	5850
	Adam HUNTER	(Scot)	69	69	71	74	283	5850
	Anders FORSBRAND	(Swe)	69	70	71	73	283	5850
40	Jon ROBSON	(Eng)	72	71	70	71	284	4675
	Angel CABRERA	(Arg)	70	68	68	78	284	4675
	Paul BROADHURST	(Eng)	72	70	72	70	284	4675
	Michele REALE	(It)	69	71	73	71	284	4675
	Miguel Angel MARTIN	(Sp)	68	71	71	74	284	4675
	Steen TINNING	(Den)	74	67	73	70	284	4675
46	Van PHILLIPS	(Eng)	69	73	66	77	285	3700
	Richard BOXALL	(Eng)	71	71	70	73	285	3700
	Steven RICHARDSON	(Eng)	73	69	66	77	285	3700
	Retief GOOSEN	(SA)	75	68	66	76	285	3700
	Sven STRÜVER	(Ger)	70	72	76	67	285	3700
	Pierre FULKE	(Swe)	70	73	68	74	285	3700
	Mark MOULAND	(Wal)	69	67	74	75	285	3700
53	Peter HEDBLOM	(Swe)	69	68	73	76	286	2844
	Per HAUGSRUD	(Nor)	70	72	67	77	286	2844
	Dean ROBERTSON	(Scot)	70	73	68	75	286	2844
	Mark DAVIS	(Eng)	70	72	70	74	286	2844
	Peter MITCHELL	(Eng)	73	70	68	75	286	2844
58	Jay TOWNSEND	(USA)	73	70	69	75	287	2280
	Miles TUNNICLIFF	(Eng)	71	72	66	78	287	2280
	Prayad MARKSAENG	(Thai)	73	70	70	74	287	2280
	Sam TORRANCE	(Scot)	71	72	67	77	287	2280
	Rolf MUNTZ	(Hol)	69	70	72	76	287	2280
	Andrew SHERBORNE	(Eng)	73	69	70	75	287	2280
64	Raymond BURNS	(N.Ire)	71	71	67	79	288	1352
	Craig HAINLINE	(USA)	73	70	71	74	288	1352
	Lian-Wei ZHANG	(Chi)	71	72	75	70	288	1352
	Padraig HARRINGTON	(Ire)	72	69	68	79	288	1352
	Anthony WALL	(Eng)	71	68	70	79	288	1352
	Paul EALES	(Eng)	71	71	68	78	288	1352
	Tse-Peng CHANG	(Tai)	70	73	66	79	288	1352
	Thomas GÖGELE	(Ger)	73	68	72	75	288	1352
72	Steven BOTTOMLEY	(Eng)	70	72	77	70	289	1139
	Rodrigo CUELLO	(Phil)	73	70	71	75	289	1139
	Gordon BRAND JNR.	(Scot)	70	72	73	74	289	1139
	Patrik SJÖLAND	(Swe)	70	70	69	80	289	1139
	Ian GARBUTT	(Eng)	71	70	79	69	289	1139
77	Nicolas JOAKIMIDES	(Fr)	71	72	72	75	290	1133
78	David TAPPING	(Eng)	69	71	70	82	292	1129
	Paolo QUIRICI	(Swi)	71	69	67	85	292	1129
	Thammanoon SRIROJ	(Thai)	68	70	73	81	292	1129
81	Ross MCFARLANE	(Eng)	71	72	73	77	293	1125
82	Olle KARLSSON	(Swe)	72	71	71	81	295	1123
83	Wayne RILEY	(Aus)	72	71	66	87	296	1121

Robert Karlsson

UNISYS

computerised scoring systems keep

PGA European Tour spectators, players and

media around the world up to the second.

But, for us, that's par for the course.*

nisys custom-designed software and networked servers have been scoring golf tournaments for the past 18 years. And now ese powerful servers are running Windows NT®.

sit www.unisys.com/sports for further information.

Coltart is desert master

Andrew Coltart secured his first

European Tour victory with a

convincing performance in Qatar

Once a land of bedouins and pearl divers, the tiny Gulf peninsular of Qatar, just 100 miles long by 50 miles wide, now boasts the world's largest gas field and a network of oil wells which in the last 50 years have transformed both the landscape and the economy.

The new industries had a further impact on the country. The westerners who arrived in their thousands to help develop the energy resources came not only to work, but to rest and play as well – and for some that meant golf. By the late 1940s Qatar's first course, only nine holes to start with, was laid out in the sand, with players putting on browns rather than greens. Two more followed, but the wheels of progress were to move only slowly and not until the early 1990s were plans unveiled for a grass course. When it came, though, it was a beauty. Doha Golf Club is a complex any nation would be proud to have. So impressive, in fact, that PGA European Tour officials, invited to see the project taking shape, were only

too glad to agree to another stop onto their early season globetrotting.

Executive Director Ken Schofield said: 'In January, February and into March the reality is that we have to play outside Europe. The world has become a smaller place and our aim is to add opportunity for our members. Yes, we're asking them

to travel widely, but if you look at world sport that is what is happening. Tim Henman and Greg Rusdski did not make it into tennis's top 20 by winning tournaments in England, Scotland, Ireland and Wales. The condition of courses has rightly been a focal point for the last couple of seasons and here in Qatar we have a truly excellent facility. I think the guys will enjoy it.'

For the first Qatar Masters, Severiano Ballesteros, Ian Woosnam and José Maria Olazábal were the main attractions. Olazábal, of course was seeking a desert double after his Dubai triumph.

The main feature, meanwhile, was the wind. Ballesteros and Woosnam, 40 at the start of the week and given a walking stick by his caddie Phil 'Wobbly' Morbey to mark the occasion, both opened with level par 72s and Olazábal a 71 comprising 17 pars and one solitary birdie.

For much of the day it looked as though none of the 132 starters would do better than 69 – 12 of them managed that

– on a course with two par fives over 600 yards, two par threes over 200 yards and a total length of 7,273 yards. But then Anders Forsbrand and Andrew Coltart produced storming finishes. Coltart birdied three of the last four holes for a 68, Forsbrand the last three for a 67.

One of those on 69, Bristol's Andrew Sherborne, was up at 4.30 am the following morning, practised under floodlights and, in far calmer weather, proceeded to trim three strokes off Forsbrand's newly-established course record. Sherborne, six years on from his last Tour victory in the Spanish Open and a worrying 104th on the 1997 Volvo Ranking, had six birdies and an eagle on the 521-yard tenth, where with only the top half of the flag in sight from the bottom of the bank fronting the green he chipped in from 25 yards. 'It's just about the earliest I've ever got up to play golf, but conditions were absolutely perfect and you've got to make the best of these days,' said the 36-year-old. His 11 under par total of 133 remained untouched all day and at halfway in the race for the £101,006 first prize, Sherborne led by two from Switzerland's Paolo Quirici and by three from Forsbrand and his fellow Swede, Patrik Sjöland.

There were others coming to terms with the course as the week progressed. Chesterfield's David Carter,

José Maria Olazábal (left) levitates. Ian Woosnam (right) didn't gain birthday honours.

Doha Golf Club, March 5-8, 1998 · Yardage 7273 · Par 72

Pos	Name	Country	Rnd 1	Rnd 2	Rnd 3	Rnd 4	Total	Prize Money £
1	Andrew COLTART	(Scot)	68	70	65	67	270	101006
2	Patrik SJÖLAND	(Swe)	70	66	67	69	272	52636
	Andrew SHERBORNE	(Eng)	69	64	68	71	272	52636
4	Van PHILLIPS	(Eng)	70	71	66	66	273	30303
5	Rolf MUNTZ	(Hol)	72	68	66	68	274	21696
	Retief GOOSEN	(SA)	70	72	66	66	274	21696
	David CARTER	(Eng)	69	75	64	66	274	21696
8	Paolo QUIRICI	(Swi)	69	66	71	70	276	15151
9	Darren CLARKE	(N.Ire)	73	67	69	68	277	11796
	Ian WOOSNAM	(Wal)	72	65	69	71	277	11796
	Per-Ulrik JOHANSSON	(Swe)	72	70	67	68	277	11796
	Roger WESSELS	(SA)	69	70	70	68	277	11796
13	Miguel Angel JIMÉNEZ	(Sp)	72	67	69	70	278	9118
	Sven STRÜVER	(Ger)	72	68	68	70	278	9118
	Jay TOWNSEND	(USA)	69	68	74	67	278	9118
	Anders FORSBRAND	(Swe)	67	69	72	70	278	9118
17	José Maria OLAZÁBAL	(Sp)	71	69	69	70	279	7696
	Padraig HARRINGTON	(Ire)	74	70	67	68	279	7696
	Ross DRUMMOND	(Scot)	69	70	68	72	279	7696
	Angel CABRERA	(Arg)	71	70	69	69	279	7696
21	Ian GARBUTT	(Eng)	69	71	69	71	280	6636
	Paul MCGINLEY	(Ire)	70	69	68	73	280	6636
	Lee WESTWOOD	(Eng)	73	70	66	71	280	6636
	Alex CEJKA	(Ger)	72	71	69	68	280	6636
	Mark ROE	(Eng)	70	73	68	69	280	6636
	David HOWELL	(Eng)	73	65	69	73	280	6636
27	Peter MITCHELL	(Eng)	72	72	68	69	281	5386
	Fernando ROCA	(Sp)	71	72	69	69	281	5386
	Paul EALES	(Eng)	71	71	68	71	281	5386
	Jean VAN DE VELDE	(Fr)	73	70	66	72	281	5386
	Mark DAVIS	(Eng)	75	69	67	70	281	5386
	Dean ROBERTSON	(Scot)	73	71	70	67	281	5386
	Paul BROADHURST	(Eng)	73	67	69	72	281	5386
	Michele REALE	(It)	69	69	72	71	281	5386
35	Miles TUNNICLIFF	(Eng)	69	69	73	71	282	4484
	Clinton WHITELAW	(SA)	71	70	71	70	282	4484
	Heinz P THÜL	(Ger)	70	70	72	70	282	4484
	Seve BALLESTEROS	(Sp)	72	70	68	72	282	4484
	David GILFORD	(Eng)	69	71	67	75	282	4484
40	Steen TINNING	(Den)	70	68	72	73	283	3696
	Miguel Angel MARTIN	(Sp)	70	70	71	72	283	3696
	Ignacio GARRIDO	(Sp)	72	71	70	70	283	3696
	Joakim HAEGGMAN	(Swe)	71	71	71	70	283	3696
	Philip WALTON	(Ire)	71	67	73	72	283	3696
	Derrick COOPER	(Eng)	69	71	70	73	283	3696
	Robert KARLSSON	(Swe)	74	69	70	70	283	3696
	Michael JONZON	(Swe)	74	67	68	74	283	3696
48	Paul LAWRIE	(Scot)	71	72	70	71	284	2787
	Daniel CHOPRA	(Swe)	71	68	72	73	284	2787
	Wook-Soon KANG	(S.Kor)	72	71	69	72	284	2787
	Tony JOHNSTONE	(Zim)	73	71	70	70	284	2787
	Sam TORRANCE	(Scot)	72	71	68	73	284	2787
	Fredrik JACOBSON	(Swe)	73	70	68	73	284	2787
	David THOMSON	(Scot)	72	72	66	74	284	2787
55	Eduardo ROMERO	(Arg)	72	72	71	70	285	2072
	Phillip PRICE	(Wal)	71	72	73	69	285	2072
	Gary ORR	(Scot)	76	67	70	72	285	2072
	Klas ERIKSSON	(Swe)	72	72	72	69	285	2072
	Jeev Milkha SINGH	(Ind)	74	70	68	73	285	2072
60	Knud STORGAARD	(Den)	72	71	73	70	286	1727
	Costantino ROCCA	(It)	75	68	73	70	286	1727
	Søren KJELDSEN	(Den)	75	67	74	70	286	1727
	Steve WEBSTER	(Eng)	74	70	68	74	286	1727
64	Des SMYTH	(Ire)	75	69	73	70	287	1226
	Roger CHAPMAN	(Eng)	72	72	73	70	287	1226
	Bob MAY	(USA)	73	69	71	74	287	1226
	Stuart CAGE	(Eng)	72	72	69	74	287	1226
68	Russell CLAYDON	(Eng)	73	71	73	71	288	905
69	Jarmo SANDELIN	(Swe)	72	68	72	77	289	903
70	Mats HALLBERG	(Swe)	69	75	71	76	291	901
71	Jim PAYNE	(Eng)	74	70	75	73	292	899
72	Mark MOULAND	(Wal)	76	68	78	73	295	897

Steen Tinning

Leaney knocks them sideways

Stephen Leaney cruised to victory for his first European Tour title

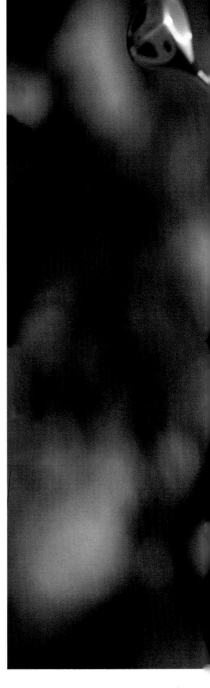

*E*uropean Tour rookie, Stephen Leaney can vouch for the truth of the old adage that it's an ill wind that blows nobody any good after his runaway eight strokes Moroccan Open victory.

The tall Australian flew in from Sydney on his 29th birthday: 'It was the longest birthday I ever had because of getting back through the time zones'. And he discovered he had an early tee-off time at Royal Agadir.

It meant he played in calm conditions instead of having to combat the wind the locals call the 'cherki', which whistled in off the Atlantic to batter the afternoon starters. He recalled, 'It was a big break and it was a

double bonus because I'd woken very early owing to jetlag after the 36-hour journey and was raring to go. It carried over to the following day when I managed to complete my second round before bad light stopped play, which gave me a big advantage, for instance, over Des Smyth, who had to go out to finish one hole, which he bogeyed, then hang around for hours to start round three.'

The luck of the draw was certainly a boost to the former Eisenhower Trophy amateur, a plus four handicapper when he turned professional in 1992, but his victory, following three West Australian Open wins and back to back Victorian Open successes, owed much more to skilled shotmaking, clever course management and wonderful putting on subtle and slippery seaside greens.

It was the high point of a career that suffered a major body-blow – literally – in 1993 when he was discovered to have a blood clot in his right shoulder. He explained: 'The first rib was pushing up against the collar bone and surgeons had to remove about seven centimetres of it to relieve the pressure. It set me back about 18 months.'

Leaney, who ended 12th behind

Andrew Coltart in the PGA Tour of Australasia Order of Merit, invested £40 in a new 'bullseye' putter in Canberra the week before flying to London and it paid an instant £58,330 dividend with his first European Tour triumph. 'I'd been getting frustrated at striking the ball well and scoring badly and decided it was time for a change,' confessed the man who earned his European Tour card with half a dozen

top ten finishes, including two seconds, in as many weeks on the European Challenge Tour after playing on a sponsor's invite in last year's Volvo German Open.

The new club in the bag helped him end the only man in the field to shoot in the sixties on all four days – 68,67,69,67 – for a tournament best 17 below par tally and the biggest Tour winning margin since Nick Price took the Dimension Data

Pro-am title over a year earlier at Sun City, Bophuthatswana.

A birdie hat-trick from the third in round four – two putts dropped from over 20 feet – effectively slammed the door tight shut on his rivals. Stephen frankly admitted: 'I was so far ahead (ten shots) I fell asleep on my drive at the long 15th and lost a ball. I did well to make six from 12 feet – it was only my fourth

bogey of the week and it's as good as I've played tee to green. Securing my Tour card so swiftly was beyond my wildest dreams. Royal Agadir reminded me a lot of some of the courses back home in Western Australia and it was a big advantage coming over with a run of tournaments under my belt.'

No one was able to put the squeeze on Leaney, who led by four at the start of round four from Robert Karlsson and Mark Davis, who bravely birdied five of the last seven holes for a 72 after a second day 65.

There was no way back for many victims of the Thursday afternoon gales,

including Severiano Ballesteros. Europe's triumphant Johnnie Walker Ryder Cup captain, after tasting defeat when his European side lost 3-1 to Tony Johnstone's Africa eight in the Sahara Cup match on the eve of the championship, was 13

Robert Karlsson claimed second place.

It had to be victor Stephen Leaney's six iron to the third in round four. He had 163 yards to go down-hill through a stiff left to right breeze to a pin close to the right hand side of the undulating green close to the sea shore, with trouble left, right and beyond. He hit it to six feet and his birdie was the first of three in a row to kickstart his victory gallop.

over par through 12 holes when play was suspended overnight and a stomach upset forced him to retire hurt.

Davis, a double winner in Austria, held second place with nine to play, only to run up a quadruple bogey nine at the tenth after his 'almost perfect' three wood second struck a rock and ricocheted into a

Sweden's Mathias Grönberg (left) and England's Mark Davis (right) took top ten placings.

bush, from where he twice hacked into a pond to pick up two penalty strokes.

Swedes Karlsson and Matthias Grönberg overtook him, but tied fourth place was his best since finishing runner-up in the 1996 Linde German Masters.

Karlsson mixed five birdies with two sixes for a closing 71 and 279, while Grönberg, ended on 282.

Ireland's Smyth, whose first day 64 matched Darren Cole's 12 month old course record (no record this time because preferred lies were used) slipped to 14th after closing rounds of 77 and 75 to end 17 strokes behind the magnificent Leaney.

Gordon Richardson

THE COURSE

Royal Agadir was designed by Robert Trent Jones inside the pastel-shaded turreted walls of King Hassan II's palace. Narrow fairways and small, sharply-sloping greens put a premium on accuracy as the links meanders between dense clumps of eucalyptus trees and scrub and bullrush-filled ponds. The 'cherki' wind off the Atlantic can make life very difficult as so many found during the Open.

Golf Royal D'Agadir, March 12-15, 1998 · Yardage 6657 · Par 72

Pos	Name	Country	Rnd 1	Rnd 2	Rnd 3	Rnd 4	Total	Prize Money £
1	Stephen LEANEY	(Aus)	68	67	69	67	271	58330
2	Robert KARLSSON	(Swe)	70	71	67	71	279	38880
3	Mathias GRÖNBERG	(Swe)	67	74	67	74	282	21910
4	Miguel Angel MARTIN	(Sp)	69	78	68	69	284	16165
	Mark DAVIS	(Eng)	71	65	72	76	284	16165
6	Tom GILLIS	(USA)	79	64	73	69	285	10500
	Olle KARLSSON	(Swe)	72	69	70	74	285	10500
	Tony JOHNSTONE	(Zim)	72	68	73	72	285	10500
9	Roger CHAPMAN	(Eng)	72	71	69	74	286	7410
	Wayne RILEY	(Aus)	73	69	71	73	286	7410
11	Heinz P THÜL	(Ger)	77	70	70	70	287	6030
	Daniel CHOPRA	(Swe)	70	71	74	72	287	6030
	Bob MAY	(USA)	69	70	76	72	287	6030
14	Miguel Angel JIMÉNEZ	(Sp)	82	68	69	69	288	5036
	Pedro LINHART	(Sp)	67	74	75	72	288	5036
	Thomas GÖGELE	(Ger)	70	67	74	77	288	5036
	Clinton WHITELAW	(SA)	73	71	72	77	293	2835
35	Silvio GRAPPASONNI	(It)	71	75	78	70	294	2555
	Dennis EDLUND	(Swe)	73	74	68	79	294	2555
	Raymond BURNS	(N.Ire)	68	79	73	74	294	2555
	Thomas BJÖRN	(Den)	70	76	76	72	294	2555
	Jesus Maria ARRUTI	(Sp)	72	73	69	80	294	2555
	Eduardo ROMERO	(Arg)	71	73	75	75	294	2555
41	Nic HENNING	(SA)	76	71	70	78	295	2205
	Darren COLE	(Aus)	76	71	73	75	295	2205
	Emanuele CANONICA	(It)	71	76	74	74	295	2205
	Peter MITCHELL	(Eng)	73	71	74	77	295	2205
45	Steve ALKER	(NZ)	74	72	74	76	296	1960
	Greg OWEN	(Eng)	74	75	74	73	296	1960
	Ross DRUMMOND	(Scot)	79	71	71	75	296	1960
48	Adam HUNTER	(Scot)	76	71	71	79	297	1715
	Francisco CEA	(Sp)	76	71	74	76	297	1715
	Raymond RUSSELL	(Scot)	74	75	74	74	297	1715
	Jeff HAWKES	(SA)	74	76	72	75	297	1715

A bridge too far for Thomas Gögele in the final round.

Pos	Name	Country	Rnd 1	Rnd 2	Rnd 3	Rnd 4	Total	Prize Money £
	Des SMYTH	(Ire)	64	72	77	75	288	5036
18	José COCERES	(Arg)	69	74	76	70	289	4515
19	Fabrice TARNAUD	(Fr)	79	71	70	70	290	4102
	Paul BROADHURST	(Eng)	71	79	70	70	290	4102
	Raphoël JACQUELIN	(Fr)	74	67	74	75	290	4102
	Diego BORREGO	(Sp)	69	72	75	74	290	4102
	Alex CEJKA	(Ger)	68	70	74	78	290	4102
24	Mathew GOGGIN	(Aus)	77	71	70	73	291	3675
	John BICKERTON	(Eng)	76	68	74	73	291	3675
	Anders FORSBRAND	(Swe)	72	71	71	77	291	3675
27	Ola ELIASSON	(Swe)	75	72	71	74	292	3202
	Stephane TALBOT	(Can)	74	74	72	72	292	3202
	Angel CABRERA	(Arg)	71	75	74	72	292	3202
	Scott HENDERSON	(Scot)	78	68	74	72	292	3202
	Michele REALE	(It)	70	75	73	74	292	3202
	Phil GOLDING	(Eng)	71	73	75	73	292	3202
33	Greg CHALMERS	(Aus)	75	75	70	73	293	2835
52	Sven STRÜVER	(Ger)	81	69	77	71	298	1505
	Olivier EDMOND	(Fr)	75	70	76	77	298	1505
54	Henrik NYSTROM	(Swe)	77	73	74	75	299	1365
	David A RUSSELL	(Eng)	75	69	76	79	299	1365
56	Mårten OLANDER	(Swe)	70	76	84	70	300	1163
	Craig HAINLINE	(USA)	75	73	71	81	300	1163
	Andrew BEAL	(Eng)	79	70	80	71	300	1163
	Francis HOWLEY	(Ire)	75	70	77	78	300	1163
60	Fredrik HENGE	(Swe)	83	67	72	79	301	1050
61	Tjaart VAN DER WALT	(SA)	77	69	76	80	302	997
	Stephen BENNETT	(Eng)	75	75	77	75	302	997
63	Carl SUNESON	(Sp)	78	71	78	76	303	945
64	Greig HUTCHEON	(Scot)	72	76	80	76	304	910
65	Gordon J BRAND	(Eng)	77	73	74	82	306	700
	Daren LEE	(Eng)	70	80	75	81	306	700
67	Marc FARRY	(Fr)	75	73	83	77	308	523
68	Birgir HAFTHORSSON	(Ice)	74	73	85	79	311	521

Mitchell is king in Cotton country

Peter Mitchell enjoyed a family

holiday and a victory at

Sir Henry Cotton's Penina

As you fall asleep at Penina, lulled into slumber by the croaking music of a thousand bullfrogs going about their nocturnal business at the foot of the fountain in the gardens below, you cannot but be touched by the ghost that still walks the fairways and woods and greens of this special place. This is Cotton coun-try, and when the Portuguese Open returned there in April, the influence of the patriarch of Penina, for all that he died more than a decade earlier, was still thick in the air.

The European Tour, such as it was in Sir Henry Cotton's great days of the 1930s and 1940s, was a vastly different entity to the global circuit it has become in the 1990s. No more is the Tour a loosely and almost randomly con-nected series of isolated tournaments in diverse out-posts; the world, rather than the narrow and constricting confines of the small village that is the Europe of today, is its oyster.

You get the feeling that Cotton would have approved of what European professional tournament golf has become. Cotton was the most liberal of free spirits; there is nothing more certain that he would have loved the multi-cultural, multi-Continental world that is inhabited by the modern European Tour professional. True, not many of them have Bentleys, as Cotton did; certainly, they do not take their skills onto the stage of the London Coliseum, as Cotton did; assuredly, they do not make a habit of lifetime habit of cocking a snook at officialdom, as Cotton did; the impression is still strong in the mind that they, and he, would have liked

THE COURSE

Penina, a mile inland from the Atlantic coast of the Algarve, is a course moulded in the image of Sir Henry Cotton, its creator. It sets a fascinating examination of a golfer's skill right through the bag and is a layout that has stood the test of time. Although Mitchell was 18 below par in winning, he and his fellow competitors could never take the magnificently tree-lined course, with its narrow fairways and subtly contoured greens, for granted. A fortune is being spent on it by the present owners; already splendid, it is certain to get even better.

each other.

It was against this background that the Open championship of the country, where Cotton made his home for the last quarter-century of his life, returned to the course that he built for the first time in sixteen years. Four days of lively competition in the glorious springtime of the Algarve brought a deserved winner who claimed his triumph against one of the more daring and brilliant attacks from behind that the Tour would see all season. Cotton would have loved the cut and thrust of it.

In the end, victory went to Peter Mitchell, who won with a total of 274, eighteen under par, but he was pushed to the bitter end by Jarmo Sandelin, who

David Gilford (above) shared second place. Seve Ballesteros (opposite).

launched his bid for glory as early as the Saturday morning of the tournament and was still slugging it out when he holed his last putt on Sunday afternoon.

There is no doubting the fact that Mitchell earned his moment in the sun. He was on a family holiday with his wife

and two daughters, but there was no holidaymaking to be had on the golf course. He was sometimes inspired, sometimes merely steady, but from first to last he was consistent, and that, no matter what degree of brilliance accompanies it, is what wins golf tournaments.

Being the fair man that he his, Mitchell would not cavil with the verdict that the player of the weekend was Sandelin. The rangy, big-hitting Swede started the weekend in a distant share of 41st place on two under par, then played 32 holes in fifteen under par before dropping his next shot.

On Saturday morning Sandelin's mission had seemed, if not impossible, then at least ludicrously unlikely; in the event,

SHOT OF THE WEEK

Peter Mitchell claimed from the start that the man who mastered the five par fives at Penina would win the tournament. Instead, he made a speciality of the four par threes, with the 16th being his particular favourite. On the final day, he was level with Jarmo Sandelin coming to the 16th, but then struck a magnificent five iron to leave him with an eight feet uphill putt for his fourth birdie of the week at the hole. He made the putt, but it was the tee shot that set him up for victory.

he was beaten by a mere one shot to finish joint second alongside David Gilford with Eduardo Romero, Sam Torrance and Jonathan Lomas a further stroke behind. To Mitchell went the spoils of victory, but Sandelin's part in the drama of the final day should never be forgotten.

Mitchell played good if not eye-catching golf in the first three days. Never out of contention, he waited for his moment like a champion miler coming off the last bend. When his sprint came, it was perfectly timed, but others who enjoyed the spotlight as the tournament progressed all played their part in a memorable four days.

In the first round, it was the sturdy frame of Darren Clarke that thrust itself to the fore. The Ulsterman's seven under par 66 put him a shot ahead of Mitchell, who picked up four shots in the last four holes, but with a scintilla of luck on the greens, Clarke might have been much closer to 60.

In the days of his youth, he often came to Penina for training sessions with the senior Irish amateur squad; it remained, he said, one of his favourite courses in mainland Europe.

Happy Darren was he who walked off the final green on that first day; sad, ailing Darren was he who tottered onto his first tee the next morning. He had been out for dinner with some fellow players the night before and ate a crab of such dubious provenance that he was up all night rackingly unwell. He barely made it to the tee, but was glad that he did in the end. After playing like the sick man he undoubtedly was for fifteen holes, he birdied the last three to stay in the picture with a 74. He eventually finished four strokes behind Mitchell.

It was a picture that was dominated early on by Wayne Riley. Winner of the title two years before, the stubby little Australian followed his first-round 68 with

a 66 that put him two strokes clear of Paul Lawrie with Mitchell and Gilford three back.

Mitchell made his first big move on Saturday, when his second 67 in three days put him a shot ahead of Lawrie on 15 under par with Gilford three back and Sandelin sharing fourth place on 11 under. It was far from all over; anybody in the first dozen or so could still do it.

As it transpired, Mitchell did not give them the chance as he kept his head on the final day. It was only afterwards that he told a small story against himself that had echoes of his last victory, in the Madeira Island Open at Santo da Serra in 1997. There, he had to birdie the last hole and did so in spite of believing he needed no more than a par, and this time he thought he needed a birdie and required only a par for a closing, and winning, 70. Sometimes ignorance really is bliss.

Mel Webb   67

PORTUGUESE OPEN, MERIDIEN PENINA, MARCH 19-22 1998 · YARDAGE 6903 · PAR 73

Pos	Name	Country	Rnd 1	Rnd 2	Rnd 3	Rnd 4	Total	Prize Money £
1	Peter MITCHELL	(Eng)	67	70	67	70	274	58330
2	Jarmo SANDELIN	(Swe)	73	71	64	67	275	30395
	David GILFORD	(Eng)	70	67	70	68	275	30395
4	Eduardo ROMERO	(Arg)	68	75	68	65	276	14860
	Sam TORRANCE	(Scot)	74	66	70	66	276	14860
	Jonathan LOMAS	(Eng)	71	69	69	67	276	14860
7	Peter BAKER	(Eng)	72	70	67	68	277	9625
	Wayne RILEY	(Aus)	68	66	74	69	277	9625
9	Darren CLARKE	(N.Ire)	66	74	69	69	278	7820
10	Tony JOHNSTONE	(Zim)	68	73	70	68	279	6720
	David CARTER	(Eng)	73	66	71	69	279	6720
12	Raphaël JACQUELIN	(Fr)	76	67	70	67	280	5535
	Francisco CEA	(Sp)	71	72	69	68	280	5535
	Jeev Milkha SINGH	(Ind)	69	73	68	70	280	5535
	Alex CEJKA	(Ger)	72	72	66	70	280	5535
16	David HOWELL	(Eng)	71	72	71	67	281	4723
	John BICKERTON	(Eng)	73	71	70	67	281	4723
	Ian GARBUTT	(Eng)	72	68	71	70	281	4723
19	Van PHILLIPS	(Eng)	70	74	73	65	282	4211
	Fredrik HENGE	(Swe)	71	71	71	69	282	4211
	Miguel Angel MARTIN	(Sp)	70	72	69	71	282	4211
22	Thomas GÖGELE	(Ger)	73	73	68	69	283	3780
	Henrik NYSTROM	(Swe)	72	68	73	70	283	3780
	Domingo HOSPITAL	(Sp)	68	75	70	70	283	3780
	Angel CABRERA	(Arg)	75	68	67	73	283	3780
	Santiago LUNA	(Sp)	71	67	71	74	283	3780
27	Peter HEDBLOM	(Swe)	72	67	75	70	284	3412
	Tom GILLIS	(USA)	71	74	69	70	284	3412
29	Stephen LEANEY	(Aus)	76	70	71	68	285	3052
	Adam HUNTER	(Scot)	72	72	73	68	285	3052
	Mark JAMES	(Eng)	71	71	72	71	285	3052
	Steve ALKER	(NZ)	74	69	70	72	285	3052
	Raymond BURNS	(N.Ire)	76	69	68	72	285	3052
34	Darren COLE	(Aus)	71	74	71	70	286	2625
	Michele REALE	(It)	74	69	72	71	286	2625
	Daniel CHOPRA	(Swe)	74	69	71	72	286	2625
	José RIVERO	(Sp)	73	70	71	72	286	2625
	Malcolm MACKENZIE	(Eng)	74	70	70	72	286	2625
	Patrik SJÖLAND	(Swe)	72	72	69	73	286	2625
40	Des SMYTH	(Ire)	73	68	74	72	287	2170
	Jeff REMESY	(Fr)	70	68	77	72	287	2170
	Cameron CLARK	(N Ire)	74	71	72	70	287	2170
	Derrick COOPER	(Eng)	73	71	73	70	287	2170
	Steen TINNING	(Den)	72	71	74	70	287	2170
	Paul EALES	(Eng)	75	71	72	69	287	2170
	Paul LAWRIE	(Scot)	72	64	69	82	287	2170
47	Jean VAN DE VELDE	(Fr)	68	73	74	73	288	1785
	Iain PYMAN	(Eng)	73	71	72	72	288	1785
	Gary EVANS	(Eng)	74	71	72	71	288	1785
	Craig HAINLINE	(USA)	77	68	72	71	288	1785
51	Stephen BENNETT	(Eng)	74	68	74	73	289	1505
	Johan RYSTRÖM	(Swe)	73	71	74	71	289	1505
	Fredrik JACOBSON	(Swe)	72	70	76	71	289	1505
	Greg OWEN	(Eng)	72	70	76	71	289	1505
55	Richard BOXALL	(Eng)	71	72	72	75	290	1172
	Jamie SPENCE	(Eng)	74	72	72	72	290	1172
	Howard CLARK	(Eng)	77	67	74	72	290	1172
	Miguel Angel JIMÉNEZ	(Sp)	75	71	73	71	290	1172
	Fabrice TARNAUD	(Fr)	75	69	70	76	290	1172
	Seve BALLESTEROS	(Sp)	72	73	69	76	290	1172
61	Andrew OLDCORN	(Scot)	71	71	74	75	291	962
	Jim PAYNE	(Eng)	74	72	71	74	291	962
	John HAWKSWORTH	(Eng)	75	71	73	72	291	962
	Russell CLAYDON	(Eng)	75	71	74	71	291	962
65	Joakim RASK	(Swe)	74	71	72	75	292	611
	David THOMSON	(Scot)	76	67	74	75	292	611
	Dean ROBERTSON	(Scot)	73	73	73	73	292	611
	Roger CHAPMAN	(Eng)	72	74	79	67	292	611
69	Maarten LAFEBER	(Hol)	73	73	74	73	293	519
70	Ola ELIASSON	(Swe)	73	71	74	76	294	516
	José COCERES	(Arg)	69	71	74	80	294	516
72	Antonio GARRIDO	(Sp)	72	73	71	79	295	513
73	Mark DAVIS	(Eng)	75	71	74	76	296	511
74	David LYNN	(Eng)	71	73	74	79	297	509
75	Stuart CAGE	(Eng)	73	70	81	74	298	507

Jeev Milkha Singh of India.

Levet scores historic victory

Thomas Levet's maiden Tour win

was the first by a Frenchman

on home soil since 1969

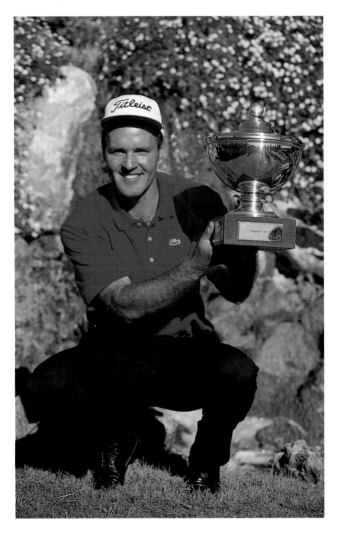

Cannes, mid-May, and the girls are strutting their stuff, hopeful young things wanting so hard to be discovered at the world-renowned film festival that it almost hurts. They wear bright smiles and the briefest of costumes, for here on the Croisette the body beautiful goes with the job. If they had been there a month earlier, they would have needed fur-lined overcoats and thermal undies. It was the week of the Cannes Open, and boy, was it cold.

Anybody making their first visit to Cannes that week would have wondered what all the fuss was about. This was the French Riviera, for Pete's sake, where the sun was supposed to shine; surly clouds, rain and frigid temperatures driven even lower by a blustery wind were not the idea at all. Cannes? This was more like Skegness in November. At one stage in the tournament the players probably could not wait until the following Monday. At least it was only snowing in England.

To be absolutely fair to Cannes, the meteorological nasties thrown at it during the tournament were decidedly untypical. The Cote d'Azur in April is usually delightful, with the blossom on the trees coming out to play, the hundreds of restaurants offering dining *al fresco* and the designer boutiques on the Rue d'Antibes offering refuge for the visitor grimly intent on some serious retail therapy of the platinum plastic variety. Cannes is a haven for the hedonistic; on this week it was more suitable for the masochistic.

Meanwhile, up there in the hills behind the town, a story unfolded that if touted around as a screenplay would have been dismissed out of hand. The plot of this story made Tin Shack look like gritty cinema verité, involving as it did the life of a man who had tasted dizzy heights and sudden decline, happiness and despair. His name was Thomas Levet, and he was the undisputed star of this particular show.

Levet came to Cannes with almost no status, except that his family loved him. He had no playing rights on any major circuit of the world, and he was expecting his summer to consist of playing European Challenge Tour golf. Yet a few years before he had been a coming man, a player who had won his card to play on the United States Tour while keeping his precious European credentials safe and sound. By 1998 it had all gone.

The Frenchman played in the tournament only because of a special exemption granted him by his home federation. He

THE COURSE

Royal Mougins is a troublesome, tricky course that places a premium on accurate driving, astute second and third shots and a magician's touch on the heavily contoured greens. With its par of 71, it is no pushover; it was not due solely to the chilly conditions that the winning score was only six under par. The green on the closing hole is a minefield – Colin Montgomerie once putted across it and straight into the lake at its side. It is easier to do than you might think.

had about him something of the actor who knows there is a great performance inside him just waiting to be pulled out if only he were allowed the chance; and Levet chose this one, wonderful week to grab his opportunity, winning the tournament with a total of 278, six under par. It may have been cold out there; Levet was so suffused by the warm glow of victory that he did not notice it.

There were one or two other intriguing little sub-plots in the peice. Like David Lynn, a confident young fellow from Billinge, in the North Midalnds, having the first hole-in-one of his career on the first day to share the lead on 67. Lynn's

brother, Simon, also a professional, had had five aces before David slotted his seven iron home on the par three fifth hole to make the score 5-1.

Lynn was in his first full season on the European Tour, unlike Christy O'Connor Junior who was in his last. O'Conner, on a valedictory final lap of the Tour before joining the ranks of the European Seniors Tour when he passed his 50th birthday on August 19, took over the baton at the halfway point after a 64 that included only 25 putts had driven him to the top of the leaderboard on six under par.

O'Connor faded from the scene on Saturday, leaving his fellow veteran and

lifelong friend, Eamonn Darcy, to step forward to wave the flag for the Irish fortysomethings. Darcy had his best round of the year, a 66, leaving him to breathe a sigh of relief that he had emerged from the perils of Royal Mougins unscathed. 'This course can bounce up and catch you,' he said. 'You can come out of the seventh, eighth, and ninth on a stretcher.' A stretcher might not have been needed if he had managed to maintain his challenge on the final day, but a Zimmer frame might have come in handy. Darcy finished that third day sharing second place with four other players on 209, four under par, four behind the leader,

Thomas Levet was being pressured by players already in the clubhouse as he approached the end of his final round. He was wavering just a bit, his resolve was being tested to its limits. He was a shot ahead of a group of three as he lined up a 40-feet putt across the 17th green. He did not look likely to hole it, but hole it he did, a cool, calm stroke sending ball diving in the front door for a birdie. As later events proved, it was the shot that won him the tournament.

who was, guess who? Correct – Thomas Levet.

Levet had played his part *sotto voce* thus far, but now, he felt, was the time to do something dramatic. With the continuing chilly weather and the difficulty of the Royal Mougins greens keeping scoring on the high side, Levet had a splendid 65 to leave clear daylight between himself and Darcy, Peter Lonard, Andrew Sherborne and Pierre Fulke. The scene was set for a combative last day.

And that is exactly what it turned out to be. Levet's nerves sent him spinning to an occasional deviation from the straight and narrow, but by and large he kept his head admirably. He had to tell himself repeatedly that this was no fluke, he was up there because he deserved to be; his biggest enemy on the day his own damaged psyche.

Still, he did not complete his victory without a few nerve-wracking moments on the last hole. He had just birdied the 17th with a monster putt to give himself an two-shot cushion, and as it transpired needed the shot he gained there to avoid putting himself into a four-man play-off.

He hit his second shot into a bunker then watched in horror as his attempted escape saw the ball fly straight up into the air and land at his feet. 'I had no idea where the ball had gone,' he admitted. 'It

Christy O'Connor Junior (left) and David Lynn (above) had their moments.

could have hit me on the head or dropped in to my pocket for all I knew.' If it had done either of those things, he would have lost the tournament.

Eventually on the green in four although still 45 feet from the flag, he had two shots to win. A double-breaking putt left him eight feet from the pin, and amid a deafening crescendo of silence, he calmly rolled the ball into the heart of the hole for the best bogey six he will ever have. His compatriots erupted, Levet raised his hands in unalloyed joy; in four days his life had changed, maybe for ever.

Mel Webb

CANNES OPEN, ROYAL MOUGINS GC, APRIL 16-19, 1998 · YARDAGE 6594 · PAR 71

Pos	Name	Country	Rnd 1	Rnd 2	Rnd 3	Rnd 4	Total	Prize Money £		Pos	Name	Country	Rnd 1	Rnd 2	Rnd 3	Rnd 4	Total	Prize Money £
1	Thomas LEVET	(Fr)	69	71	65	73	278	50000		32	Mathias GRÖNBERG	(Swe)	73	71	68	74	286	2400
2	Greg TURNER	(NZ)	70	73	67	69	279	22370			Steve ALKER	(NZ)	73	71	71	71	286	2400
	Phillip PRICE	(Wal)	74	66	72	67	279	22370			Santiago LUNA	(Sp)	69	68	77	72	286	2400
	Sven STRÜVER	(Ger)	69	72	69	69	279	22370			Olivier EDMOND	(Fr)	72	71	74	69	286	2400
5	Steve WEBSTER	(Eng)	70	71	70	69	280	11600			Gordon BRAND JNR.	(Scot)	75	69	71	71	286	2400
	Clinton WHITELAW	(SA)	72	71	72	65	280	11600		37	David LYNN	(Eng)	67	75	76	69	287	2070
7	Ross MCFARLANE	(Eng)	76	68	70	67	281	9000			Andrew CLAPP	(Eng)	73	72	71	71	287	2070
8	Mark DAVIS	(Eng)	69	69	73	71	282	6730			Christophe POTTIER	(Fr)	74	71	72	70	287	2070
	Peter LONARD	(Aus)	68	71	70	73	282	6730			Jean VAN DE VELDE	(Fr)	73	72	72	70	287	2070
	Andrew SHERBORNE	(Eng)	73	68	68	73	282	6730			Peter MITCHELL	(Eng)	71	74	70	72	287	2070
11	Mark ROE	(Eng)	70	75	70	68	283	4902			Pedro LINHART	(Sp)	72	71	69	75	287	2070
	Joakim HAEGGMAN	(Swe)	70	73	68	72	283	4902		43	David GILFORD	(Eng)	70	74	74	70	288	1710
	Alex CEJKA	(Ger)	72	73	68	70	283	4902			Jay TOWNSEND	(USA)	70	72	72	74	288	1710
	Jeff REMESY	(Fr)	67	74	69	73	283	4902			Philip WALTON	(Ire)	72	71	73	72	288	1710
	Paul LAWRIE	(Scot)	74	71	67	71	283	4902			Fabrice TARNAUD	(Fr)	70	74	71	73	288	1710
16	Mark MOULAND	(Wal)	71	71	71	71	284	3561			Jonathan LOMAS	(Eng)	71	70	76	71	288	1710
	Ian GARBUTT	(Eng)	74	71	74	65	284	3561			Tom GILLIS	(USA)	73	67	73	75	288	1710
	Miguel Angel MARTIN	(Sp)	69	74	76	65	284	3561		49	Patrik SJÖLAND	(Swe)	72	69	72	76	289	1470
	Michael LONG	(NZ)	69	72	70	73	284	3561			Andrew SANDYWELL	(Eng)	69	74	72	74	289	1470
	Michael CAMPBELL	(NZ)	70	75	72	67	284	3561			David MONTESI (AM)	(Fr)	70	73	75	71	289	
	Eamonn DARCY	(Ire)	71	72	66	75	284	3561		51	Robert ALLENBY	(Aus)	67	75	73	75	290	1350
	Andrew OLDCORN	(Scot)	72	72	70	70	284	3561			Chris VAN DER VELDE	(Hol)	71	72	72	75	290	1350
	David HOWELL	(Eng)	73	70	72	69	284	3561		53	Dean ROBERTSON	(Scot)	73	70	76	72	291	1200
	Pierre FULKE	(Swe)	73	65	71	75	284	3561			Stephen BENNETT	(Eng)	72	73	73	73	291	1200
	Steen TINNING	(Den)	70	74	69	71	284	3561			Stephen ALLAN	(Aus)	71	67	72	81	291	1200
	David HIGGINS	(Ire)	69	69	75	71	284	3561		56	Wayne WESTNER	(SA)	68	77	76	71	292	997
27	Christy O'CONNOR JNR	(Ire)	72	64	75	74	285	2790			Marc FARRY	(Fr)	70	73	71	78	292	997
	Raphaël JACQUELIN	(Fr)	69	73	70	73	285	2790			Jeev Milkha SINGH	(Ind)	67	74	79	72	292	997
	Craig HAINLINE	(USA)	71	72	71	71	285	2790			Stephane LAHARY	(Fr)	72	71	77	72	292	997
	Miguel Angel JIMÉNEZ	(Sp)	75	69	66	75	285	2790		60	Alberto BINAGHI	(It)	71	74	74	74	293	885
	Bob MAY	(USA)	74	71	71	69	285	2790			Jon ROBSON	(Eng)	71	74	76	72	293	885
										62	David TAPPING	(Eng)	75	70	76	73	294	825
											Pascal EDMOND	(Fr)	76	69	72	77	294	825
										64	Daniel CHOPRA	(Swe)	69	73	77	76	295	780
										65	Rolf MUNTZ	(Hol)	74	69	76	79	298	750

Michael Campbell (below) in a sea of sand.

Ready for BUSINESS

Professional golfers must be 100% fit to perform at the highest level. The 3M Mobile Physio Unit, with its team of physiotherapists and stocks of 3M Health Care products helps PGA European Tour professionals play to their true potential.

With over 50,000 products spanning the breadth of science, and 75,000 creative minds all over the world, we are equally well placed to help your business reach its true potential.

To find out more, visit our web site on www.3M.com/uk

3M - Official sponsors of the PGA European Tour and the Physio unit

3M *Innovation*

Björn is double first

Victory in Spain made Thomas Björn
the first man to win twice on
the 1998 European Tour

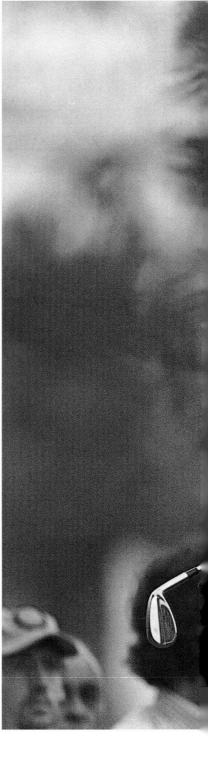

There was a temptation to believe after the Peugeot Open de España that spectators had been given a glimpse into the future. For there was a distinct feeling during that week at the El Prat course, near Barcelona, that something new was happening.

Perhaps, it was the much-heralded appearance of the brightest amateur to emerge in Europe since José Maria Olazábal 15 years ago. Or maybe the rare sight of a previously unknown left-hander leading the field and playing well enough to suggest that he had the talent to develop into a top-class player. Or perhaps it was the way events finally unfolded to reveal a Johnnie Walker Ryder Cup hero winning for only the third time but in such a manner as to suggest that he could be destined for greater glory.

Thomas Björn walked off with the champion's cheque for £91,660 at the end of a thoroughly entertaining week's golf, which provided followers of the European scene with plenty of food for thought.

But first, centre stage was taken by 18-year-old Sergio Garcia, the European Amateur Champion for whom an outstanding future was being predicted. The Costa Brava professional's son had been the talk of the amateur scene for the past year without reaching the attention of the general public. This was the week when he became big news, was given the high-profile treatment and emerged as a star in the making. The way the teenager handled his introduction to a wider fame gave all the indications that he would develop into the player so many people want him to be.

Not everyone would easily accept being dubbed El Nino and described as the next Tiger Woods, while being lauded by such celebrated compatriots as Severiano Ballesteros and the aforementioned Olazábal. Ballesteros called the youngster, studying at a US college, 'the player of the 21st century', who could even beat all the professionals that week. Olazábal

conceded that the newcomer was a better player than he had been at the same age.

Faced with living up to such praise Garcia promptly took advantage of the benign conditions around the flat, parkland course to shoot an opening 66, which put him in sixth place alongside the favourite Olazábal. What made Garcia's appeal so instantly recognisable was his distance off the tee. In line with the mod-

ern trend his ability to strike his drives in excess of 300 yards enabled him to over-power the course and set up scoring opportunities.

Nothing exemplified this quality bet-ter than his eagle at his final hole, the 490-yard ninth, which he devoured with a drive and an eight iron before holing a putt of 12 feet.

Although he was to fade from con-

tention over the following three rounds to finish in a tie for 34th, Garcia conducted himself well enough – on and off the course – to keep the fires of expectation burning.

As the low scoring continued beneath the noisy flightpath of the adjacent Barcelona airport he was to be outscored – if not completely overshadowed – by another interesting character in the form

77

THE COURSE

El Prat is an excellent parkland course south of Barcelona, where the repeated interruptions of planes taking off from the nearby international airport are a test of the players concentration. Designed by Spanish architect Javier Arana in 1954 it hosted the 1956 Spanish Open, which was won by Peter Alliss. In calm conditions which the players enjoyed this time it invites low scoring but the pines and palms which line several fairways demand accuracy, particularly from the tee.

of Greg Chalmers. The 24-year-old from Perth, Western Australia, is one of a small minority in tournament golf – a left-hander. Quite why there are so few, who stand on the wrong side of the ball, in the professional ranks remains one of the mysteries of the 20th century.

Chalmer's fellow-countryman Richard Green did prove that lefties can be champions when he upstaged Greg Norman and Ian Woosnam to win a play-off for the 1997 Dubai

Greg Chalmers (left) Robert Allenby (right above), and José Maria Olazábal (right below).

Desert Classic.

Although Chalmers did not win in Barcelona he suggested that he might stick around long enough to prove that seriously talented Antipodean left-handers did not end with Bob Charles, the New Zealander who won the 1963 Open Championship. Apart from creating a good impression as a personable character, Chalmers, a graduate of the European Challenge Tour, featured from the start to the bitter end of the event.

He was still sharing the lead, with compatriot Robert Allenby, after the second round when the halfway cut, at a demanding four under par, sent such luminaries as Bernhard Langer, Costantino Rocca, Padraig Harrington and David Gilford heading for the early flight home. By the end of the third round Chalmers had the chance to draw away from his challengers, only to drive into the woods on the 18th hole, take a double-bogey six and see his three-shot lead cut to only one.

The final round seemed to be set up perfectly for Olazábal to win his national title for the first time. He wanted it badly and had pulled himself into contention with a thrilling third round of 64, even though he admitted he had not hit the ball to his own satisfaction. Nonetheless, as he began his final round on Sunday urged on by a large Spanish gallery, Olazábal was a threatening presence two shots off the lead.

Yet nobody had told his playing companion Björn how the story was supposed to end. While Olazábal played well

The timing and execution of Thomas Björn's chip at the 435-yard par four 16th on the final day could not have ben better. At that moment he was tied with José Maria Olazábal and Australian Greg Chalmers for the lead. Olazábal was in pole position, having struck an immaculate approach shot to within ten feet of the hole. But Björn chipped out of light rough, slightly downhill into the hole for his birdie, putting the pressure on the Spaniard, who left his putt short. And in those moments the title was decided.

enough to win on most occasions with a five-under par 67, Björn played even better. The Dane who proved his merit in the Ryder Cup had taken a five-week break from golf to sort out his personal life. On his return he reckoned he was swinging the club as well as he had ever done in his career. Like a racing thoroughbred he timed his late burst to the finishing line to perfection. For two-thirds of the day he did not look the likely winner until birdies at two of the most difficult holes, the 14th and 16th, took him into the lead from where he could not be caught. The turning point was the 435-yard par four 16th where Björn, after missing the green on the right, chipped in from 20 feet for birdie. Olazábal subsequently left his ten-feet birdie putt short and could not recover.

To Björn went the spoils of victory. But for many others, Chalmers, Garcia and even Olazábal, it was a week of encouraging achievement.

Peter Higgs   79

El Prat, Barcelona, Spain, April 23-26, 1998 • Yardage 6639 • Par 72

Pos	Name	Country	Rnd 1	Rnd 2	Rnd 3	Rnd 4	Total	Prize Money £
1	Thomas BJÖRN	(Den)	68	67	66	66	267	91660
2	Greg CHALMERS	(Aus)	64	66	69	69	268	47765
	José Maria OLAZÁBAL	(Sp)	66	71	64	67	268	47765
4	Eduardo ROMERO	(Arg)	66	67	70	67	270	25400
	Mark JAMES	(Eng)	68	66	70	66	270	25400
6	Roger WESSELS	(SA)	71	69	66	65	271	19250
7	Stephen ALLAN	(Aus)	66	72	69	65	272	14176
	Mathias GRÖNBERG	(Swe)	69	67	71	65	272	14176
	Katsuyoshi TOMORI	(Jpn)	67	67	66	72	272	14176
10	Phillip PRICE	(Wal)	67	66	71	69	273	11000
11	David HOWELL	(Eng)	65	68	67	74	274	8223
	Olle KARLSSON	(Swe)	70	70	67	67	274	8223
	Angel CABRERA	(Arg)	67	70	69	68	274	8223
	Gordon BRAND JNR.	(Scot)	67	66	73	68	274	8223
	Roger CHAPMAN	(Eng)	68	71	66	69	274	8223
	Andrew COLTART	(Scot)	69	70	68	67	274	8223
	Miguel Angel MARTIN	(Sp)	69	70	70	65	274	8223
	Eamonn DARCY	(Ire)	68	71	65	70	274	8223
	Robert ALLENBY	(Aus)	66	64	70	74	274	8223
20	Miles TUNNICLIFF	(Eng)	67	69	69	70	275	6187
	Daniel CHOPRA	(Swe)	66	72	70	67	275	6187
	Sam TORRANCE	(Scot)	70	69	65	71	275	6187
	Ivo GINER	(Sp)	67	70	67	71	275	6187
	Paul LAWRIE	(Scot)	68	66	73	68	275	6187
	Jay TOWNSEND	(USA)	64	69	70	72	275	6187
26	David CARTER	(Eng)	68	69	66	73	276	5039
	Malcolm MACKENZIE	(Eng)	69	67	74	66	276	5039
	Domingo HOSPITAL	(Sp)	67	68	72	69	276	5039
	Robert KARLSSON	(Swe)	72	67	73	64	276	5039
	Peter HEDBLOM	(Swe)	69	67	74	66	276	5039
	Patrik SJÖLAND	(Swe)	66	71	69	70	276	5039
	Miguel Angel JIMÉNEZ	(Sp)	67	67	69	73	276	5039
	Craig HAINLINE	(USA)	68	71	67	70	276	5039
34	Wayne RILEY	(Aus)	73	67	70	67	277	4180
	Ian WOOSNAM	(Wal)	69	70	72	66	277	4180
	Peter MITCHELL	(Eng)	69	71	71	66	277	4180
	Paul EALES	(Eng)	68	72	71	66	277	4180
	Mark ROE	(Eng)	69	67	68	73	277	4180
	Sergio GARCIA (AM)	(Sp)	66	70	70	71	277	
39	Klas ERIKSSON	(Swe)	69	71	66	72	278	3630
	Ignacio GARRIDO	(Sp)	70	66	72	70	278	3630
	Iain PYMAN	(Eng)	71	68	72	67	278	3630
	Santiago LUNA	(Sp)	68	67	71	72	278	3630
	José RIVERO	(Sp)	71	69	69	69	278	3630
44	Marc FARRY	(Fr)	69	68	69	73	279	2970
	Paul BROADHURST	(Eng)	72	67	70	70	279	2970
	Joakim HAEGGMAN	(Swe)	69	70	70	70	279	2970
	José COCERES	(Arg)	70	68	69	72	279	2970
	Thomas LEVET	(Fr)	68	71	69	71	279	2970
	Stephen LEANEY	(Aus)	70	69	71	69	279	2970
	Van PHILLIPS	(Eng)	69	71	69	70	279	2970
51	Jeff REMESY	(Fr)	68	69	73	70	280	2010
	Dennis EDLUND	(Swe)	69	70	70	71	280	2010
	Silvio GRAPPASONNI	(It)	70	66	72	72	280	2010
	Mark MOULAND	(Wal)	72	65	71	72	280	2010
	Jose Manuel LARA	(Sp)	69	71	67	73	280	2010
	Kalle BRINK	(Swe)	67	73	71	69	280	2010
	Seve BALLESTEROS	(Sp)	69	71	71	69	280	2010
	Ian GARBUTT	(Eng)	67	71	71	71	280	2010
	Ruben GONZALEZ	(Sp)	71	68	69	72	280	2010
	Francisco CEA	(Sp)	70	69	69	72	280	2010
	José Manuel CARRILES	(Sp)	64	70	74	72	280	2010
62	Bradley DREDGE	(Wal)	69	68	76	68	281	1512
	Jean VAN DE VELDE	(Fr)	65	69	72	75	281	1512
64	Jarmo SANDELIN	(Swe)	68	71	67	76	282	1210
	Jonathan LOMAS	(Eng)	68	70	70	74	282	1210
	Clinton WHITELAW	(SA)	68	68	71	75	282	1210
67	Des SMYTH	(Ire)	69	69	72	73	283	823
68	Gary ORR	(Scot)	71	69	73	71	284	821
69	Brian DAVIS	(Eng)	69	71	74	71	285	817
	Peter BAKER	(Eng)	69	71	70	75	285	817
	Jim PAYNE	(Eng)	70	69	72	74	285	817
72	Fernando ROCA	(Sp)	71	68	69	80	288	813

Eduardo Romero shared fourth place.

HEREDEROS DEL
MARQUES DE RISCAL

*V*inos de los *H*erederos del *M*arqués de *R*iscal, S.A.

Elciego
01340 Álava

Oficina Comercial:
Juan Ramón Jiménez, 8
28036 Madrid
Tlf: (91) 345 28 67
Fax: (91) 345 45 82

It's Patrik's day in May

Patrik Sjöland claimed his
first European Tour title
in convincing fashion

José Maria Olazábal made it perfectly clear at the Peugeot Open de España that he is not a fan of finishing second in golf tournaments. But even the major championship winners do not get their own way on the European Tour, the pool of talent is too deep for that.

While Olazábal was upset at losing in Barcelona to Denmark's Thomas Björn at the Italian Open another Sandinavian, Patrik Sjöland, never gave the Spaniard the chance to lose the tournament.

Despite a determined last round charge by Olazábal, who closed with a 65, and an even stronger one from his own countryman, Joakim Haeggman, who shot a 63, Sjöland was never deterred from winning his maiden title at Castelconturbia. Even Björn, continuing his fine form, was unable to make an impression and fell from second with a round to go to fourth place. Sjöland started the last 18 holes – the tournament was reduced to 54 holes due to heavy rain earlier in the week – with a three-stroke lead, never saw it diminish to less than two, and eventually won by three from Olazábal and Haeggman at 195, 21 under par.

Olazábal had seen this coming. The Spaniard was Sjöland's playing companion for the first two rounds. Despite sitting around in the clubhouse for virtually all of Thursday and more than half of Friday watching first the rain fall and then the noble efforts of the greenkeeping staff to get the course playable. Sjöland opened with a 64. Then he added a 65 in a round which began on Saturday evening and completed on Sunday morning.

It was a performance combining high-class talent and extreme patience and maturity. Olazábal knew what he had seen. 'I turned to my manager, Sergio Gomez, and said that if he kept playing the same way, his first win would come very soon.' Olazábal added later: 'It was quicker than I thought.' Olazábal opened up his last round with three birdies in a row, while Haeggman came home in 29. Sjöland was never fazed as he compiled his 66. It contained not one dropped shot. In fact, the 26-year-old only made one bogey in 54 holes, at the 15th hole in

SHOT OF THE WEEK

Klas Eriksson holed-in-one with a wedge at the short fourth hole in the first round, moments after Martin Gates had achieved the same feat in the previous group. 'We had to wait for several moments as the cup was repaired, 'Eriksson, who had scored one ace already in the season said. 'There was a TV cameraman there who said he had missed Martin's hole-in-one – and then he missed mine as well!'

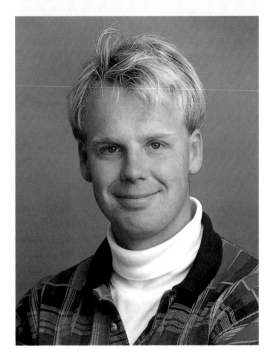

THE COURSE

Nestling into the foothills of the Alps, the Castelconturbia course is regarded as one of Robert Trent Jones Senior's finest pieces of work. And rightly so. The course had staged the Italian Open seven years previously, but was not helped by torrential rain. When play was finally possible, four tees had to be moved forward, shaving 234 yards off the 6,826-yard layout, including 135 yards at the par five eighth. The hole gave up 221 birdies and 70 eagles helping to make for spectacular scoring.

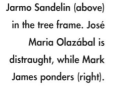

Jarmo Sandelin (above) in the tree frame. José Maria Olazábal is distraught, while Mark James ponders (right).

the first round. It was at the same hole in the final round that he claimed his fourth two and clinched his victory.

'This is definitely the best I have hit the ball in my life,' Sjöland, who hardly missed a fairway or green in the tournament, said. 'Today I was nine out of ten, but for the first two rounds I was 11 out of ten.'

Sjöland was helped by a tip from his follow countryman and Tour player Ola Eliasson, who noticed he was slightly too closed at impact earlier in the week. 'We have been friends for ten years and he knows my game,' Sjöland said.

His other inspiration was his girl-friend, Ulrika, who has taken to caddieing for him this season. 'It is great to have her around because it is so hard to be away for long spells,' he said.

'She does not play golf but helps me mentally. She helps me focus on shots and then we talk about other things in-between.'

Sjöland, now based in Marbella, was involved in a serious car crash six years ago on icy roads in Sweden when he was taking his sister to an indoor driving range. 'The car rolled over and I went out of the sun-roof, even though it was not open at the time,' Sjöland said. He spent a

month in hospital and had his spleen removed.

Trying to win his maiden title was not easy either. Two years before, he bogeyed the final hole at Bergamo to lose the Italian Open to Jim Payne. Earlier in the same year, he faced a birdie putt on the final green which could have given him victory in the Madiera Island Open. But the final hole pin placement was exeptionally demanding. While players three and four-putted, Sjöland was the only one to five-putt.

But the number of times he has appeared in the top ten of tournaments suggested he was near a maiden victory. Already in the 1998 season he had finished third in the Alfred Dunhill South African PGA Championship and second in the Qatar Masters to Andrew Coltart.

'After finishing second two years ago, this means an awful lot, 'Sjöland said. 'I knew I had to make some birdies because Olazábal got off to a good start, too.'

Which just left Olazábal as the runner-up again. 'This was different to last week. I was never really close enough, although I thought if I could get within a shot of him I might have a chance,' he said.

Andrew Farrell

Castelconturbia, Milan, April 30-May 3, 1998 · Yardage 6820 · Par 72

Pos	Name	Country	Rnd 1	Rnd 2	Rnd 3	Rnd 4	Total	Prize Money £
1	Patrik SJÖLAND	(Swe)	64	65	66		195	81853
2	José Maria OLAZÁBAL	(Sp)	68	65	65		198	42655
	Joakim HAEGGMAN	(Swe)	67	68	63		198	42655
4	Thomas BJÖRN	(Den)	66	66	68		200	24557
5	Peter BAKER	(Eng)	67	67	67		201	20824
6	Steen TINNING	(Den)	68	65	69		202	13788
	Lee WESTWOOD	(Eng)	68	67	67		202	13788
	Sven STRÜVER	(Ger)	67	69	66		202	13788
	Bob MAY	(USA)	69	68	65		202	13788
10	Mark JAMES	(Eng)	65	69	69		203	9095
	David LYNN	(Eng)	71	65	67		203	9095
	Jean VAN DE VELDE	(Fr)	67	70	66		203	9095
13	Phillip PRICE	(Wal)	68	67	69		204	7237
	Paul MCGINLEY	(Ire)	63	72	69		204	7237
	Retief GOOSEN	(SA)	70	67	67		204	7237
	Greg TURNER	(NZ)	66	71	67		204	7237
	Jarmo SANDELIN	(Swe)	68	70	66		204	7237
18	Gordon BRAND JNR.	(Scot)	70	66	69		205	5932
	Paul BROADHURST	(Eng)	68	68	69		205	5932
	Jay TOWNSEND	(USA)	71	66	68		205	5932
	Robert KARLSSON	(Swe)	67	70	68		205	5932
	Andrew CLAPP	(Eng)	72	67	66		205	5932
23	Silvio GRAPPASONNI	(It)	68	68	70		206	4935
	Emanuele CANONICA	(It)	69	67	70		206	4935
	Massimo FLORIOLI	(It)	67	70	69		206	4935
	Michael CAMPBELL	(NZ)	68	69	69		206	4935
	Andrew COLTART	(Scot)	70	68	68		206	4935
	Thomas LEVET	(Fr)	69	69	68		206	4935
	Robert ALLENBY	(Aus)	68	71	67		206	4935
	Roger CHAPMAN	(Eng)	69	70	67		206	4935
31	Marc FARRY	(Fr)	68	67	72		207	3687
	Klas ERIKSSON	(Swe)	66	70	71		207	3687
	Pierre FULKE	(Swe)	67	70	70		207	3687
	Wayne WESTNER	(SA)	69	68	70		207	3687
	Fredrik HENGE	(Swe)	68	69	70		207	3687
	Costantino ROCCA	(It)	69	69	69		207	3687
	Ignacio GARRIDO	(Sp)	69	69	69		207	3687
	Steve WEBSTER	(Eng)	72	66	69		207	3687
	Stephen LEANEY	(Aus)	68	71	68		207	3687
	Miguel Angel MARTIN	(Sp)	72	68	67		207	3687
	Paolo QUIRICI	(Swi)	74	66	67		207	3687
	Rolf MUNTZ	(Hol)	69	71	67		207	3687
43	Mathias GRÖNBERG	(Swe)	70	67	71		208	2897
	Padraig HARRINGTON	(Ire)	70	69	69		208	2897
	Nicolas VANHOOTEGEM	(Bel)	71	68	69		208	2897
	Michael JONZON	(Swe)	74	66	68		208	2897
47	Robert COLES	(Eng)	71	65	73		209	2504
	Eamonn DARCY	(Ire)	68	70	71		209	2504
	Gary EVANS	(Eng)	69	71	69		209	2504
	Anssi KANKKONEN	(Fin)	70	70	69		209	2504
51	Darren CLARKE	(N.Ire)	65	71	74		210	1871
	Martin GATES	(Eng)	70	68	72		210	1871
	David CARTER	(Eng)	68	70	72		210	1871
	Chris VAN DER VELDE	(Hol)	73	66	71		210	1871
	Eduardo ROMERO	(Arg)	72	67	71		210	1871
	Rodger DAVIS	(Aus)	70	70	70		210	1871
	Dennis EDLUND	(Swe)	70	70	70		210	1871
	Michael LONG	(NZ)	70	70	70		210	1871
	Dean ROBERTSON	(Scot)	70	70	70		210	1871
60	David GILFORD	(Eng)	69	68	74		211	1375
	Stephen ALLAN	(Aus)	69	70	72		211	1375
	Angel CABRERA	(Arg)	73	67	71		211	1375
	Steven RICHARDSON	(Eng)	72	68	71		211	1375
	Jamie SPENCE	(Eng)	68	72	71		211	1375
65	Thomas GÖGELE	(Ger)	71	67	74		212	1227
66	Raymond BURNS	(N.Ire)	71	66	76		213	735
	Van PHILLIPS	(Eng)	70	69	74		213	735
	Raphaël JACQUELIN	(Fr)	72	67	74		213	735
69	Ronan RAFFERTY	(N.Ire)	67	72	76		215	729
	Federico BISAZZA	(It)	71	69	75		215	729
	Malcolm MACKENZIE	(Eng)	73	67	75		215	729
72	Scott HENDERSON	(Scot)	69	69	78		216	725

Thomas Björn

World class turf care.

We have the edge.

Over 200 years experience in developing and manufacturing grass cutting equipment is undoubtedly a key factor in Ransomes' worldwide success.

Ransomes has continued to identify customers ongoing needs and respond with continuous improvement, vision and innovation to stay ahead of the competition. Which is why the current range offers unbeatable features, toughness and value for money.

But delivering the equipment is only the first part of our service. We have also worked extremely hard in developing a Textron worldwide dealer network which offers support right through to after sales.

There is one more thing that experience has taught us at Ransomes. Our passion and commitment to serve our customers at all times and at all levels is what differentiates us from the competition.

For a free demonstration or the name of your nearest dealer call freephone **0500 026208** for details.

Ransomes and E-Z-GO are Official Suppliers to the PGA European Tour.

RANSOMES TEXTRON TURF CARE AND SPECIALTY PRODUCTS

RANSOMES JACOBSEN LTD., RANSOMES WAY, IPSWICH, ENGLAND IP3 9QG
TEL: (01473) 270000 FAX: (01473) 276300

Jiménez hits the £2 million mark

Victory in Majorca took Miguel Angel Jiménez's

career earnings to a new milestone

Miguel Angel Jiménez ignored a troublesome kidney stone complaint, and the excitement of the lead changes over the final day's play, to clinch the Turespana Masters Open Baleares, in Majorca.

Europe's Johnnie Walker Ryder Cup vice-captain recorded his third professional Tour win in 16 years, carding a final even par round 72 around the Santa Ponsa course for a two-shot victory over compatriot Miguel Angel Martin.

Jiménez described his win as 'magical', coming six days after news that his wife, Monserrat, had learnt that the couple are expecting their second child. 'I have been waiting a long time to win again,' said Jiménez who became the 24th European

THE COURSE

For the professionals, Santa Ponsa at 7,155 yards, is a long course, well-protected by bunkers and a number of strategically placed water hazards on some holes. The closeness of the course to the ocean means, too, that sea-breezes will often dictate scoring trends. Santa Ponsa features a number of uphill and downhill dog-leg holes, plus a monster par five, the tenth, that measures a whopping 645 yards, one of the longest on the European Tour. The course is laid out over 700,000 square metres of a natural amphitheatre, and is the finishing touch to a large number of sports that tourists and residents alike can enjoy in the Santa Ponsa area. Santa Ponsa staged its first major international event with the running of the 1992 Turespana Open Baleares won by Severiano Ballesteros. The course was designed by Folco Nardi, designer of many Spanish courses, though there has been some slight modifications since it was opened in March 1977.

Tour player to top the £2 million mark in prize-money. 'This has been a magic victory because of the what has surrounded me this week, so much so that I feel that I have seven or eight new white hairs in my head.' Martin, who shared the opening round lead, could only muster a 72 on the last day to eventually finish two

Seve Ballesteros (left) in aquatic recovery at the second. Paul McGinley (right above), and Anders Forsbrand (right).

strokes behind Jiménez.

The 26-year-old Madrid born player looked a likely winner when he eagled the 492 yard, sixth hole but a two over par back nine effort undid his chance for tournament win number three.

Irishman Paul McGinley came awfully close to sinking the 'Spanish Armada', claiming his best result of the season with a superb third place finish.

McGinley, with a six under par total, tied in third place with Japan's Katsuyoshi Tomori, who recorded his best-ever finish in the 16 months he's been competing full-time on the European Tour.

From the outset, Spanish golfers virtually turned the event into a local affair, pinning-up the 'Private Party' sign early in the tournament when Martin and Santiago Luna grabbed the first round lead with five under par 67s. Martin in particular showed no ill-effects of missing the tournament's official pro-am, after local Majorcan doctors took a series of blood tests and x-rays to reveal he too had a kidney stone. He was advised to relax, take a hot bath, drink lots of water, and prescribed a herbal drink that Martin described as tasting 'awful'.

A Scotsman, an Englishman, an Italian and an Australian were one shot back but four other Spaniards, Jiménez, José Rivero, Ivo Giner and the amateur Raul Quiros, were only two shots off the lead.

At the halfway stage, it remained an all-Spanish affair at the top of the leader board with Luna and Jiménez tied at seven under par and Martin and Rivero at five under.

Jiménez's kidney stone complaint

SHOT OF THE WEEK

It seemed inevitable with ten lead changes over the last round that it would always be one remarkable shot that would separate the ultimate victor from those nine other golfers looking to win. Jiménez, who'd gone bogey-birdie on three occasions over the first 15 holes of the final day had just bogeyed the par four 16th to lead by just one shot with two to play. But disaster looked to be looming for the Spaniard when his pulled his drive left off the 350 yard par four penultimate tee. The ball cannoned off a tree and came to rest between two clumps of bushes some 120-yards from the green. His next shot would be crucial. To protect his leading cushion, Jiménez now needed to place the ball in exactly the right position to attack the pin which he did in dazzling fashion. He courageously threaded his sand-wedge shot between the bushes and breathed a big sigh of relief when the ball pulled-up six feet from the flagstick. Jiménez then holed out for a birdie and a two-shot lead with one to play.

flared early in round three. He started feeling pain on the third hole and by the sixth he was forced to swallow two pain-killing tablets. But the pills had no effect and by the ninth, a doctor was called. The doctor gave Jiménez a pain-killing injection on the 11th tee which seemed to do the trick as the Spaniard was in no pain when he walked off the last delighted to be enjoying a two shot leading cushion, at nine under par, over Martin and Luna.

Luna's Turespana challenge peaked when he grabbed a share of the lead, at ten under par, after 11 holes of the second round. But the long-time Tour campaigner lost concentration over the remaining seven holes, dropping three shots. A disappointing four-over par, last round 76, sent Luna into a share of sixth place.

McGinley looked set to snatch an improbable victory from the under the nose of the leading Spanish players when he holed birdies at Santa Ponsa's 11th and 13th holes, though in a repeat of the scenario of earlier rounds, McGinley took bogeys over the handful of final holes to ruin what chance he had of victory.

But looking at the bigger picture, McGinley could feel pleased that he was getting back to 100% fitness after suffering a rib cartilage injury in February whilst playing in Malaysia.

A five-hour post-second round putting session paid dividends for long-sleeved Englishman Van Phillips, who finished in fifth place.

Bernie McGuire

Santa Ponsa I, Mallorca, May 7-10, 1998 · Yardage 7155 · Par 72

Pos	Name	Country	Rnd 1	Rnd 2	Rnd 3	Rnd 4	Total	Prize Money £
1	Miguel Angel JIMÉNEZ	(Sp)	69	68	70	72	279	58330
2	Miguel Angel MARTIN	(Sp)	67	72	70	72	281	38880
3	Paul MCGINLEY	(Ire)	71	73	67	71	282	19705
	Katsuyoshi TOMORI	(Jpn)	74	67	73	68	282	19705
5	Van PHILLIPS	(Eng)	75	69	67	73	284	14830
6	Michael LONG	(NZ)	71	71	72	71	285	11375
	Santiago LUNA	(Sp)	67	70	72	76	285	11375
8	Paul BROADHURST	(Eng)	71	72	69	76	288	7502
	Massimo FLORIOLI	(It)	72	70	72	74	288	7502
	Angel CABRERA	(Arg)	71	69	73	75	288	7502
	Michele REALE	(It)	68	72	70	78	288	7502
12	Andrew BEAL	(Eng)	72	73	70	74	289	5666
	Andrew SANDYWELL	(Eng)	70	74	73	72	289	5666
	Richard JOHNSON	(Wal)	71	72	72	74	289	5666
15	Alberto BINAGHI	(It)	72	76	68	74	290	4827
	Greig HUTCHEON	(Scot)	70	76	70	74	290	4827
	David HOWELL	(Eng)	72	72	72	74	290	4827
	Diego BORREGO	(Sp)	70	73	74	73	290	4827
19	Francisco CEA	(Sp)	73	75	66	77	291	4156
	Michael CAMPBELL	(NZ)	74	72	73	72	291	4156
	Malcolm MACKENZIE	(Eng)	72	71	73	75	291	4156
	John BICKERTON	(Eng)	70	72	73	76	291	4156
23	Roger WESSELS	(SA)	73	75	77	67	292	3727
	Peter MITCHELL	(Eng)	72	74	72	74	292	3727
	Anders HANSEN	(Den)	73	71	73	75	292	3727
	Anthony WALL	(Eng)	70	72	76	74	292	3727
27	John MELLOR	(Eng)	72	75	72	74	293	3155
	Raphaël JACQUELIN	(Fr)	71	75	74	73	293	3155
	Pedro LINHART	(Sp)	72	73	73	75	293	3155
	Daren LEE	(Eng)	70	75	73	75	293	3155
	Stephen BENNETT	(Eng)	70	74	75	74	293	3155
	Andrew CLAPP	(Eng)	72	71	74	76	293	3155
	José RIVERO	(Sp)	69	70	78	76	293	3155
	Sergio GARCIA (AM)	(Sp)	70	75	76	72	293	
34	Robert LEE	(Eng)	71	75	76	72	294	2520
	Mathew GOGGIN	(Aus)	73	73	77	71	294	2520
	Anders FORSBRAND	(Swe)	72	74	72	76	294	2520
	Tom GILLIS	(USA)	76	72	74	72	294	2520
	Greg OWEN	(Eng)	77	71	72	74	294	2520
	Ross DRUMMOND	(Scot)	75	73	71	75	294	2520
	Marc PENDARIES	(Fr)	72	74	74	74	294	2520
	John HAWKSWORTH	(Eng)	68	78	76	72	294	2520
	Bernhard LANGER	(Ger)	72	73	74	75	294	2520
43	Heinz Peter THÜL	(Ger)	73	73	71	78	295	2100
	Jeev Milkha SINGH	(Ind)	72	75	74	74	295	2100
	Emanuele CANONICA	(It)	77	70	72	76	295	2100
46	Marco GORTANA	(It)	74	72	74	76	296	1750
	Francisco VALERA	(Sp)	75	72	75	74	296	1750
	Stuart CAGE	(Eng)	73	74	75	74	296	1750
	Domingo HOSPITAL	(Sp)	72	75	74	75	296	1750
	Matthew BLACKEY	(Eng)	76	72	74	74	296	1750
	Paul CURRY	(Eng)	74	74	72	76	296	1750
	John WADE	(Aus)	68	75	73	80	296	1750
53	Ivo GINER	(Sp)	69	77	77	74	297	1295
	Fernando ROCA	(Sp)	72	75	75	75	297	1295
	Birgir HAFTHORSSON	(Ice)	72	75	71	79	297	1295
	Robert Jan DERKSEN	(Hol)	72	76	72	77	297	1295
	Brian DAVIS	(Eng)	71	75	75	76	297	1295
	Yago BEAMONTE	(Sp)	74	72	77	74	297	1295
59	Neal BRIGGS	(Eng)	74	74	76	74	298	1085
60	Stephen SCAHILL	(NZ)	73	74	75	77	299	980
	Ola ELIASSON	(Swe)	72	75	78	74	299	980
	Alvaro SALTO	(Sp)	73	74	73	79	299	980
	Olivier EDMOND	(Fr)	74	74	70	81	299	980
	Andrew MCKENNA	(Scot)	68	78	72	81	299	980
	Raul QUIROS (AM)	(Sp)	69	76	77	77	299	
65	Gary NICKLAUS	(USA)	76	71	76	77	300	611
	Dennis EDLUND	(Swe)	74	74	74	78	300	611
	Søren KJELDSEN	(Den)	73	75	76	76	300	611
	Bernardo SOLANES	(Sp)	75	73	77	75	300	611
69	Jon ROBSON	(Eng)	72	75	77	77	301	517
	Francisco DE PABLO	(Sp)	75	72	76	78	301	517
	Daniel WESTERMARK	(Swe)	73	75	79	74	301	517
72	Paul STREETER	(Eng)	73	74	79	76	302	512
	Ruben GONZALEZ	(Sp)	75	73	78	76	302	512
74	Mark DAVIS	(Eng)	73	75	82	73	303	509
75	Steven RICHARDSON	(Eng)	74	74	76	81	305	507
76	Mark MOULAND	(Wal)	74	71	77	85	307	505

Michael Campbell sparkled in the second round.

The sun shines on Clarke

The rain departed from The Oxfordshire

and left Darren Clarke bathed

in the glow of victory

*B*enson and Hedges can be forgiven for believing their event could not have had worse weather over the years had Michael Fish been the Tournament Director. Fish, Suzanne Charlton and Ian McCaskill would have had to trawl deep through the meteorological archives to discover why this idyllic piece of Oxfordshire countryside close to Thame can experience all four seasons in one round. Imagine the relief of Benson and Hedges's Director Jim Elkins when this year's Pro-Am was played under skies more associated with the Costa del Sol. 'What's all this about writing that if it's the Benson and Hedges it must be time for bad weather,' chided a smiling Elkins. 'Just you wait,' was the reply. Sure enough – cometh the tournament, cometh the rain. And when it rains at The Oxfordshire, it does not pour with birdies and eagles, but cats and dogs. If any sponsor on the European Tour – and Benson and Hedges have been around longer than any other – deserves four days of sun, it is the tobacco giants.

But if you cannot get four then three

will do and that's what came their way to everybody's surprise and relief. The first day clouds were chased away by a comparative heat wave... and the smile on Darren Clarke's face. The Ulsterman had had to deal with a few storms of his own over the previous 18 months since he last won a tournament. It is never easy when results do not live up to achievements and Clarke was not the first golfer on earth to wonder if he was the unluckiest to have ever swung a club.

Whatever was attacking Clarke's confidence, it was nothing compared to the pressure heading his way from close friend Lee Westwood. The Worksop 25-year-old was fast emerging as the leader of the new breed – those quickly aligning themselves alongside Colin Montgomerie and José Maria Olazábal and elbowing the Famous Five, Nick Faldo, Severiano Ballesteros, Sandy Lyle, Bernhard Langer and Ian Woosnam into the margins of European golf for the first time.

Clarke had been spurred by Westwood's amazing achievements. He did not want to be left behind. And so it was a different personality to the unsure and highly self-critical one which arrived to tackle course designer Rees Jones's magnificent creation. A short session with American sports psychologist Bob Rotella plus a top ten finish in only his first visit to the US Masters finally convinced Clarke that he was capable of achieving his goals. Clarke could see clearly now the rain had gone, not to mention the fog from a suspicious mind.

Others would enjoy the early

95

spotlight while Clarke waited in the fringe. Scots Dean Robertson and Paul Lawrie, Swede Patrik Sjöland and England's Gary Evans signalled their intentions with first-round 67's spread over two days. None would stay the course over four intense and enthralling days of competition.

Clarke's 70–69 start did not announce him as a serious contender, but he was content. Others were punching more impressive numbers. None more so than Barry Lane, back in the media limelight he had been long gone from. A 66 for a nine under-par halfway aggregate would set experienced observers wondering if Lane was back in the form which made him a Ryder Cup player. For Lane it

SHOT OF THE WEEK

Put a wedge in a professional's hands from the middle of the fairway 110 yards out and he would comfortably hit nine out of ten to within 20 feet of the target. This was where Darren Clarke found himself on the 16th during the last round trying to protect a small lead. Given the day, the circumstances and the fact that Clarke had not won for 18 months, to put it to one foot of the pin was a magnificent shot which won him the title.

would prove to be a short trip down Memory Lane. The weekend would not prove kindly although a top 20 finish was more like the old self.

Others would make their bids for attention and the spotlight started to shine so strongly on Clarke he could have done with sunglasses. If tournaments do not start properly until the back nine on last-day afternoon, Clarke posted his entry form to join the decision makers with a third-round 67. Clarke's best of the day would ensure not only the lead, but also a last-day pairing with his close friend Colin Montgomerie. Few opponents, if any, come more intimidating. Montgomerie, whom Clarke would graciously record afterwards, had always been available to him for advice and help, was expected to be the dominating force. After the first nine holes of the last round, Clarke had

Santiago Luna captured runner-up spot for the largest prize of his career.

The Oxfordshire: created by one of the world's great designers, this Rees Jones course is one of his best. It nestles in some prime areas of Oxfordshire and offers not only an outstanding test, but marvellous views. Professionals enjoy the courses where every club is needed and this is true of The Oxfordshire. But the most important weapon in the artillery needed to negotiate the undulations of both fairways and greens is imagination.

Massimo Florioli (left) enjoyed the week.
Robert Allenby (right) watches a pitch darkly.

reduced the record breaking, five-time European Number One to a supporting role. Indeed, there would be neither opportunity nor mercy for anybody.

There have been bigger winning margins than the three strokes he enjoyed over Spain's Santiago Luna, but for most of a sunny Sunday, Clarke could have been recruited to the force of Elliot Ness. The 29-year-old was simply untouchable. Others made contributions. Massimo Florioli showed what inspiration he has gained from Italian compatriot Costantino Rocca by finishing joint third and 17-year-old amateur Justin Rose, from Hampshire, proved what an addition to the European Tour he is going to be when he turns professional.

But this was Clarke's day and the one which could ultimately prove to be the one when he finally broke through the clouds of self-doubt to spread sunlight on his career – and on the Benson and Hedges International Open.

Martin Hardy

The Oxfordshire GC, May 14-17, 1998 · Yardage 7205 · Par 72

Pos	Name	Country	Rnd 1	Rnd 2	Rnd 3	Rnd 4	Total	Prize Money £
1	Darren CLARKE	(N.Ire)	70	69	67	67	273	125000
2	Santiago LUNA	(Sp)	69	71	69	67	276	83320
3	Thomas BJÖRN	(Den)	68	74	68	67	277	42220
	Massimo FLORIOLI	(It)	68	67	71	71	277	42220
5	Retief GOOSEN	(SA)	71	68	71	68	278	29010
	Colin MONTGOMERIE	(Scot)	69	68	69	72	278	29010
7	Rodger DAVIS	(Aus)	70	70	70	69	279	18247
	Mark MOULAND	(Wal)	70	70	70	69	279	18247
	Greg TURNER	(NZ)	72	67	69	71	279	18247
	Patrik SJÖLAND	(Swe)	67	72	68	72	279	18247
11	José Maria OLAZÁBAL	(Sp)	72	70	70	68	280	12560
	Paul LAWRIE	(Scot)	67	73	70	70	280	12560
	Brian DAVIS	(Eng)	69	70	72	69	280	12560
	Gary EVANS	(Eng)	67	71	69	73	280	12560
15	Bob MAY	(USA)	71	67	71	72	281	10571
	Per HAUGSRUD	(Nor)	69	68	71	73	281	10571
	Phillip PRICE	(Wal)	69	67	73	72	281	10571
18	Peter MITCHELL	(Eng)	74	68	69	71	282	8937
	Russell CLAYDON	(Eng)	69	73	67	73	282	8937
	Andrew SHERBORNE	(Eng)	69	75	70	68	282	8937
	Ian WOOSNAM	(Wal)	71	70	70	71	282	8937
	Stuart CAGE	(Eng)	69	71	71	71	282	8937
	Barry LANE	(Eng)	69	66	75	72	282	8937
24	Paul MCGINLEY	(Ire)	69	73	73	68	283	7200
	David CARTER	(Eng)	69	73	68	73	283	7200
	Pierre FULKE	(Swe)	71	72	70	70	283	7200
	Gordon BRAND JNR.	(Scot)	70	71	69	73	283	7200
	Søren KJELDSEN	(Den)	70	71	71	71	283	7200
	Paul AFFLECK	(Wal)	68	73	71	71	283	7200
	Robert ALLENBY	(Aus)	71	69	69	74	283	7200
	Scott HENDERSON	(Scot)	69	71	70	73	283	7200
	Peter BAKER	(Eng)	73	66	73	71	283	7200
33	Carl SUNESON	(Sp)	69	73	72	70	284	5850
	Paul CURRY	(Eng)	69	73	68	74	284	5850
	Katsuyoshi TOMORI	(Jpn)	72	70	72	70	284	5850
	Greg OWEN	(Eng)	73	71	72	68	284	5850
	Jamie SPENCE	(Eng)	70	69	70	75	284	5850
38	Jim PAYNE	(Eng)	73	69	70	73	285	5025
	Jonathan LOMAS	(Eng)	70	72	71	72	285	5025
	Peter O'MALLEY	(Aus)	69	73	73	70	285	5025
	Fabrice TARNAUD	(Fr)	71	72	69	73	285	5025
	Mathias GRÖNBERG	(Swe)	70	74	71	70	285	5025
	Bradley DREDGE	(Wal)	68	72	76	69	285	5025
44	Dean ROBERTSON	(Scot)	67	74	71	74	286	4275
	Stephen LEANEY	(Aus)	70	71	71	74	286	4275
	Andrew COLTART	(Scot)	72	69	71	74	286	4275
	Sven STRÜVER	(Ger)	70	71	72	73	286	4275
	Justin ROSE (AM)	(Eng)	72	68	72	74	286	
48	Wayne WESTNER	(SA)	70	72	74	71	287	3675
	David LYNN	(Eng)	69	74	71	73	287	3675
	Greg CHALMERS	(Aus)	71	73	70	73	287	3675
	Dennis EDLUND	(Swe)	74	67	76	70	287	3675
52	David HOWELL	(Eng)	71	71	70	76	288	2850
	Des SMYTH	(Ire)	69	74	73	72	288	2850
	Gary ORR	(Scot)	69	74	73	72	288	2850
	Michael CAMPBELL	(NZ)	72	71	71	74	288	2850
	Mats HALLBERG	(Swe)	69	72	71	76	288	2850
	Stephen BENNETT	(Eng)	73	68	75	72	288	2850
	Robert Jan DERKSEN	(Hol)	71	69	74	74	288	2850
59	Padraig HARRINGTON	(Ire)	70	72	74	73	289	2325
60	Eamonn DARCY	(Ire)	74	70	70	76	290	2250
61	Chris VAN DER VELDE	(Hol)	70	74	75	72	291	2137
	Thomas GÖGELE	(Ger)	73	71	70	77	291	2137
63	Carl WATTS	(Eng)	69	74	76	73	292	1987
	Adam HUNTER	(Scot)	72	72	73	75	292	1987
65	Carl MASON	(Eng)	73	70	73	77	293	1500
	Lee WESTWOOD	(Eng)	71	69	77	76	293	1500
67	Miles TUNNICLIFF	(Eng)	71	73	74	78	296	1123
68	Wayne RILEY	(Aus)	71	72	78	76	297	1121
69	Anders FORSBRAND	(Swe)	76	68	78	85	307	1119

Colin Montgomerie waits for a sign.

Montgomerie's grandstand finish

Vital putts on the last two greens
enabled Colin Montgomerie to capture
the biggest title of his career

Colin Montgomerie is
fairly familiar with
coming to the final hole of
an event with the weight of
expectation resting heavily
on his broad shoulders. Such
is his astonishing consistency
and dogged determination
that it is almost inevitable
that he will be involved in
the denouement.

Pressure, of course, is
relative whether it's the
Guildford Winter Alliance
or the final hole of a major
championship, but it is
doubtful if Montgomerie has
experienced anything more
taxing than last year's Ryder
Cup by Johnnie Walker
when he came to the final
hole at Valderrama in his
singles match with Scott
Hoch knowing that a half
would keep the Cup in
European hands. He did it
with a rock solid tee shot and a secure second shot into the heart of the green. He
had done it before on the same course in
the 1995 Volvo Masters when he needed
to par the last to hold off Sam Torrance

for the Volvo Ranking title.

But gremlins abound in golf and for
all Montgomerie's experience, every final
hole scenario is fraught with dangerous
possibilities.

Such was the case in the Volvo PGA Championship, the European Tour's flagship event with a prize fund of £1,200,000, when Montgomerie came to Wentworth's renowned 18th hole needing a birdie four to avoid going into a play-off. The orthodox way to achieve this is to hit a long, fading drive round the dog-leg and then find the green with a long iron. Indeed, the hole is perfectly set up for Montgomerie's stock fade shot.

This time, however, he slightly over-did the stock shot and the ball plummeted down into a thick clump of rough. From there he could only nudge the ball up the fairway within 105 yards of the green.

As it happened, this was the optimum distance for a hard lob-wedge and Montgomerie duly dispatched the ball to within nine feet of the pin. The putt crept into the hole and the £200,000 first prize was his.

'This is the strongest tournament on the European Tour, only the majors are

There were two candidates for this honour and both were executed by Colin Montgomerie at the vital stage of the Championship. On the 71st hole he faced a putt of nine feet for his par knowing that if he missed he would have to birdie the last hole to get into a play-off. Having passed that test, he then arrived on the 18th green with a putt of similar distance to take the title. That went in as well. Both shots carried equal importance, both were played under extreme pressure and both were successful. What might be termed a split decision.

more important,' said the champion afterwards. 'I am delighted to add this title to my list of European victories.'

In fact, it was Montgomerie's first win at Wentworth. In 1991 he had lost a play-off to Severiano Ballesteros in the same event and in 1994 he had lost in the final of the World Match-Play Championship to Ernie Els.

There was a moment in the preliminary stages when it looked as though Montgomerie would draw another blank over the West course. In the first round he had compiled 26 putts for the first 13 holes and was not full of joie de vivre. He managed to complete the round in 70 but trailed leader Michael Jonzon by four strokes when the Swede picked up six birdies in a pretty flawless display. On 67 came Brian Davis with a host of other players under 70, including the dangerous Els on 69.

Jonzon added a 70 in the second round to retain the lead but taking close order were Australia's Peter Lonard with a 65 and Sweden's Mats Hallberg with a 69. They lay one stroke of Jonzon's pace while Els lurked ominously two behind.

Meanwhile, Montgomerie was in the midst of a crisis. With the cut predicted at one under par, he had driven into the trees on the 15th and had to take a penalty drop. A six would take him to

one over par for the Championship, two beyond the limit. However, he fashioned a marvellous recovery, escaped with a bogey five, and then played the remaining three holes in birdie, birdie, eagle, to post another 70 and lie four shots off the lead.

The morning of the third day was nostalgia before noon. Having made the cut on the mark, Severiano Ballesteros began to turn back the years. An eagle at the fourth was followed by three birdies

Andrew Coltart (above left) in purple haze. (Right from top), third round renaissance from Seve Ballesteros. A score of greens staff, the 3M physio unit, buggies from E-Z Go and the Mizuno unit were all fully utilised during the week.

Things looked up for Seve Ballesteros in the third round (above), while Thomas Björn (right) and Paul McGinley (below) see the funny side

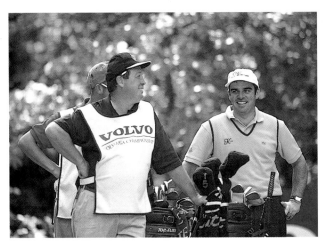

in the next four holes and the news spread like wildfire across the Wentworth environs. By the time he reached the turn in 31, he had a following that took one back to his halcyon days. He did not disappoint them, visiting the trees three times in the last six holes but still effecting those magical recoveries. None more so than at the 18th where, after a pushed drive, he hit his second straight left but then pitched up to five feet for a second consecutive birdie and a scintillating 65. It put him in the clubhouse on 208, eight under par, and the speculation grew as to whether he could win the title. 'Ask me when I've won,' was the Spaniard's response. 'I don't like to sell the skin before I've killed the rabbit.'

The rest of the day belonged to Montgomerie. He matched Ballesteros's 65 to take sole possession of the lead on 205, one stroke ahead of Hallberg and Dean Robertson, who posted a 67, with Els, Gary Orr and David Gilford two strokes off the pace.

The stage was set for a pulsating finish as over 20,000 people swarmed onto the course in anticipation. Would Ballesteros turn back the years, would Els ease his way to the front, would Montgomerie lay the ghosts of Wentworth's past or would one of the new young bloods surge forward? These were the questions, who would provide the answers?

First to show was Orr

E-Z-GO
Consistent high quality driving

E-Z-GO TXT

E-Z-GO WORKHORSE

**Official supplier
of Golf Cars to the
European Tour**

Ransomes Way, Ipswich, England IP3 9QG
Telephone: (01473) 270000 Fax: (01473) 276300

TURF CARE AND SPECIALITY PRODUCTS

Dean Robertson
(right), footloose
from the rough.
Patrick Sjöland
(opposite) finds
that time is on
his side.

who raced to the turn in 31 to take a one shot lead as Montgomerie could only find one birdie in an outward 34. Robertson was right in the thick of it after turning in 33 as was Patrik Sjöland who also turned in 31. Ballesteros could make no inroads on par and Els was emerging as a big threat after turning in 33 and then collaring a birdie at the tenth.

Robertson took the lead when Montgomerie dropped a shot at the 11th and the two Scots shared birdies on the 12th. The 13th was crucial as Robertson holed from 14 feet for a birdie and Montgomerie had to follow him in from nine feet to avoid going two shots behind. The dogged determination came through again and the putt went in. Both three-putted the 14th but then Montgomerie atoned with a wonderful second shot to the 15th for a

THE COURSE

It was a slightly different West course which greeted the players in 1998. The tee at the 11th had been moved back 22 yards, lengthening the hole to 398 yards and the 12th had also received the same treatment, being extended by 27 yards to 510 yards. The fairway bunkers on the 18th had been deepened. Chris Kennedy, Golf Courses Manager at Wentworth, said: 'We have aimed to improve the course to a test of golf which can live up to the challenges coming from modern equipment. The West course is already a difficult test and we want to keep it that way.' That mission was certainly accomplished.

Clockwise: Sandy Lyle for his supporters, Peter Hedblom in Palmeresque finish, José Maria Olazábal and Costantino Rocca couldn't win again. Rivals for the title, Colin Montgomerie and Ernie Els (right).

birdie.

Ahead of them, Orr and Els had both stumbled and although they rallied at the end to finish with 68s and totals of 275, the same as Sjöland, it still looked as though the outcome would be decided from the final pairing.

Robertson was the first to feel the pinch with a hooked drive into the trees on the 16th which resulted in an ugly six. Montgomerie parred and now needed one birdie from the last two holes to win. He struggled down the 17th, not finding the green in three and chipping to around

nine feet in four: once again his resolve was undiminished and the ball was safely holed.

Whether that putt was more crucial than the similar one he holed for victory on the final green is debatable, but he acknowledged the part the Ryder Cup had

played in tempering his approach in such situations. He was also fulsome in his praise of Robertson and paid tribute to Els, twice his nemesis in the US Open. 'I believe Ernie is the best player in the world, so any time you finish ahead of him you've had a good tournament.' said

the new champion.

It was the end of a memorable week at Wentworth: the sun shone, the course was immaculate, the crowds poured in and Colin Montgomerie staged a grandstand finish in a showpiece setting.

Chris Plumridge 109

WENTWORTH CLUB, MAY 22-25, 1998 • YARDAGE 7006 • PAR 72

Pos	Name	Country	Rnd 1	Rnd 2	Rnd 3	Rnd 4	Total	Prize Money £
1	Colin MONTGOMERIE	(Scot)	70	70	65	69	274	200000
2	Patrik SJÖLAND	(Swe)	72	71	66	66	275	89433
	Ernie ELS	(SA)	69	69	69	68	275	89433
	Gary ORR	(Scot)	70	69	68	68	275	89433
5	Dean ROBERTSON	(Scot)	70	69	67	70	276	37160
	Peter LONARD	(Aus)	72	65	71	68	276	37160
	Andrew COLTART	(Scot)	72	66	70	68	276	37160
	Thomas BJÖRN	(Den)	70	69	69	68	276	37160
	Mats HALLBERG	(Swe)	68	69	69	70	276	37160
10	Paul MCGINLEY	(Ire)	72	69	68	68	277	24000
11	Phillip PRICE	(Wal)	71	72	68	67	278	20100
	Gordon BRAND JNR.	(Scot)	71	69	72	66	278	20100
	David GILFORD	(Eng)	70	69	68	71	278	20100
	Padraig HARRINGTON	(Ire)	70	69	69	70	278	20100
15	Costantino ROCCA	(It)	71	70	70	68	279	17600
16	Lee WESTWOOD	(Eng)	71	71	69	69	280	15564
	Sam TORRANCE	(Scot)	70	71	71	68	280	15564
	Stephen LEANEY	(Aus)	69	73	71	67	280	15564
	José Maria OLAZÁBAL	(Sp)	72	71	70	67	280	15564
	Jean VAN DE VELDE	(Fr)	71	71	69	69	280	15564
21	Seve BALLESTEROS	(Sp)	72	71	65	73	281	12780
	Robert KARLSSON	(Swe)	71	71	71	68	281	12780
	Massimo FLORIOLI	(It)	75	68	67	71	281	12780
	David HOWELL	(Eng)	68	71	71	71	281	12780
	Wayne WESTNER	(SA)	73	69	68	71	281	12780
	Per-Ulrik JOHANSSON	(Swe)	70	71	72	68	281	12780
	Rodger DAVIS	(Aus)	73	69	69	70	281	12780
	Van PHILLIPS	(Eng)	70	73	68	70	281	12780
29	José COCERES	(Arg)	73	69	68	72	282	10620
	Darren CLARKE	(N.Ire)	71	68	75	68	282	10620
	Bernhard LANGER	(Ger)	69	70	72	71	282	10620
	Domingo HOSPITAL	(Sp)	69	69	74	70	282	10620
33	Fabrice TARNAUD	(Fr)	73	69	72	69	283	9480
	Greg TURNER	(NZ)	70	68	70	75	283	9480
	Michael JONZON	(Swe)	66	70	72	75	283	9480
	Roger WESSELS	(SA)	71	71	71	70	283	9480
37	Mark MCNULTY	(Zim)	69	72	72	71	284	8520
	Peter SENIOR	(Aus)	72	70	69	73	284	8520
	Mark ROE	(Eng)	71	71	69	73	284	8520
	Tony JOHNSTONE	(Zim)	69	73	73	69	284	8520
41	Clinton WHITELAW	(SA)	69	74	72	70	285	6960
	Peter BAKER	(Eng)	74	69	73	69	285	6960
	Russell CLAYDON	(Eng)	71	72	70	72	285	6960
	Katsuyoshi TOMORI	(Jpn)	70	70	72	73	285	6960
	Malcolm MACKENZIE	(Eng)	68	71	74	72	285	6960
	Jonathan LOMAS	(Eng)	71	71	71	72	285	6960
	Santiago LUNA	(Sp)	71	71	73	70	285	6960
	Thomas GÖGELE	(Ger)	71	71	72	71	285	6960
	Dennis EDLUND	(Swe)	71	71	74	69	285	6960
50	Mark JAMES	(Eng)	69	73	69	75	286	5400
	Brian DAVIS	(Eng)	67	75	72	72	286	5400
	Rolf MUNTZ	(Hol)	72	71	71	72	286	5400
	Andrew SHERBORNE	(Eng)	71	70	74	71	286	5400
54	Ian WOOSNAM	(Wal)	73	70	74	70	287	4320
	Sven STRÜVER	(Ger)	73	69	75	70	287	4320
	Eduardo ROMERO	(Arg)	70	72	70	75	287	4320
	Sandy LYLE	(Scot)	69	74	72	72	287	4320
	Peter HEDBLOM	(Swe)	70	70	75	72	287	4320
59	Carl WATTS	(Eng)	71	69	71	77	288	3660.
	Chris VAN DER VELDE	(Hol)	68	75	76	69	288	3660
61	Raymond BURNS	(N.Ire)	70	72	74	73	289	3480
62	Howard CLARK	(Eng)	70	73	74	73	290	3360
63	Diego BORREGO	(Sp)	71	72	74	76	293	3240
64	Steven RICHARDSON	(Eng)	70	73	74	78	295	3060
	David TAPPING	(Eng)	69	74	78	74	295	3060

Tree trouble for Gary Orr.

BRUT IMPÉRIAL
MOËT & CHANDON
CHAMPAGNE
Official Suppliers to the
PGA European Tour

Westwood wins in great style

A third round course record 61

set Lee Westwood on the road

to victory in Hamburg

*I*f ever one word could be used to sum up the European Tour it would have to be competition. Everywhere you look it is present, repeated like a mantra so no-one can escape its underlying message: fail to improve and accept the consequences.

It is there among sponsors as they vie with each other to provide the quality of venue, prize-money and facilities that will attract the leading players. It is there among the golfers in the lower reaches of the Volvo Ranking as they try to climb over one another and keep their cards.

Most of all, of course, it is present among the elite, that special breed of player for whom only winning is good enough. It is not much of an exaggeration to say the European Tour was built upon the competition that existed in the mid-1980s between five players whose names are familiar to us all.

Now we are seeing it again, a competition among the rookies who performed so well at Valderrama in the Johnnie

Walker Ryder Cup but who see that as merely a springboard to more success not as the highlight of their careers. And in particular we are witnessing it between two of those rookies who are both man-

BRUT IMPÉRIAL

MOËT & CHANDON

CHAMPAGNE

*Official Suppliers to the
PGA European Tour*

Westwood wins in great style

A third round course record 61

set Lee Westwood on the road

to victory in Hamburg

*I*f ever one word could be used to sum up the European Tour it would have to be competition. Everywhere you look it is present, repeated like a mantra so no-one can escape its underlying message: fail to improve and accept the consequences.

It is there among sponsors as they vie with each other to provide the quality of venue, prize-money and facilities that will attract the leading players. It is there among the golfers in the lower reaches of the Volvo Ranking as they try to climb over one another and keep their cards.

Most of all, of course, it is present among the elite, that special breed of player for whom only winning is good enough. It is not much of an exaggeration to say the European Tour was built upon the competition that existed in the mid-1980s between five players whose names are familiar to us all.

Now we are seeing it again, a competition among the rookies who performed so well at Valderrama in the Johnnie

Walker Ryder Cup but who see that as merely a springboard to more success not as the highlight of their careers. And in particular we are witnessing it between two of those rookies who are both man-

aged by the same ex-professional, Andrew 'Chubby' Chandler. It is only an opinion but the belief is that Darren Clarke would not be half the golfer he is now were it not for Lee Westwood. And that Westwood would not have improved so quickly, so rapidly, were it not for Clarke.

It has been wonderful to watch their progress. First Westwood wins a tournament. On the sidelines you study Clarke's face. You see he is thrilled for his mate but there is also something more: he is saying to himself that next week it is going to be my turn.

At the Deutsche Bank – SAP Open Tournament Players' Championship of Europe, they went one better. We witnessed the pair going at it hammer and tongs in the same tournament. Few events this year will top the experience.

First, a word of praise for the sponsors, who took the decision to upgrade their event this year and were handsomely rewarded with a field that would grace any

THE COURSE

A considerable investment programme has realised its reward at Gut Kaden, which has improved over each of the seven years that it has held a European Tour event. The new front nine will blend better with the inward half as it matures and the aesthetics of the venue are all the better for the burying of overhead power cables which used to be present on the final four holes.

tournament. In addition to the cream of Europe, the Masters champion Mark O'Meara was in attendance, and four rounds of nothing worse than 70 enabled this popular and gracious visitor to claim third spot on his own.

At the halfway stage it looked as if we were in for a reprise of the Benson and Hedges International Open. Clarke and Colin Montgomerie were disputing things at the summit. Then Montgomerie shot 72 in the third round and there was that mantra, swirling around his head: fail to keep pace and accept the consequences.

And where was Westwood at this stage? He was

LEE WESTWOOD'S RECORD 61

Hole	Yards	Metres	Par	Score	Clubs Used
1	400	366	4	4	Driver, sand wedge 2 putts from 8ft
2	185	169	3	3	7 iron, 2 putts from 5ft
3	537	491	5	4	Driver, 6 iron, sand wedge to 12ft
4	432	395	4	4	Driver, sand wedge, 2 putts from 12ft
5	200	183	3	2	5 iron to 15ft
6	540	494	5	3	Driver, 3 wood to 35ft
7	449	411	4	3	3 wood, 4 iron to 5ft
8	361	330	4	4	2 iron, sand iron 2 putts from 6ft
9	375	343	4	4	2 iron, 9 iron 2 putts from 12ft
OUT	3479	3182	36	31	
10	422	386	4	3	Driver, wedge to 2ft
11	412	377	4	4	Driver, wedge to 2½ ft, 2 putts
12	415	380	4	3	Driver, 7 iron to 15ft
13	372	340	4	4	3 iron, 9 iron, 2 putts from 30ft
14	181	165	3	3	2 iron, sand wedge to 6ft
15	566	518	5	4	Driver, driver, sand wedge to 25ft
16	167	153	3	2	6 iron to 15ft
17	564	516	5	4	Driver, 5 iron, sand iron to 4ft
18	450	411	4	3	Driver, 5 iron to 40ft
IN	3550	3246	36	30	
TOTAL	7029	6428	72	61	

on the sidelines, feeling happy for Clarke no doubt but waiting for the third round, waiting for his turn.

One of the glories of golf is that you never know what will happen next. Westwood was frustrated with his putting at the halfway stage. In the third round he could not miss. A small adjustment here, a holed putt there, suddenly the confidence is back and Westwood is the most dangerous of competitors when the mood is upon him, entirely fearless. He finished his third round with a course record 61.

Clarke and Westwood have now reached the stage where either can beat the

SHOT OF THE WEEK

For all the brilliant golf that Westwood played over the last two days one shot during the first two rounds meant that he retained any interest in winning. That was a holed nine iron shot from 138 yards at his second hole, the 11th on the card, during the second round. It was the first time that he had holed a full iron

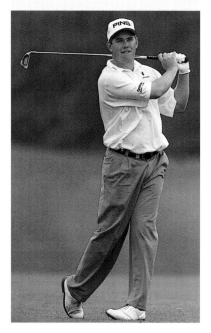

other on any given day. The competition has driven them to this pinnacle. This time it was Westwood's turn - well, it was only fair given that Clarke had won two weeks earlier - although even a final round 66 was merely good enough for a one shot victory.

Next year the event moves to another course, which will not thrill Clarke. In

seven years at Gut Kaden he never finished worse that fourth, an extraordinary level of consistency.

But at the prize-giving, as he shook his friend's hand and congratulated him on a notable success - it did not prevent him from plotting in the back of his mind how next time things would be different.

Derek Lawrenson

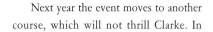

José Maria Olazábal (left) and Ian Woosnam (right) finished well back but US Masters champion Mark O'Meara (below) took third place.

GUT KADEN, HAMBURG, MAY 29 - JUNE 1, 1998 · YARDAGE 7029 · PAR 72

Pos	Name	Country	Rnd 1	Rnd 2	Rnd 3	Rnd 4	Total	Prize Money £
1	Lee WESTWOOD	(Eng)	69	69	61	66	265	183340
2	Darren CLARKE	(N.Ire)	67	66	65	68	266	122210
3	Mark O'MEARA	(USA)	67	69	63	70	269	68860
4	Philip WALTON	(Ire)	69	70	65	67	271	46713
	Bernhard LANGER	(Ger)	67	66	70	68	271	46713
	Peter SENIOR	(Aus)	69	67	64	71	271	46713
7	David HOWELL	(Eng)	69	68	66	69	272	28343
	Miguel Angel JIMÉNEZ	(Sp)	69	69	65	69	272	28343
	Jim PAYNE	(Eng)	70	68	69	65	272	28343
10	Paul LAWRIE	(Scot)	68	72	66	67	273	20370
	Bob MAY	(USA)	67	68	68	70	273	20370
	Colin MONTGOMERIE	(Scot)	67	67	72	67	273	20370
13	Paul BROADHURST	(Eng)	68	65	65	76	274	16547
	Peter MITCHELL	(Eng)	66	70	67	71	274	16547
	Thomas BJÖRN	(Den)	69	68	71	66	274	16547
	Joakim HAEGGMAN	(Swe)	69	70	63	72	274	16547
17	Costantino ROCCA	(It)	70	71	66	68	275	13750
	Ian WOOSNAM	(Wal)	69	71	64	71	275	13750
	Gary ORR	(Scot)	71	68	69	67	275	13750
	Paolo QUIRICI	(Swi)	68	70	67	70	275	13750
	Jean VAN DE VELDE	(Fr)	67	67	67	74	275	13750
22	Jeev Milkha SINGH	(Ind)	69	70	67	70	276	11880
	Retief GOOSEN	(SA)	68	68	69	71	276	11880
	Paul MCGINLEY	(Ire)	65	74	66	71	276	11880
	Nick PRICE	(Zim)	70	68	68	70	276	11880
	Ian GARBUTT	(Eng)	70	68	67	71	276	11880
27	Greg CHALMERS	(Aus)	67	71	69	70	277	9915
	Emanuele CANONICA	(It)	67	71	68	71	277	9915
	Scott HENDERSON	(Scot)	70	66	66	75	277	9915
	Marc FARRY	(Fr)	72	66	68	71	277	9915
	Alex CEJKA	(Ger)	68	70	70	69	277	9915
	José Maria OLAZÁBAL	(Sp)	69	71	67	70	277	9915
	Jarmo SANDELIN	(Swe)	69	70	71	67	277	9915
34	Phillip PRICE	(Wal)	70	71	68	69	278	8360
	Sam TORRANCE	(Scot)	68	69	69	72	278	8360
	Pierre FULKE	(Swe)	72	67	69	70	278	8360
	Brian DAVIS	(Eng)	69	68	70	71	278	8360
	Katsuyoshi TOMORI	(Jpn)	68	69	70	71	278	8360
39	Wayne WESTNER	(SA)	70	66	70	73	279	7040
	Per HAUGSRUD	(Nor)	71	66	67	75	279	7040
	Mark JAMES	(Eng)	67	68	72	72	279	7040
	Mats HALLBERG	(Swe)	70	70	67	72	279	7040
	Eamonn DARCY	(Ire)	72	69	67	71	279	7040
	Mark ROE	(Eng)	68	70	70	71	279	7040
	Peter O'MALLEY	(Aus)	67	70	71	71	279	7040
46	Wayne RILEY	(Aus)	72	69	67	72	280	5390
	José COCERES	(Arg)	70	69	72	69	280	5390
	Jamie SPENCE	(Eng)	67	73	72	68	280	5390
	Domingo HOSPITAL	(Sp)	72	69	69	70	280	5390
	David GILFORD	(Eng)	70	71	69	70	280	5390
	Miles TUNNICLIFF	(Eng)	70	69	69	72	280	5390
	Carl WATTS	(Eng)	73	67	69	71	280	5390
	Mark MOULAND	(Wal)	70	69	69	72	280	5390
54	Russell CLAYDON	(Eng)	71	67	72	71	281	3868
	David CARTER	(Eng)	70	71	69	71	281	3868
	Steve WEBSTER	(Eng)	72	69	66	74	281	3868
	Kalle BRINK	(Swe)	71	68	72	70	281	3868
	Peter HEDBLOM	(Swe)	73	68	68	72	281	3868
	Derrick COOPER	(Eng)	72	69	70	70	281	3868
60	Padraig HARRINGTON	(Ire)	69	72	72	69	282	3190
	Andrew COLTART	(Scot)	68	68	74	72	282	3190
	Thomas GÖGELE	(Ger)	70	68	70	74	282	3190
63	Thomas HENNIG	(Ger)	73	68	71	71	283	2557
	Dennis EDLUND	(Swe)	67	72	71	73	283	2557
	Santiago LUNA	(Sp)	72	69	72	70	283	2557
	Paul EALES	(Eng)	68	70	73	72	283	2557
67	Dean ROBERTSON	(Scot)	73	68	70	73	284	1644
	Adam HUNTER	(Scot)	70	69	72	73	284	1644
	Roger CHAPMAN	(Eng)	71	69	71	73	284	1644
	Daniel CHOPRA	(Swe)	72	67	72	73	284	1644
	Raymond RUSSELL	(Scot)	69	69	72	74	284	1644
72	Craig HAINLINE	(USA)	73	68	72	72	285	1635
	Malcolm MACKENZIE	(Eng)	71	68	74	72	285	1635
	Andrew OLDCORN	(Scot)	70	71	69	75	285	1635
	Per-Ulrik JOHANSSON	(Swe)	70	71	72	72	285	1635
76	Stephen ALLAN	(Aus)	67	74	67	78	286	1627
	Mark DAVIS	(Eng)	70	70	70	76	286	1627
	Raymond BURNS	(N.Ire)	70	70	73	73	286	1627
	Gary EVANS	(Eng)	73	68	72	73	286	1627
80	Anthony WALL	(Eng)	71	70	70	76	287	1621
	Yusuf KAYA	(Tur)	72	69	72	74	287	1621
82	Richard BOXALL	(Eng)	71	70	72	75	288	1618

Darren Clarke

Welcome TPC fans!

Deutsche Bank SAP Open

TOURNAMENT PLAYERS' CHAMPIONSHIP OF EUROPE

May 21 - 24, 1999
Golf Club St.Leon-Rot near Heidelberg.

For further information please contact the
Deutsche Bank - SAP Tournament office
Tel. + 49 (0) 4193 9 000 0
Fax + 49 (0) 4193 9 000 111

Internet address: http://www.deutschebank-sap-open.de

Westwood drives to consecutive victories

There was no stopping Lee Westwood

as he completed another four rounds in the 60s

for a second successive win

Lee Westwood, the winner of the National Car Rental English Open, is one of the most successful golf talents to emerge on the British scene since Nick Faldo was a lanky lad with a Beatles haircut. Only time will tell if this pleasant young man from Worksop can match Faldo's phenomenal success story, but all his steps so far are in the right direction.

His two strokes victory over the Australian Greg Chalmers and Sweden's Olle Karlsson highlighted the super qualities of his game – bold when he had to be, patient when that was necessary. Three rounds of 68 and one of 67 gave him a 17-under par aggregate of 271 and that was good enough for the first prize of £108,330. It was his first win in Britain since turning pro in 1993 and it took him to the number one spot on the Volvo Ranking for the first time in his spectacular career.

Yet when the tournament began very few follow-

ers were ready to bet against Colin Mont-gomerie, winner of the Volvo PGA Championship a couple of weeks previ-ously. Montgomerie had been praying that a combination of fertiliser and heavy spring rain would toughen-up the Marriott Hanbury Manor course, US Open style, with heavy rough waiting to punish the wayward hitters. And when his first tee shot of the tournament disappeared in to the thick stuff, he knew he had got what he wanted. A hack out, a flick onto the green, one putt for his par and then he was off and running for an eight-birdie 64.

But there the plot was lost for Mont-gomerie, five times leading money winner in Europe and desperate to make the US Open the first major victory of his career.

It was all he could do over the next two days to keep his head above water as the bright young men of the European Tour threw birdies at him from every direction. Westwood had a second succes-sive 68, Sweden's Patrik Sjöland a 67, and day three saw a stunning 61 from Chalmers that lifted him out of the pack and into second place. Chalmers said afterwards: 'I felt I could do no wrong. No matter what I did the ball flew straight at the flag. It was frightening in a way but it was great at the same time. It was like being outside yourself. Weird but what-ever it is, I wish I could bottle it.'

Chalmers took his aggressive play into the fourth round and opened with three straight birdies to go two strokes clear of Westwood. But Westwood, who had won his previous tournament, the Deutsche Bank - SAP Open TPC of Europe, refused to hit the panic button. Westwood clawed his way back with birdies at eight and nine and then pulled clear again with birdies at the 12th and 13th.

A minor scare at the short 16th where both men missed the green but Westwood then holed an eye-popping putt of 30 feet for par while Chalmers missed from only eight feet. 'That was the tournament right there,' said Westwood.

Last day 66 took Olle Karlsson (left) into joint second place.

The putt from 30 feet at the 16th which Westwood sank on the final day. Both he and Chalmers had missed the green with their tee shots and Westwood, whose ball was in a bad lie, could only hit it and hope. It raced ten yards past the hole, Chalmers hit his second shot to eight feet and then stared aghast as Westwood holed his putt, calm as you like, to save par. Almost inevitably, Chalmers missed his putt.

Balancing act from Costantino Rocca.

THE COURSE

The Hanbury Manor course near Ware in Hertfordshire, some 25 miles north of London, boasts some of the finest greens in England. It was originally designed by former Open champion Harry Vardon but has since been renovated and improved by Jack Nicklaus Junior.

'If I had missed I'm sure he'd have holed. It was a classic match-play situation.'

Chalmers sportingly held up his hands and said: 'I was beaten by a better player. Simple as that. He holed the important putts and showed what a

tremendous competitor he is.'

As Westwood slipped away for a Concorde flight to the US Open, he said: 'It's lovely to see my name at the top of the Volvo Ranking for the first time and to have won in Britain. This has put me in

the right frame of mind to go to the United States. It's great to have shot my last ten rounds in a row in the 60s and to be 40 under par for the last two events.'

Montgomerie said disconsolately: 'To finish fourth is very disappointing. After

Greg Chalmers (left) threatened to break 60 at one stage in his dazzling third round. Top ten finish for Jeev Milkha Singh (right).

GREG CHALMER'S RECORD 61					
HOLE	YARDS	METRES	PAR	SCORE	CLUBS USED
1	400	366	4	4	Driver, sand wedge 2 putts from 8ft
2	185	169	3	3	7 iron, 2 putts from 5ft
3	537	491	5	4	Driver, 6 iron, sand wedge to 12ft
4	432	395	4	4	Driver, sand wedge, 2 putts from 12ft
5	200	183	3	2	5 iron to 15ft
6	540	494	5	3	Driver, 3 wood to 35ft
7	449	411	4	3	3 wood, 4 iron to 5ft
8	361	330	4	4	2 iron, sand iron 2 putts from 6ft
9	375	343	4	4	2 iron, 9 iron 2 putts from 12ft
OUT	3479	3182	36	31	
10	422	386	4	3	Driver, wedge to 2ft
11	412	377	4	4	Driver, wedge to 21⁄2 ft, 2 putts
12	415	380	4	3	Driver, 7 iron to 15ft
13	372	340	4	4	3 iron, 9 iron, 2 putts from 30ft
14	181	165	3	3	2 iron, sand wedge to 6ft
15	566	518	5	4	Driver, driver, sand wedge to 25ft
16	167	153	3	2	6 iron to 15ft
17	564	516	5	4	Driver, 5 iron, sand iron to 4ft
18	450	411	4	3	Driver, 5 iron to 40ft
IN	3550	3246	36	30	
TOTAL	7029	6428	72	61	

shooting a 64 in the first round I should have gone on and won but I left dozens of shots out on the golf course.'

Frank Clough

MARRIOTT HANBURY MANOR HOTEL, JUNE 4-7, 1998 • YARDAGE 7029 • PAR 72

Pos	Name	Country	Rnd 1	Rnd 2	Rnd 3	Rnd 4	Total	Prize Money £
1	Lee WESTWOOD	(Eng)	68	68	67	68	271	108330
2	Greg CHALMERS	(Aus)	70	73	61	69	273	56450
	Olle KARLSSON	(Swe)	70	70	67	66	273	56450
4	Colin MONTGOMERIE	(Scot)	64	72	69	69	274	32500
5	Patrik SJÖLAND	(Swe)	68	67	70	70	275	27530
6	Phillip PRICE	(Wal)	73	71	67	65	276	22750
7	Robert ALLENBY	(Aus)	67	71	70	69	277	19500
8	Roger WESSELS	(SA)	68	69	70	71	278	15380
	Jeev Milkha SINGH	(Ind)	71	69	67	71	278	15380
10	Christy O'CONNOR JNR	(Ire)	71	70	68	71	280	11650
	Mark MCNULTY	(Zim)	73	68	66	73	280	11650
	Stephen LEANEY	(Aus)	66	69	70	75	280	11650
	Knud STORGAARD	(Den)	71	70	72	67	280	11650
14	Gary EVANS	(Eng)	70	73	68	70	281	8978
	Paul EALES	(Eng)	69	72	70	70	281	8978
	Andrew COLTART	(Scot)	67	72	67	75	281	8978
	Van PHILLIPS	(Eng)	69	72	71	69	281	8978
	Michael CAMPBELL	(NZ)	71	72	71	67	281	8978
	Bob MAY	(USA)	71	69	69	72	281	8978
20	Nicolas VANHOOTEGEM	(Bel)	66	72	72	72	282	7410
	Jon ROBSON	(Eng)	66	73	73	70	282	7410
	Russell CLAYDON	(Eng)	71	70	72	69	282	7410
	Peter BAKER	(Eng)	69	72	70	71	282	7410
	Thomas GÖGELE	(Ger)	70	73	70	69	282	7410
25	Derrick COOPER	(Eng)	68	76	68	71	283	6240
	Ian GARBUTT	(Eng)	70	72	70	71	283	6240
	Steve WEBSTER	(Eng)	72	68	70	73	283	6240
	Philip WALTON	(Ire)	74	69	70	70	283	6240
	Padraig HARRINGTON	(Ire)	74	69	70	70	283	6240
	Michael JONZON	(Swe)	72	68	72	71	283	6240
	Nicolas JOAKIMIDES	(Fr)	65	74	72	72	283	6240
32	José RIVERO	(Sp)	69	73	69	73	284	5265
	Mats HALLBERG	(Swe)	72	72	66	74	284	5265
	Pierre FULKE	(Swe)	72	70	69	73	284	5265
	Gary ORR	(Scot)	75	69	68	72	284	5265
36	Mark MOULAND	(Wal)	72	72	72	69	285	4680
	Dean ROBERTSON	(Scot)	68	73	71	73	285	4680
	Eamonn DARCY	(Ire)	71	72	71	71	285	4680
	Paul AFFLECK	(Wal)	74	65	74	72	285	4680
	Anthony WALL	(Eng)	75	68	68	74	285	4680
41	Mathias GRÖNBERG	(Swe)	73	70	72	71	286	3835
	Fabrice TARNAUD	(Fr)	70	66	75	75	286	3835
	Miguel Angel JIMÉNEZ	(Sp)	68	72	70	76	286	3835
	Jeff REMESY	(Fr)	70	71	71	74	286	3835
	David HOWELL	(Eng)	74	69	70	73	286	3835
	Ronan RAFFERTY	(N.Ire)	69	72	72	73	286	3835
	Thomas BJÖRN	(Den)	73	70	70	73	286	3835
	Raphaël JACQUELIN	(Fr)	69	71	73	73	286	3835
49	Greg OWEN	(Eng)	72	72	71	72	287	2795
	Michael LONG	(NZ)	71	70	72	74	287	2795
	Peter MITCHELL	(Eng)	70	73	73	71	287	2795
	Paul BROADHURST	(Eng)	75	69	70	73	287	2795
	Steve ALKER	(NZ)	70	71	73	73	287	2795
	Ignacio GARRIDO	(Sp)	70	74	71	72	287	2795
	Darren CLARKE	(N.Ire)	72	72	75	68	287	2795
	Michele REALE	(It)	71	71	72	73	287	2795
57	Craig HAINLINE	(USA)	71	69	75	73	288	2063
	Steen TINNING	(Den)	74	70	71	73	288	2063
	David GILFORD	(Eng)	72	71	76	69	288	2063
	Rolf MUNTZ	(Hol)	69	72	76	71	288	2063
61	Steven RICHARDSON	(Eng)	70	71	74	74	289	1787
	Andrew SANDYWELL	(Eng)	74	70	68	77	289	1787
	Massimo FLORIOLI	(It)	72	68	74	75	289	1787
	Tom GILLIS	(USA)	71	73	71	74	289	1787
65	Ivo GINER	(Sp)	75	68	73	74	290	1080
	Andrew SHERBORNE	(Eng)	72	70	70	78	290	1080
	Wayne RILEY	(Aus)	68	73	76	73	290	1080
	Paul CURRY	(Eng)	73	71	68	78	290	1080
	Jay TOWNSEND	(USA)	70	73	75	72	290	1080
	Stephen ALLAN	(Aus)	73	70	73	74	290	1080
71	Roger CHAPMAN	(Eng)	71	72	73	76	292	963
	Carl WATTS	(Eng)	68	75	74	75	292	963
	John BICKERTON	(Eng)	74	70	72	76	292	963
74	Howard CLARK	(Eng)	71	72	74	79	296	959
75	Rodger DAVIS	(Aus)	73	71	79	77	300	957

Colin Montgomerie couldn't maintain his first round pace.

Monty's delighted with his 64. It's his favourite room.

What could be more relaxing for Colin Montgomerie than a golf break? If playing golf is your profession, quite a lot actually.

At Marriott Hotel & Country Clubs, as well as a minimum of one superb golf course, you'll find a whole range of leisure facilities. If you're looking for a golf break, or even a break from golf, there are 27* Marriott Hotels throughout the UK, 10^ of which are hotel & country clubs offering golf breaks for players at any level. For reservations or our 1998/99 Golf Breaks brochure, call 0800 221 222.

ITV Teletext
p387

When you're comfortable you can do anything.

Marriott
HOTELS · RESORTS · SUITES

PIERRE, CHEPSTOW • BREADSALL PRIORY, DERBY • TUDOR PARK, MAIDSTONE • HOLLINS HALL, BRADFORD • GOODWOOD PARK, CHICHESTER
DALMAHOY, EDINBURGH • MEON VALLEY, SOUTHAMPTON • FOREST OF ARDEN, BIRMINGHAM • MANCHESTER • HANBURY MANOR, WARE.

*Manchester opens Autumn 1998 and new London Heathrow early 1999. ^Manchester & Hollins Hall courses open spring 1999.

Slaley Hall looks to the future

Despite the abandonment of the 1998 Compaq

European Grand Prix, the tournament

is set fair towards the millennium

Colin Montgomerie, winner of the 1997 Compaq European Grand Prix (left). Retief Goosen (right) was the winner in 1996.

The birth of a new event on the European Tour is always exciting, and with victories by Retief Goosen and Colin Montgomerie, the Compaq European Grand Prix was given the perfect start to life.

So it was more than a little frustrating when in 1998 the tournament was officially cancelled on the Sunday following excessive rain which waterlogged the course at the superb De Vere Slaley Hall complex in Northumberland.

Even so the determination of the organisers and sponsors to advance the tournament towards the new millennium

THE COURSE

Dave Thomas enthused over the stunning setting of the Tyne Valley when he first saw the 1,000-acre Slaley Hall estate, and he has good reason to feel proud of his design which has become the flagship course in the north east alongside the five star hotel. A spectacular mix of imposing pines, rolling moorland and water makes for a typical Thomas course with massive bunkers and raised greens. The 452-yards ninth hole, described by Ronan Rafferty as an 'Augusta-like' par four, is Slaley's signature hole played as it is over water through an avenue of towering pines and dense rhododendrons to a sloping green.

Peter Hedblom (left).

was emphasised with the early announcement that in 1999 the Compaq European Grand Prix would be played on June 24-27.

Paul Dermody, the Managing Director of Greenalls Hotels and Leisure, which operate Slaley Hall as part of the De Vere Hotel portfolio, said: 'Through our work on other tournaments at The Belfry and other De Vere Hotels, we enjoy a very good relationship with the European Tour and look forward to continuing to use our experience and expertise to ensure the tournament is one of the very best.'

The foundation of this outlook is clearly based on the success of the first two tournaments at Slaley Hall which is recognised as the 'Gleneagles of the North'. In 1996 the South African Goosen, then 27, led from the start to the finish for his debut win on the European Tour.

Goosen set the tone for the tournament with an opening 66 which gave him a two-stroke lead over Juan Carlos Pinero. 'I like it on the European Tour and enjoy it over here,' said Goosen. He liked it all the more as with further scores of 69, 70 and 72 for an 11-under-par aggregate of 277, he won by two shots from Ross Drummond with Robert Lee two strokes further back in third place.

Roger Chapman at picturesque Slaley Hall (above left). Colin Montgomerie, winner of the 1997 trophy (above right).

In golf, the adage 'horses for courses' frequently applies, and Goosen proved the point 12 months later when he strung together scores of 69, 69, 68 and 69 for a total of 275 which was two shots lower than his winning score in 1996. The only problem for Goosen was that a certain Colin Montgomerie chose the 1997 Compaq European Grand Prix to demonstrate to the 'Toon-Army' of spectators the magnificence of his game. Montgomerie had edged into a one-shot lead, ahead of Lee Westwood and Goosen, with scores of 69, 68 and 68. Out in 35 on the last day, he was caught by Westwood, with Goosen hanging in, but Montgomerie really cut loose on the back nine.

The Scot had birdies at the tenth and 12th then showed the rest of the field the way home with further birdie putts at the 14th, 16th and 17th and, at the last, his

ball toppled into the hole to equal the course record of 65 and bring a smile to his face as wide as the Tyne Bridge. His total of 270 - 18 under par - won him the £108,330 first prize by five shots from Goosen and six from Westwood.

Montgomerie insisted: 'This tournament has proved there is golfing life north of Watford' after being presented with the impressive trophy by Joe McNally, the Managing Director of Compaq UK. 'We need tournaments like this, sponsors like Compaq and venues like Slaley Hall.'

Frustrating, then, that the 1998 tournament, with Severiano Ballesteros in the field, was compelled to be cancelled although, as Tournament Director Mike Stewart explained, it was remarkable that any play whatsoever was possible. He said: 'The conditions were due to the excessive rainfall over the previous two weeks (61.4mm over the 14 days com-

pared to the average of 50.2mm for the month of June). It was very disappointing because the golf course was quite clearly in the best condition it had ever been which speaks volumes for the superb efforts of the greenkeepers and the staff.'

Meanwhile Slaley Hall continues to show its commitment to golf with investment on the course, strengthening the test for Europe's finest players, and Brendan Foster, Managing Director of Nova International, organisers of the Compaq European Grand Prix, says: 'We have an excellent relationship with De Vere Hotels who already possess a second to none reputation for hosting major golf tournaments at their hotels. Their enthusiasm and support to ensure the North of England's biggest tournament continues to grow quickly, just as it has since its beginning in 1996, has been fantastic.'

Mitchell Platts   131

Emotional return for Lanner

Mats Lanner returned to the site
of his last European Tour victory
and emerged from the wilderness

He had won the
Alfred Dunhill
Cup for Sweden, pocketed
two European Tour titles
and banked more than £1
million along the way. Yet
nothing could rival the ela-
tion felt by Mats Lanner on
sinking a putt of two feet on
Santo da Serra's 72nd green.

The putt did more than
assure victory in the Madeira
Island Open, the first repeat
winner of a fiercely con-
tested tournament. More,
too, than earn the 37-year-
old Swede a £50,000 wel-
come payday. He put it best:
'This feels like getting my
job back,' in the form of a
priceless two-year Tour
exemption.

Lanner, a winner in
Madeira four years earlier,
returned in search of his
ticket to rejoin the big-time;
a passport to escape the
wilderness into which his
career had drifted since losing his playing rights 18
months before.

He did not need the dreamy backdrop of the Auld Grey Toon, packed Open grandstands, even the glint of the Ryder Cup, to lift himself for that putt. Simply, it was win or bust.

Madeira served up golf at the sharp end with some players grafting for survival rather than posterity; taking a further throw of the dice in the hope their number would come up.

There was Englishman David Tapping, who had enjoyed his fifteen minutes of fame when challenging for the halfway lead at the 1997 Open Championship, rediscovering his touch to lead the first round by two shots. A six under par 66 betrayed a formline which showed 12 cuts missed in his previous 15 starts.

Then there was Stephen Scahill, a New Zealander who had left behind a golden amateur memory in Vancouver six years ago. There he combined with Michael Campbell and Phil Tataurangi to sensationally win the World Team Cham-

THE COURSE

Idyllic Santo da Serra has switched its nines, but that did not bother Stephen Scahill during his course record score of 61. Situated 1,800 feet above sea level, the 6,606-yard course offers one of golf's great views, stretching down from the clubhouse to an Atlantic Ocean dotted with desert islands. Beautiful it might be, but there is a beastly side to Robert Trent Jones's redesigned layout. Wickedly undulating, peppered with pine, Mimosa and eucalyptus trees, the Santo da Serra claimed scores ranging from one (Rudi Sailer and Katsuyoshi Tomori) to ten (Stephen Ames) during the tournament.

pionship: overhauling a star-studded American side which included Justin Leonard, David Duval and Jay Sigel, after trailing by seven shots with nine holes remaining.

Lounging 178th on the Volvo Ranking and playing only his third Tour event of the year (another to have lost his card), Scahill was way down the list of likely candidates to follow the 61s posted by Lee Westwood (Deutsche

New Zealander Stephen Scahill (left). Andrew Beal views a putt (right).

Bank - SAP Open TPC of Europe) and Greg Chalmers (National Car Rental English Open) in the preceding Tour stops. Yet there it was on day two, an 11 under par 61 which clipped two strokes off Peter Mitchell's record low round and rocketed the 28-year-old into a three-stroke lead at the halfway point.

Containing an eagle and ten birdies, Scahill's spectacular effort was the best of the week by four strokes. And when he followed up with a 69, including birdies at the last two holes, to ensure a two-stroke cushion entering the final round, the London-based player was threatening a maiden Tour triumph.

But Lanner, who had sized up the task when he moved briefly alongside Scahill at 12 under par on the 15th green, was ready to make his move and while low cloud, which put back the start of the final round by almost three hours, delayed

Mats Lanner vowed to remember 'for the rest of my life' the sand shot he played to the 72nd hole. No wonder. Leading by one, the Swede had carved his approach into greenside sand and had to up-and-down to win. He responded by splashing to within two feet of the pin.

his assault on the summit, he would not be denied.

A product of windy Wellington, Scahill would not have been too down-hearted by the stiff breeze which accompanied him to the first tee. As befits US Open week, par would be achievement enough. Indeed, of the 71 who played the final round only Englishman John Bickerton bettered regulation.

It was a day for keeping your head and waiting for others to lose theirs. Lanner, rich in experience, did precisely that, patiently reeling off 17 pars whilst the disappointed Scahill, who never got out of first gear, carded five bogey figures. Still, only one stroke separated the pair coming up the last, with Salisbury's Andy Beal only one further back.

And when Lanner found sand with his approach the door was swinging open. Scahill could not capitalise, however, over-shooting the green and whilst he executed a smart save, the spoils of victory deservedly went to Lanner after he followed suit, coolly splashing to within two feet of the stick.

Alex Spink

SANTO DA SERRA, JUNE 18-21, 1998 · YARDAGE 6606 · PAR 72

Pos	Name	Country	Rnd 1	Rnd 2	Rnd 3	Rnd 4	Total	Prize Money £
1	Mats LANNER	(Swe)	70	66	68	73	277	50000
2	Stephen SCAHILL	(NZ)	72	61	69	76	278	33330
3	Andrew BEAL	(Eng)	71	68	67	73	279	18780
4	Thomas GÖGELE	(Ger)	68	68	73	73	282	13850
	Francisco CEA	(Sp)	69	69	71	73	282	13850
6	Carl SUNESON	(Sp)	70	72	69	72	283	9750
	Rudi SAILER	(Aut)	70	68	70	75	283	9750
8	John MELLOR	(Eng)	69	70	73	72	284	7095
	Christian CÉVAER	(Fr)	70	71	69	74	284	7095
10	Katsuyoshi TOMORI	(Jpn)	70	72	68	76	286	5377
	Ivo GINER	(Sp)	72	67	70	77	286	5377
	Tom GILLIS	(USA)	70	69	69	78	286	5377
	Fredrik JACOBSON	(Swe)	71	71	65	79	286	5377
14	John BICKERTON	(Eng)	73	69	74	71	287	4230
	Maarten LAFEBER	(Hol)	76	68	71	72	287	4230
	Adam HUNTER	(Scot)	71	72	71	73	287	4230
	Ross DRUMMOND	(Scot)	71	71	70	75	287	4230
	Roger WINCHESTER	(Eng)	68	73	69	77	287	4230
19	Mathew GOGGIN	(Aus)	73	73	69	73	288	3242
	Stephen AMES	(T&T)	68	78	69	73	288	3242
	Paul AFFLECK	(Wal)	76	68	72	72	288	3242
	John WADE	(Aus)	76	70	70	72	288	3242
	Robert LEE	(Eng)	73	71	70	74	288	3242
	Pedro LINHART	(Sp)	70	69	74	75	288	3242
	Mårten OLANDER	(Swe)	72	68	73	75	288	3242
	Steve ALKER	(NZ)	71	74	68	75	288	3242
	Joakim RASK	(Swe)	71	69	72	76	288	3242
	Greig HUTCHEON	(Scot)	71	69	71	77	288	3242
	Michael CAMPBELL	(NZ)	71	67	70	80	288	3242
30	Stephen BENNETT	(Eng)	72	72	72	73	289	2572
	Andrew SHERBORNE	(Eng)	74	69	73	73	289	2572
	David TAPPING	(Eng)	66	73	73	77	289	2572
	Andre STOLZ	(Aus)	72	69	70	78	289	2572
34	John HAWKSWORTH	(Eng)	73	72	72	74	291	2220
	Scott WATSON	(Eng)	74	71	72	74	291	2220
	Gordon J BRAND	(Eng)	71	69	73	78	291	2220
	Gary NICKLAUS	(USA)	72	71	70	78	291	2220
	Greg OWEN	(Eng)	73	72	68	78	291	2220
	Daniel CHOPRA	(Swe)	73	72	67	79	291	2220
	Santiago LUNA	(Sp)	68	71	72	80	291	2220
41	Olivier EDMOND	(Fr)	73	70	72	77	292	1890
	Brian NELSON	(USA)	69	76	72	75	292	1890
	Sören KJELDSEN	(Den)	73	73	71	75	292	1890
	Jeev Milkha SINGH	(Ind)	75	72	74	71	292	1890
45	Jeff REMESY	(Fr)	71	76	68	78	293	1650
	Jean Louis GUEPY	(Fr)	70	76	73	74	293	1650
	Robert MOSS	(USA)	71	73	76	73	293	1650
	Gary EMERSON	(Eng)	72	71	66	84	293	1650
49	Robert WRAGG	(Eng)	72	72	73	77	294	1470
	Ged FUREY	(Eng)	71	74	69	80	294	1470
51	Paul STREETER	(Eng)	75	69	74	77	295	1260
	Steven BOTTOMLEY	(Eng)	69	75	74	77	295	1260
	David HIGGINS	(Ire)	73	71	74	77	295	1260
	Ola ELIASSON	(Swe)	77	69	74	75	295	1260
	Daren LEE	(Eng)	72	71	71	81	295	1260
56	Craig HAINLINE	(USA)	72	72	75	77	296	960
	Michele REALE	(It)	72	75	72	77	296	960

Joint sixth for Rudi Sailer of Austria.

	Stephen HAMILL	(N.Ire)	73	74	72	77	296	960
	Stephen DODD	(Wal)	76	71	72	77	296	960
	Mauricio MOLINA	(Arg)	72	73	76	75	296	960
	Henrik NYSTROM	(Swe)	73	73	77	73	296	960
62	António SOBRINHO	(Port)	73	74	71	79	297	840
63	David LYNN	(Eng)	74	69	75	80	298	697
	Darren COLE	(Aus)	71	72	75	80	298	697
	Phil GOLDING	(Eng)	70	73	79	76	298	697
	Johan RYSTRÖM	(Swe)	74	70	71	83	298	697
67	Brian DAVIS	(Eng)	73	72	76	79	300	448
	Stephane FERRIERA (AM)	(Port)	74	73	73	80	300	
68	Anthony WALL	(Eng)	72	74	74	81	301	445
	Daniel SILVA	(Port)	71	75	77	78	301	445
70	Francis HOWLEY	(Ire)	73	74	77	80	304	442

You want to

be sure they

can keep

in touch.

That's why Cellnet

cover over

80 countries

worldwide.

Network quality is our first priority, which is why we were the first to offer coverage across the US. Even with unbeaten coverage across the UK, we continue to develop our network throughout the world so that you can be contacted wherever you are.

We run the network so you can run your life. 0800 21 4000

cellnet network

cellnet it's in your hands

Return of the warrior

Nearly three years had passed since Sam Torrance

tasted victory and his 21st European Tour title

was one of the sweetest

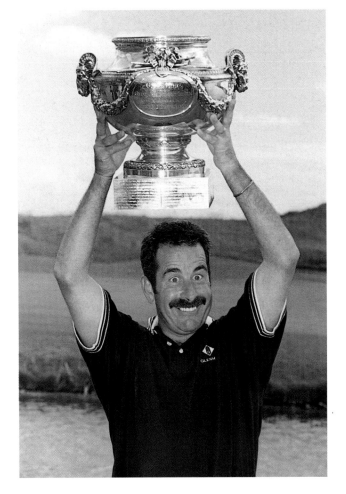

The week started badly for Scotland's finest at Le Golf National. After an early Tuesday morning practice round for the Peugeot Open de France, Andrew Coltart, Adam Hunter and Dean Robertson drove the 580 kilometres to St. Etienne and back to watch the Scottish football team lose to Morocco in the Group A decider of the World Cup.

It was not the result golf's tartan trio had hoped for. But they remained sanguine. 'Seeing 20,000 Scottish fans, two thirds of them dressed in kilts, marching and singing in the streets, was a fantastic experience,' said Robertson on his return at 5 o'clock the following morning.

Five days later one of their countrymen, dressed in his Sunday best of dark blue, was to triumph in another sporting field of France.

But the golfers' every spare moment was spent watching the World Cup on television, either in their room at the Novotel alongside the first tee or in the many brasseries in and around Versailles.

Everywhere there were reminders that France during this third week in June had been taken over by la Coupe du Monde. Even the room normally used as an interview area by the press was taken over as a dining room by the footballers of South Korea.

However, there was a golf championship to be played and a highly prestigious one at that. This was the 92nd playing of the French Open, first won in 1906 by Arnaud Massy. Colin Montgomerie was the favourite, but he had come straight from the US Open in San Francisco. Jet-lag was his enemy, and in an effort to combat the worst of its effects he flew by private jet from Farnborough to the nearby airstrip. He had one passenger, Sam Torrance. Six days earlier Sam had not intended to play, but a 63 at Sunningdale followed by a 65 at Wentworth had persuaded him that to disregard such a seam of form would indeed be foolish. This was his 589th European Tour event, but his appetite was undiminished. After all, he still was not exempt for the Open Championship at Royal Birkdale three weeks later.

Inside 24 hours Torrance's late change-of-mind was vindicated, a stunning eight under par 64 opening up a two-shot gap over the field. Had it not been for an even better one in the closing moments of the last round, the 44-year-old Scot's third shot at the 18th hole would have merited being shot-of-the-week.

Caught between a seven and an eight

THE COURSE

iron for his approach over the water almost surrounding the 'island' green, he selected the seven then watched his ball scuttle over the putting surface and finally come to rest on a narrow wooden bridge. While it was a fortunate break, Torrance was confronted with a 30-yard chip that could have gone anywhere because the ball was lodged in a half-inch gap between the planks.

Astonishingly, he almost holed it for an eagle three, and with his trusty broomhandle putter he did not miss the birdie opportunity from eight feet. It was Torrance's lowest round since a 63 in Switzerland in September 1995, just days before his last tournament win in the British Masters at Collingtree.

Pedro Linhart and Eduardo Romero from Argentina were in close touch on 66. Of Montgomerie, however, there was scarcely a sign, a 74 – which contained 36 putts – consigning him to also-

Peter Mitchell in semi-silhouetted sandscape

ran status. But resilience is one of Colin's greatest assets and he came back the next day with a 68 to make the cut comfortably.

Still, a Montgomerie round is rarely without its dramas, and this was no exception. Six under par with three holes to play, his second shot with a nine iron bounded from the edge of the green into knee-high rough from which he took two attempts to extricate himself.

A six was the result, and as he walked off the green he jabbed the offending piece of hard turf with is putter, whereupon the head fell off and he was obliged to putt on the two remaining greens with his eight iron.

A threat of discipline hung over him. But his explanation satisfied Tournament Director, David Garland. 'No way was it done in anger', said Garland after collecting evidence. 'This was confirmed by the caddie of one of his playing companions. This is the last of three putters he had specially made which have broken.'

Montgomerie, having escaped the yel-

SHOT OF THE WEEK

There can be no doubt, Sam Torrance's seven wood second shot to within 18 inches of the hole for a birdie three at the 470-yard 17th hole. At the time he knew he needed to birdie one of the last two holes to have a chance of winning. But there was a strong breeze blowing straight into the players which turned the hole into a par four and a half. The previous day Sam hooked his drive into thick rough on the left, an error which cost him a five. 'This time I had to commit myself 100 per cent to the tee shot, so I hit it very hard,' he said later. 'It turned out perfectly.' But not quite as perfect as his second shot. Selecting the seven wood he has carried for more than two years, he made the perfect swing and the perfect contact, the ball soaring straight through the wind to land less than 18 inches from the hole. 'The shot measured 207 yards and I hit it exactly 207 yards, a foot so so to the right,' he said. 'Under the cosh, that"s the best I've ever played.'

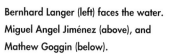

Bernhard Langer (left) faces the water. Miguel Angel Jiménez (above), and Mathew Goggin (below).

low card, Torrance preserved his two-stroke lead with a 70. Italy's Massimo Florioli was the immediate threat after two 67s, but by now Torrance was looking over his shoulder at Montgomerie. Two years earlier in the Canon European Masters at Crans-sur-Sierre Montgomerie came from eight behind to win by four shots. 'I reckon I need two 64s, but the way I am playing I can do that' said Europe's number one. 'I'm still right in there.' By Saturday night he wasn't, a 73 in windy conditions leaving him nine shots adrift.

With his fellow countryman gone, Torrance could breath slightly more easily going into a warm, but breezy, final day. However, he faced a challenge of World Cup dimensions with, among others, New Zealand's Michael Campbell, Florioli, Olivier Edmond and Marc Farry from France, Linhart and the 1984 champion, Bernhard Langer, all snapping at his heels.

It was Britain versus the rest, and Torrance had not won for 33 months. It was a major test of his nerve and the more

disciplined, alcohol-free, lifestyle which he embarked upon nine months earlier.

With less than half an hour remaining of a tense afternoon, a play-off looked inevitable. But as the pressure mounted so the Scot found his inspiration. 'Coming off the 16th green I knew I had to birdie one of the last two holes to win,' he said later. He did not delay, birdieing the 17th, and for good measure, the 18th as well to

win by two shots from Florioli, Edmond, Langer and Australia's Mathew Goggin, who eagled the last hole.

It was a time for champagne, and when he arrived home that evening a bottle was duly cracked open. But nary a drop passed his lips. 'I had a nice cup of tea instead,' he said. Truly, this was a Torrance reborn.

Jock MacVicar 141

LE GOLF NATIONAL, PARIS, JUNE 25-28, 1998 · YARDAGE 7122 · PAR 72

Pos	Name	Country	Rnd 1	Rnd 2	Rnd 3	Rnd 4	Total	Prize Money £
1	Sam TORRANCE	(Scot)	64	70	72	70	276	83330
2	Massimo FLORIOLI	(It)	69	67	75	67	278	33262
	Olivier EDMOND	(Fr)	70	70	71	67	278	33262
	Bernhard LANGER	(Ger)	71	70	68	69	278	33262
	Mathew GOGGIN	(Aus)	69	70	69	70	278	33262
6	Marc FARRY	(Fr)	70	67	73	69	279	16250
	Pedro LINHART	(Sp)	66	73	70	70	279	16250
8	Russell CLAYDON	(Eng)	69	70	70	71	280	11216
	David HOWELL	(Eng)	70	69	69	72	280	11216
	Santiago LUNA	(Sp)	75	68	67	70	280	11216
11	Søren KJELDSEN	(Den)	70	72	75	64	281	8164
	Philip WALTON	(Ire)	72	73	69	67	281	8164
	Jarmo SANDELIN	(Swe)	74	69	71	67	281	8164
	Alex CEJKA	(Ger)	70	69	73	69	281	8164
	Michael CAMPBELL	(NZ)	70	67	69	75	281	8164
16	Nicolas JOAKIMIDES	(Fr)	72	68	73	69	282	6285
	Ian GARBUTT	(Eng)	73	68	72	69	282	6285
	Retief GOOSEN	(SA)	70	70	70	72	282	6285
	Jean VAN DE VELDE	(Fr)	67	71	73	71	282	6285
	Paul MCGINLEY	(Ire)	71	72	72	67	282	6285
	Paul BROADHURST	(Eng)	73	70	68	71	282	6285
	Tom GILLIS	(USA)	72	71	66	73	282	6285
23	Francisco CEA	(Sp)	75	68	71	69	283	5175
	Miguel Angel JIMÉNEZ	(Sp)	72	73	68	70	283	5175
	Andrew CLAPP	(Eng)	72	71	70	70	283	5175
	Colin MONTGOMERIE	(Scot)	74	68	73	68	283	5175
	Eduardo ROMERO	(Arg)	66	75	72	70	283	5175
	Alexandre BALICKI	(Fr)	72	73	72	66	283	5175
29	Klas ERIKSSON	(Swe)	68	71	74	71	284	4133
	Ross DRUMMOND	(Scot)	70	71	75	68	284	4133
	Stephen SCAHILL	(NZ)	73	71	68	72	284	4133
	Gordon J BRAND	(Eng)	70	73	71	70	284	4133
	Van PHILLIPS	(Eng)	71	72	69	72	284	4133
	Gary NICKLAUS	(USA)	69	75	71	69	284	4133
	Peter MITCHELL	(Eng)	71	74	68	71	284	4133
	Thomas GÖGELE	(Ger)	74	68	69	73	284	4133
	Raphaël JACQUELIN	(Fr)	73	70	73	68	284	4133
38	Gary ORR	(Scot)	74	70	73	68	285	3450
	Wayne RILEY	(Aus)	70	68	76	71	285	3450
	Jean Louis GUEPY	(Fr)	75	70	70	70	285	3450
	Craig HAINLINE	(USA)	71	71	73	70	285	3450
42	Andre STOLZ	(Aus)	74	70	73	69	286	3050
	Adam HUNTER	(Scot)	71	74	68	73	286	3050
	Jamie SPENCE	(Eng)	72	70	69	75	286	3050
	Francis HOWLEY	(Ire)	70	72	73	71	286	3050
46	Dean ROBERTSON	(Scot)	68	75	74	70	287	2650
	Heinz Peter THÜL	(Ger)	69	74	74	70	287	2650
	Mark ROE	(Eng)	74	68	70	75	287	2650
	John WADE	(Aus)	74	71	71	71	287	2650
50	Robert LEE	(Eng)	73	71	74	70	288	2350
	Sven STRÜVER	(Ger)	72	73	73	70	288	2350
52	Darren COLE	(Aus)	70	74	72	73	289	2000
	Steve WEBSTER	(Eng)	70	73	73	73	289	2000
	Katsuyoshi TOMORI	(Jpn)	68	73	75	73	289	2000
	Greg TURNER	(NZ)	72	73	72	72	289	2000
	Diego BORREGO	(Sp)	72	72	69	76	289	2000
57	Gary EVANS	(Eng)	72	71	76	72	291	1560
	Steve ALKER	(NZ)	74	71	77	69	291	1560
	Steven BOTTOMLEY	(Eng)	70	73	72	76	291	1560
	Mårten OLANDER	(Swe)	74	71	73	73	291	1560
	Richard BOXALL	(Eng)	69	72	73	77	291	1560
62	Stephen FIELD	(Eng)	70	74	78	70	292	1325
	John HAWKSWORTH	(Eng)	71	72	72	77	292	1325
	Ola ELIASSON	(Swe)	71	72	78	71	292	1325
	Phil GOLDING	(Eng)	72	73	72	75	292	1325
66	John BICKERTON	(Eng)	67	77	77	72	293	749
	Johan RYSTRÖM	(Swe)	72	73	70	78	293	749
68	Des SMYTH	(Ire)	69	72	77	76	294	745
	Robert ALLENBY	(Aus)	70	70	75	79	294	745
	Oliver DAVID (AM)	(Fr)	74	71	77	79	301	

Colin Montgomerie.

The new Precept MC Spin

Driven by the world's greatest drivers

NEW Precept MC Spin

Newly developed thin cover.

Larger muscle-fibre molecular core.

Tour proven spin and feel for optimum control.

Precept MC Distance	Precept Tour	Precept EV Extra Spin
New muscle fibre core.	Double cover wound technology.	Super spin cover and high velocity core
Ultimate distance for all types of golfer.	The ultimate feel and distance ball.	for distance and control.

Driven by: NICK FALDO   JUMBO OZAKI   **NICK PRICE**   **MARK CALCAVECCHIA**   **STUART APPLEBY**   **LEE JANZEN**

Winner 1998 St Jude Classic   Winner 1998 Honda Classic   Winner 1998 Kemper Open   Winner 1998 US Open

Distributed by Dimensions in Sport 0181 947 6555

Carter's memorable week

David Carter's maiden European Tour
victory in Ireland gave him an
unforgettable moment

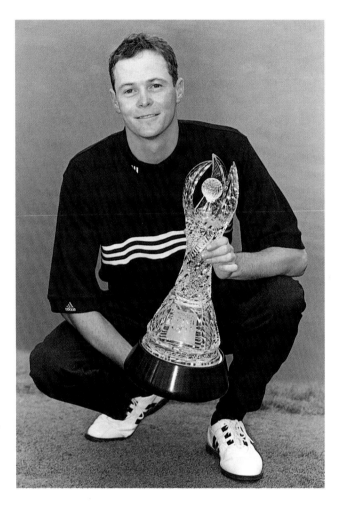

They talk about the luck of the Irish.

True, David Carter is not an Irishman but after all the nice things that broke his way in Co. Wicklow in the first week of July one was left to wonder if he was in communion with the lep- rechauns. Carter, in fact, was born in South Africa and only came to live in Chester- field in his late teens. But he is the first to agree that two huge slices of good fortune have proved crucial not only to his career but to his life as a whole.

And one of those hap- pened in Ireland on a bright, warm Sunday at Druids Glen, venue for the Mur- phy's Irish Open. Carter was in hot pursuit of his maiden European Tour title and enjoying a two stroke lead in the £1 mil- lion Championship when he arrived at the par five 16th, a hole where birdie is gener- ally anticipated if not always realised.

Carter knew as he stood on the tee that a four could virtually wrap it all up there and then. However, when he drove into a bunker on the left and then tried an over ambitious recovery with a four wood, it was the last thing on his mind. It was, instead, damage limitation time. The ball came to rest in knee high rough on the right and as the minutes slipped by, it seemed that the search would prove fruitless.

And it would have been had it not been for two curious little boys. Perhaps they looked a little more assiduously than their elders, as those of such curious age are wont to do, and with only seconds remaining on the clock came the magic shout. Eureka, we have it! Carter hacked the ball out and a very relieved man eventually signed for a six.

'It somehow felt like a birdie, not a bogey, after all the anxiety of the search,' he admitted later. Now his lead over Colin Montgomerie, champion in each of the pre- vious two years, was down to one. Montgomerie had played impeccably for a clos- ing 68 and a six under par clubhouse target. And with Carter still having to face the perilous 17th and 18th holes, nothing was guaranteed.

To his credit, Carter parred the short 17th with a seven iron and now needed a four at the last to win, just as Andrew Oldcorn, in 1996, found the left rough off the tee, the pond in front of the green with his approach and a double bogey six cost him the title. This time, Carter was in trouble on the right, but the result with the second was pre- cisely the same.

It looked as if Montgomerie had snared that third successive Irish title. But hold on a minute – the good fortune we talked about earlier was not about to desert Carter. Having dropped under penalty, he pitched on to twenty feet and then to a fanfare of a deafening cheer from

THE COURSE

Originally, Druids Glen – named after an ancient Druid altar which still stands to the right of the 12th green – was a slightly intriguing choice for the event among Irish enthusiasts when it first hosted the Championship in 1996. Now, after three years, it has clearly grown into *the* event and this time, again, attracted large, enthusiastic and knowledgeable crowds. Druids Glen made no secret of its delight at being chosen as host venue once more in 1999 and are now planning major developments including another 18 hole course and luxurious hotel as part of its bid for the 2005 Ryder Cup.

the thousands circling the green and a highly impressive Irish jig by himself and caddy Cliff Picking, knocked the putt in for a five to tie.

'I will never forget that moment,' said Carter. 'And as we drove back in the buggy to the 18th tee for the play-off, I kept telling myself this was meant to be, I was meant to win this Championship. After all, I find a ball in knee high grass at the 16th that I had no right to find to escape with a six,

It went thataway. Darren Clarke signals a wide.

146

SHOT OF THE WEEK

On Friday afternoon, Nick Faldo came to the 18th standing six over par and needing a birdie to stay in the Championship. He hit a poor drive and was left with a shot of 220 yards to the flag, uphill, through the trees and over a lake. He chose a three wood and left the ball no more than four feet from the flag before rolling in the putt. 'It was an amazing result and very important for me to stay in the tournament,' said the delighted, three times former champion.

Barry Lane (left), Colin Montgomerie (centre) and John McHenry (right) featured strongly during the week.

then I up and down it at the 18th. Fate had to be on my side.'

And so it proved. This time it was Montgomerie's turn to drive in the rough. He was happy to punch the ball out and pitch and putt for his par. To his horror, it instead scuttled along the fairway until plopping into the water with its dying gasp. Now 'all' David Carter had to do was find the green. And keeping his rhythm and his nerve, he did precisely that. When Monty pitched on and then missed his putt, he graciously conceded and a maiden Tour victory belonged to the ecstatic Carter, a young man who captured the hearts of the enormous crowds and who fully merited his triumph.

Afterwards, Carter spoke of what it all meant to him. And also, of course, of the good fortune that has followed him around over the past couple of years. Like the occasion he was severely concussed in a swimming pool accident in Sun City in March 1997 and as a result of which he collapsed in a coma in his Dubai hotel room a few days later.

'I must have been lying there for a long time when Iain Pyman came along and found me and raised the alarm,' Carter recalled. 'I was rushed to hospital and had an emergency operation on my brain. The surgeon said that if I hadn't been found for another three or four hours that I would have first of all become

paralysed and then died such was the pressure on the brain. Iain Pyman is my best friend and I have thanked him a thousand times.'

He then went on to describe how he suffered memory loss: 'It still isn't brilliant. When I was in hospital, Iain would come in to see me in the morning and when he came back in the evening I'd ask where he'd been that morning.'

You suspect, though, that nothing will prevent him remembering that very special weekend at Druids Glen in July 1998 for many years to come – and the part that fate and a little bit of Irish luck played in its execution.

Charlie Mulqueen   147

DRUIDS GLEN, DUBLIN, JULY 2-5, 1998 · YARDAGE 7012 · PAR 71

Pos	Name	Country	Rnd 1	Rnd 2	Rnd 3	Rnd 4	Total	Prize Money £
1	David CARTER	(Eng)	68	72	67	71	278	159991
2	Colin MONTGOMERIE	(Scot)	65	74	71	68	278	106631
3	Peter BAKER	(Eng)	69	75	66	70	280	53996
	John MCHENRY	(Ire)	70	68	70	72	280	53996
5	Craig HAINLINE	(USA)	70	68	72	71	281	40797
6	José COCERES	(Arg)	75	67	70	70	282	31197
	Gary ORR	(Scot)	70	69	72	71	282	31197
8	Peter LONARD	(Aus)	69	74	70	70	283	23998
9	Ian GARBUTT	(Eng)	73	69	71	71	284	17490
	Ian WOOSNAM	(Wal)	73	74	65	72	284	17490
	Russell CLAYDON	(Eng)	71	71	73	69	284	17490
	Derrick COOPER	(Eng)	73	70	72	69	284	17490
	José Maria OLAZABAL	(Sp)	73	72	71	68	284	17490
	Steve WEBSTER	(Eng)	71	70	70	73	284	17490
15	Lee WESTWOOD	(Eng)	70	73	73	69	285	14085
16	Peter O'MALLEY	(Aus)	74	70	69	73	286	11716
	Jim PAYNE	(Eng)	71	71	71	73	286	11716
	Steven RICHARDSON	(Eng)	68	71	74	73	286	11716
	Paolo QUIRICI	(Swi)	72	75	70	69	286	11716
	Klas ERIKSSON	(Swe)	71	74	72	69	286	11716
	Miguel Angel JIMÉNEZ	(Sp)	71	71	72	72	286	11716
	Paul BROADHURST	(Eng)	70	71	72	73	286	11716
	Barry LANE	(Eng)	70	75	62	79	286	11716
	Brian DAVIS	(Eng)	71	71	73	71	286	11716
25	Mark DAVIS	(Eng)	68	75	72	72	287	9935
	Eamonn DARCY	(Ire)	74	72	69	72	287	9935
27	Nick FALDO	(Eng)	75	72	67	74	288	8927
	Tony JOHNSTONE	(Zim)	71	67	77	73	288	8927
	Eduardo ROMERO	(Arg)	74	71	71	72	288	8927
	David LYNN	(Eng)	68	76	70	74	288	8927
	Anssi KANKKONEN	(Fin)	74	71	73	70	288	8927
32	Stephen ALLAN	(Aus)	69	71	78	71	289	8063
33	Ernie ELS	(SA)	71	71	70	78	290	7775
	Peter SENIOR	(Aus)	75	71	73	71	290	7775
35	Van PHILLIPS	(Eng)	71	72	71	77	291	7199
	José RIVERO	(Sp)	69	75	74	73	291	7199
	Domingo HOSPITAL	(Sp)	74	72	74	71	291	7199
	Greg CHALMERS	(Aus)	69	75	72	75	291	7199
39	Keith NOLAN	(Ire)	71	74	71	76	292	6143
	Jamie SPENCE	(Eng)	72	74	74	72	292	6143
	David GILFORD	(Eng)	73	71	72	76	292	6143
	Jarmo SANDELIN	(Swe)	69	75	76	72	292	6143
	Mark MCNULTY	(Zim)	71	74	74	73	292	6143
	Michael JONZON	(Swe)	75	70	72	75	292	6143
	Steen TINNING	(Den)	75	71	71	75	292	6143
46	Niclas FASTH	(Swe)	73	69	75	76	293	4991
	Mark ROE	(Eng)	74	71	73	75	293	4991
	Ignacio GARRIDO	(Sp)	74	69	78	72	293	4991
	Richard GREEN	(Aus)	71	73	75	74	293	4991
	Sven STRÜVER	(Ger)	72	74	75	72	293	4991
51	Paul AFFLECK	(Wal)	70	77	72	75	294	4319
	Carl SUNESON	(Sp)	72	75	74	73	294	4319
53	Carl WATTS	(Eng)	72	72	77	74	295	3647
	Dean ROBERTSON	(Scot)	74	72	74	75	295	3647
	David HIGGINS	(Ire)	75	69	72	79	295	3647
	Roger CHAPMAN	(Eng)	73	72	73	77	295	3647
	Katsuyoshi TOMORI	(Jpn)	70	73	72	80	295	3647
58	Raymond BURNS	(N.Ire)	74	71	73	78	296	3023
	Robert ALLENBY	(Aus)	73	73	77	73	296	3023
60	Alex CEJKA	(Ger)	72	70	77	78	297	2831
	Fabrice TARNAUD	(Fr)	69	74	72	82	297	2831
	Sergio GARCIA (AM)	(Sp)	68	73	75	81	297	
62	Fredrik JACOBSON	(Swe)	73	70	81	74	298	2639
	Olivier EDMOND	(Fr)	71	71	79	77	298	2639
64	Sam TORRANCE	(Scot)	71	76	76	76	299	2495
65	Stephen AMES	(T&T)	68	78	78	76	300	1919
	Phillip PRICE	(Wal)	70	72	81	77	300	1919
67	Nicolas JOAKIMIDES	(Fr)	75	72	77	77	301	1438
68	Jonathan LOMAS	(Eng)	75	72	74	81	302	1436
69	Angel CABRERA	(Arg)	75	72	77	79	303	1434
70	Andrew OLDCORN	(Scot)	74	72	80	81	307	1432

British Amateur champion Sergio Garcia

Guardian Performance Data[SM] is the official statistics service for the PGA European Tour.

Sponsored by the Guardian Royal Exchange Group, this records and reports on the seven key aspects of play, from driving distances to the average number of putts per round. So players and fans can analyse how everyone's performing.

And at the end of the tour, we'll all be able to see who the best players are in the individual categories, and overall.

Guardian Performance Data.[SM] It's the best insurance for the future of a golfer's game.

Guardian and Guardian Performance Data Servicemarks are all Registered Servicemarks of Guardian Royal Exchange plc. Guardian Royal Exchange, Group Royal Exchange, London EC3V 3LS, Tel: 0171 283 7101, www.gre-group.com

Westwood continues winning ways

Lee Westwood captured his third European Tour title of the year with another convincing performance

*T*he legendary Ben Hogan always saw himself more in competition with the golf course than with his fellow competitors and once famously remarked after a US Open at Oakland Hills that he'd brought the monster to its knees.

Though he didn't need to visit Loch Ness to tame Scotland's monster when he won the Open at Carnoustie in 1953, the guess is that Hogan would also have taken a shine to the more manicured beast created by Tom Weiskopf and Jay Morrish at

Loch Lomond. Like all outstanding golf courses, Loch Lomond has the capacity to sort out the wheat from the chaff. In its three year history of staging a European Tour event, the course on the bonnie, bonnie banks has invited only Ryder Cup players to claim the winner's laurels.

After Thomas Björn of Denmark came through in 1996 and Tom Lehman from Arizona blew away the competition in 1997, the tradition was maintained at the 1998 Standard Life Loch Lomond event when the finest English golfer since Nick Faldo produced a winning mixture of power and touch to bank the first prize of £141,660 and take another important step down the road towards establishing himself as Europe's number one.

Like any successful middle-distance runner, Lee Westwood used the first lap of the circuit to ease himself into position rather than set the pace for others. On a day when Faldo's injured elbow and Jack Nicklaus' troublesome hip made most of

THE COURSE

If anything Tom Weiskopf's masterpiece was in even better shape for the third staging of the Standard Life Loch Lomond than the previous two events. Both Colin Montgomerie and José Maria Olazábal said that the course was arguably the best of all those used on the European Tour. Attention to detail was so exact that giant fans were installed on both the putting green and the practice range to keep away midges.

the headlines – one golfer pulled out of the Open and the other was doubtful – Westwood's tidy opening salvo of 69 amounted to little more than a footnote.

The early running on the course was made by another of Westwood's colleagues at Valderrama, Ian Woosnam, who has a knack of playing well in Scotland during July. He repeated the form which won him three Scottish Opens and carded a four under par round of 67 to stake a one shot lead over Gary Orr. Hailing from nearby Helensburgh, Orr was born and bred just seven miles from Loch Lomond. Any comparison between where the hairdresser's son learned to play the game in Dunbartonshire and Weiskopf's course, however, was purely coincidental. 'I suppose they both have 18 holes,'

Halfway leader Ross Drummond.

grinned the Scot, who went to work each day on a diet of his mother's cooking.

Another Scot, one who had only taken his place in the 150 strong field after the late withdrawal of Davis Love III, the US PGA champion, moved to centre stage after the second round. Ross Drummond posted a 66 to move to the top of the

leaderboard on 137 at the halfway mark. A veteran of 20 summers on Tour, Drummond, 41, lost his card the year before and now found himself chasing invitations to tournaments and playing for his livelihood. As it turned out the strain of leading would prove too much for him, but on Thursday the man from Ayrshire rolled back the years as he covered the back nine in 31. For a stand-in, it was a stand out performance. Bulldog Drummond was only too well aware that a younger pup was snapping at his heels. After shooting a second successive round of 69, Westwood was just one stroke off the lead and feeling relaxed enough about his game to spend as much time at Loch Lomond catching trout as chasing birdies.

Refreshed by casting a rod rather than

The Feathery

1825 – The golfer's favourite ball, well, the only ball available in the year Standard Life came into being. Made of pieces of dry leather and you've guessed it, feathers.

Hand Hammered Gutta

1860 – Ball manufacturers had found that the chips made by repeated hitting enabled the ball to travel further. Incidentally Standard Life were also travelling further with 70% of their business coming from abroad.

Gutta Percha

1870 – By now this had become the choice of discerning golfers everywhere, in much the same way Standard Life was becoming the preferred choice among people who wanted a good return on their investment.

Wound Rubber Ball

1900 – This was a breakthrough in the modern game. The new style of ball had a solid core. Something that Standard Life had been enjoying for years now.

Modern Ball

1930 – Advances in materials and regularity in the construction of the ball meant that people could rely on consistent performance whatever the conditions. Now, who does that remind you of?

Leaders in our field since 1825

STANDARD LIFE

The Standard Life Loch Lomond
golf tournament
7-10 July 1999

SHOT OF THE WEEK

When Lee Westwood walked onto the 14th tee in the second round, his caddie, Mick Doran, suggested he might want to take the conservative route to the green by laying up down the left fairway of the 345-year par four. Instead the Englishman took out the driver and carried the marsh, ending just short of the green's apron. After Westwood ran the chip 15 feet past the hole, Doran slyly suggested that he could have got to his point by an easier route. The Ryder Cup player was so irked that he rammed in the putt for birdie and spoke later that risk-taking was the key to his game.

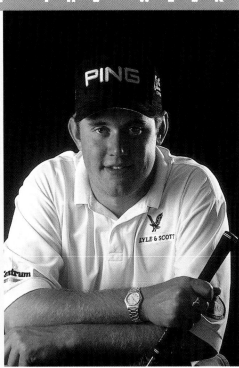

Defending champion Tom Lehman (above). Dennis Edlund punches a putt home (left).

swinging a driver, Westwood went back to work in the third round determined to make another positive move. Among the leaders who started late, Westwood was one of the golfers who had to contend with a two and a half hour delay caused by torrential rain. Frustrated by missing a short putt before play was suspended, Westwood showed why his temperament is admired just as much as his ability by making a birdie at the 14th hole after the course dried out and making par over the remaining holes for a masterly 68 and a share of the lead on 208 with Sweden's Dennis Edlund after 54 holes.

A part-time conjurer, Edlund could only look on in the final round as Westwood cast a spell over Loch Lomond and signed off with another sub-par round to win his fourth tournament of the year by four strokes from the chasing pack. The victory was not without a couple of moments of tension as the 25-year-old from Worksop shed strokes at both the tenth and 11th holes, but he set the record straight by holding a brace of long putts on the 15th and 17th greens for a closing 70 and an eight under par total of 276.

Westwood is too laid-back a fellow to warrant any sort of comparison with Hogan, but there was evidence in Scotland that the Englishman's warm demeanour hides a cold attitude to winning. At Loch Lomond, the Big Ice Man was on the march.

Mike Aitken

Loch Lomond, Glasgow, July 8-11, 1998 • Yardage 7050 • Par 71

Pos	Name	Country	Rnd 1	Rnd 2	Rnd 3	Rnd 4	Total	Prize Money £
1	Lee WESTWOOD	(Eng)	69	69	68	70	276	141660
2	Ian WOOSNAM	(Wal)	67	73	74	66	280	51180
	Eduardo ROMERO	(Arg)	71	70	71	68	280	51180
	Robert ALLENBY	(Aus)	72	72	68	68	280	51180
	David HOWELL	(Eng)	68	71	70	71	280	51180
	Dennis EDLUND	(Swe)	70	69	67	74	280	51180
7	Colin MONTGOMERIE	(Scot)	72	71	68	70	281	23375
	Gary ORR	(Scot)	68	72	71	70	281	23375
9	Tom LEHMAN	(USA)	73	68	69	72	282	17985
	Paul BROADHURST	(Eng)	69	71	71	71	282	17985
11	Clark DENNIS	(USA)	74	68	71	70	283	15130
	Derrick COOPER	(Eng)	75	68	67	73	283	15130
13	Dean ROBERTSON	(Scot)	72	72	71	69	284	12017
	Stewart CINK	(USA)	70	74	71	69	284	12017
	Klas ERIKSSON	(Swe)	73	72	65	74	284	12017
	Stephen ALLAN	(Aus)	70	68	72	74	284	12017
	Craig HAINLINE	(USA)	75	66	71	72	284	12017
	Massimo FLORIOLI	(It)	73	71	69	71	284	12017
	Sam TORRANCE	(Scot)	73	70	72	69	284	12017
20	Jamie SPENCE	(Eng)	70	71	72	72	285	9817
	Alex CEJKA	(Ger)	71	71	69	74	285	9817
	Jarmo SANDELIN	(Swe)	75	71	72	67	285	9817
	Patrik SJÖLAND	(Swe)	74	73	68	70	285	9817
24	Ian GARBUTT	(Eng)	73	69	72	73	287	8287
	Stuart APPLEBY	(Aus)	73	68	74	72	287	8287
	Stephen AMES	(T&T)	75	71	70	71	287	8287
	Jean VAN DE VELDE	(Fr)	71	72	73	71	287	8287
	Miguel Angel JIMÉNEZ	(Sp)	71	70	74	72	287	8287
	Peter BAKER	(Eng)	73	69	73	72	287	8287
	Thomas GÖGELE	(Ger)	76	69	70	72	287	8287
	Pierre FULKE	(Swe)	75	69	72	71	287	8287
32	Jim PAYNE	(Eng)	74	70	73	71	288	6885
	José Maria OLAZÁBAL	(Sp)	72	71	69	76	288	6885
	Thomas BJÖRN	(Den)	73	72	70	73	288	6885
	Paul MCGINLEY	(Ire)	72	69	72	75	288	6885
36	Ross DRUMMOND	(Scot)	71	66	72	80	289	6205
	Carl WATTS	(Eng)	74	73	73	69	289	6205
	Jesper PARNEVIK	(Swe)	71	73	72	73	289	6205
	Stephen FIELD	(Eng)	75	70	70	74	289	6205
40	Padraig HARRINGTON	(Ire)	74	69	77	70	290	5270
	Olle KARLSSON	(Swe)	74	72	69	75	290	5270
	Robert DAMRON	(USA)	70	76	73	71	290	5270
	David GILFORD	(Eng)	74	72	71	73	290	5270
	Russell CLAYDON	(Eng)	74	66	75	75	290	5270
	Thomas LEVET	(Fr)	74	71	74	71	290	5270
	Glen DAY	(USA)	75	71	72	72	290	5270
47	Greg TURNER	(NZ)	73	74	73	71	291	4250
	David CARTER	(Eng)	72	75	72	72	291	4250
	Joakim HAEGGMAN	(Swe)	73	71	69	78	291	4250
	John MCHENRY	(Ire)	73	71	75	72	291	4250
	Costantino ROCCA	(It)	68	74	77	72	291	4250
52	Mats LANNER	(Swe)	72	72	74	74	292	3740
53	Carlos Daniel FRANCO	(Para)	75	72	73	73	293	3315
	Domingo HOSPITAL	(Sp)	74	73	73	73	293	3315
	Roger CHAPMAN	(Eng)	76	70	75	72	293	3315
	Paul EALES	(Eng)	76	70	73	74	293	3315
57	Stuart CAGE	(Eng)	72	75	73	74	294	2748
	Sven STRÜVER	(Ger)	74	72	77	71	294	2748
	Andrew COLTART	(Scot)	71	69	73	81	294	2748
	Sergio GARCIA (AM)	(Sp)	71	71	76	76	294	
60	Silvio GRAPPASONNI	(It)	76	69	76	74	295	2507
	Angel CABRERA	(Arg)	72	71	76	76	295	2507
62	Ignacio GARRIDO	(Sp)	72	73	71	81	297	2057
	Stephen LEANEY	(Aus)	75	70	75	77	297	2057
	Brian DAVIS	(Eng)	73	74	72	78	297	2057
	Ross MCFARLANE	(Eng)	76	69	75	77	297	2057
	Mathias GRÖNBERG	(Swe)	75	70	76	76	297	2057
67	Gary EVANS	(Eng)	78	68	73	79	298	1273
68	Andrew OLDCORN	(Scot)	71	75	76	77	299	1269
	José COCERES	(Arg)	75	72	75	77	299	1269
	Santiago LUNA	(Sp)	74	73	77	75	299	1269

David Howell (above) shared second place.

One of the best

Royal Birkdale provided all the ingredients for
a memorable Championship and Mark O'Meara
found the mixture exactly to his liking

This is the story of how four men, Mark O'Meara, Brian Watts, Tiger Woods and Justin Rose, one magnificent golf course and a lot of wind proved one of golf's axioms to be absolutely right. The saying could have been that 'you can talk to a fade but a hook won't listen' or 'two up with five to play never wins'. In fact, what was clear from one of the most exciting Opens in recent years was that a good golf course might throw up a great champion but a great one always will.

There can be no quibbling with the name of O'Meara and the words 'Champion golfer for 1998' as he is now known after winning the Open. Quietly and unassumingly, with a swing that is repetitive even under intense pressure, O'Meara added the old claret jug to the green jacket that was put over his shoulders on a still spring evening three months earlier when he won the Masters.

The mid-life crisis is supposed to set in during a person's 40s, when they are more than halfway through the 20th century version of the Biblical lifespan of three score years and ten. Don't talk to O'Meara, who will be 42 next January, about crises. Crisis? What crisis? The only sort of crisis he had in 1998 was how to deal with all the success he was having.

O'Meara is a modest man who describes himself as a 'nice consistent player', eschewing words such as great because he believes they belong to golfers such as Jack Nicklaus, Ben Hogan, Arnold Palmer and Byron Nelson. O'Meara, though, has equalled one of the modern game's records and eclipsed another. He is the oldest man in modern times to win two major titles in one year, older than the 40-year-olds Ben Hogan in 1953 and Jack Nicklaus in 1980. He is the third man in the past 22 years to win the Masters and the Open in the same year. Tom Watson in 1977 and Nick Faldo in 1990 were the other two.

O'Meara's play was that of the solid, consistent professional he is, a man who goes out to meet whatever the challenge is and does his best to beat it. The challenge in question at the 127th Open was twofold: to tame a revitalised, par 70 Royal Birkdale on which £500,000 had been spent to upgrade the greens, install new tees and remove areas of Lancashire Weed, while coping with an extraordinary range of conditions, most of which were inclement. One windy day in practice

**Sergio Garcia casts a long shadow (left).
Tiger Woods chips in on the 71st hole
(below left). Brian Watts in a tangle (right).**

Tom Lehman lost six balls in eight holes in Birkdale's thick rough.

For four rounds of the Open the weather ranged from the benevolent opening day when 28 men were under par, to the horror of the second day when a 50 mph wind and a furious rain squall caused play to be suspended for 38 minutes, to the near gale of Saturday when Phil Mickelson had an 85, defending champion Justin Leonard and Nick Price 82s, Lee Janzen, the US Open champion, an 80, and Lee Westwood, the winner at Loch Lomond the previous week, and Fred Couples 78s. As the average score in the third round was 77.49 there must have been a few low scores. Costantino Rocca had the day's best, a 70.

Two of O'Meara's rounds were two over par, two were under par, leaving him tied after 72 holes with Watts, a little-known 32-year-old American who competes on the Japanese Tour where, prior to the Open, he had won 11 tournaments and nearly $1m annually for the past five years. Watts led after 36 holes, after 54 holes and still led after 67 holes.

In the end it took a remarkable bunker shot on the 72nd hole to get him into a play-off with O'Meara, who had finished minutes earlier and was watching from behind the green. Watts had to position his right foot on the grass at the back of the bunker and his left foot in the sand. From this uncomfortable stance he contrived to hit his ball to a foot of the hole.

O'Meara triumphed over Watts by two strokes after a four-hole play-off, which started at the 15th. Watts missed a short putt at that hole to fall one behind the Masters champion and dropped another after a bad drive on the 17th. On the 18th fairway for the second time in as many hours, O'Meara turned to Jerry Higginbotham, his caddie, and said: 'I have never been this calm. I cannot believe how calm I am.' After this he hit a safe four iron to the heart of the green and two-putted for victory.

O'Meara may have won because of an expedition he, Woods and Payne Stewart made to Ireland the week before the Open, during which they played courses such as Waterville and Ballybunion. It was on these links, where the fairways were fast-running, the greens firm and there was always a hint of a wind that the seeds were laid for O'Meara's victory. As Woods took on the wind, O'Meara stood on each tee and asked where he had to hit his ball to stand the best chance of getting a par. After the round at Waterville, O'Meara had hit two greens in regulation but gone round in 72.

O'Meara used his knowledge of Royal Birkdale gained from winning the 1987 English Open, when he holed two seven iron shots in the final round, and playing alongside Ian Baker-Finch when the Australian won the 1991 Open. He also

had his share of winner's luck when his ball appeared to be lost in thick rough on the sixth hole of the third round. O'Meara had thought it lost and begun to walk back to the tee when a spectator found it and then pocketed it. After much discussion with rules officials, O'Meara was allowed to replace the ball from where he managed a bogey five, one, perhaps two and maybe even three strokes better than it might have been.

The rounds that laid the foundations for his victory were his 68 on Friday and his 72 on Saturday. These were two strokes better than any other competitor and, incidentally, ten strokes better than Woods. These were the rounds when O'Meara's work spent practising keeping the ball low with Hank Raney, his swing coach, paid off. 'I felt if I went out and played well and kept my composure com-

ing down the stretch I'd have a chance,' O'Meara said.

This was precisely what he did and what Woods did not for a few crucial moments. Woods has yet to understand the patience that is needed to deal with the subtleties of a links course in a wind. The Open was the first major championship since the Masters in 1997 in which he was a genuine contender. He started with a 65, finished with a 66 and scored 17 birdies – more than O'Meara and four more than any other competitor. Significantly, though, he could do no better than 73 and 77 in the bad weather of the two middle rounds and he started his last round with three putts.

Woods staged a grandstand finish. Having taken 33 strokes to the turn, he birdied the 15th, which was downwind, and chipped in from 30 feet on the 17th

159

THE COURSE

Royal Birkdale's 7,018-yard course has long enjoyed a reputation as one of the fairest and toughest of all courses on the Open rota but it can hardly have been in better condition than it was this year. £500,000 was spent on improving the greens, which had been poor at the 1991 Open, on building new tees and removing thousands of bushes known as Lancashire Weed. A wet spring contributed to the growth of the rough and the fairways were wide enough to encourage a mixture of caution and aggression.

Sign language from Nick Faldo (top),
Ernie Els (centre) and Colin
Montgomerie (above).

A rare moment of good weather (above). Jesper Parnevik came close again (below).

Justin Rose's third stroke on the 72nd hole was the one that determined his future, as well as being one that was heard in Manchester. As his 45-yard pitch dropped softly onto the putting surface and drifted into the hole for a birdie, Rose knew it had answered a question: was he going to turn professional? He had wrestled with the question for days but as his ball disappeared out of sight and an enormous roar went up from the spectators, Rose knew he had to turn professional. Minutes later, he announced he had.

Final scoreboard salutes Mark O'Meara (left). Justin Rose recieves the Silver Medal for leading amateur (right).

for another birdie. The exultation with which he greeted this was matched only by that which he showed on the 18th when he holed from 35 feet for another birdie.

In this dramatic finish Woods surged past everyone except O'Meara and Watts and finished one stroke behind them. The only man who created more excitement than Woods on the last day was Rose, the 17-year-old amateur, a Walker Cup player, and he had been doing that since Friday when he had a 66 during which he fleet-ingly held the lead.

One month earlier sports enthusiasts in Britain had warmed to Michael Owen, the brilliant young footballer who had played so well for England in the World Cup. Now came Rose, a baby-faced teenager who would not be 18 for two more weeks and lay second after 36 holes. Rose looked composed on Friday, held on well during Saturday's maelstrom for a 75 and then refused to quit the scene, as amateurs are supposed to. A 69 put him level with Jim Furyk, Raymond Russell and Jesper Parnevik in joint fourth place, two strokes behind O'Meara and Watts. It was the best finish by an amateur since Frank Stranahan tied for second behind Ben Hogan at Carnoustie in 1953.

The 127th Open was a championship that had been mouthwatering in prospect and turned out to be breathtaking in reality. One of the last to be staged under the secretaryship of Sir Michael Bonallack, who is to retire by the year 2000, it was truly a Championship fit for a knight.

John Hopkins   163

ROYAL BIRKDALE, JULY 16-19, 1998 · PAR 70 · YARDS 7018

Pos	Name	Country	Rnd 1	Rnd 2	Rnd 3	Rnd 4	Total	Prize Money £
1	Mark O'MEARA	(USA)	72	68	72	68	280	300000
2	Brian WATTS	(USA)	68	69	73	70	280	188000
3	Tiger WOODS	(USA)	65	73	77	66	281	135000
4	Jim FURYK	(USA)	70	70	72	70	282	76666
	Jesper PARNEVIK	(Swe)	68	72	72	70	282	76666
	Raymond RUSSELL	(Scot)	68	73	75	66	282	76666
	Justin ROSE (AM)	(Eng)	72	66	75	69	282	
7	Davis LOVE III	(USA)	67	73	77	68	285	49500
8	Thomas BJÖRN	(Den)	68	71	76	71	286	40850
	Costantino ROCCA	(It)	72	74	70	70	286	40850
10	John HUSTON	(USA)	65	77	73	72	287	33333
	Brad FAXON	(USA)	67	74	74	72	287	33333
	David DUVAL	(USA)	70	71	75	71	287	33333
13	Gordon BRAND JNR.	(Scot)	71	70	76	71	288	29000
14	Peter BAKER	(Eng)	69	72	77	71	289	23650
	Greg TURNER	(NZ)	68	75	75	71	289	23650
	José Maria OLAZÁBAL	(Sp)	73	72	75	69	289	23650
	Des SMYTH	(Ire)	74	69	75	71	289	23650
18	Curtis STRANGE	(USA)	73	73	74	70	290	17220
	Vijay SINGH	(Fij)	67	74	78	71	290	17220
	Sandy LYLE	(Scot)	71	72	75	72	290	17220
	Robert ALLENBY	(Aus)	67	76	78	69	290	17220
	Mark JAMES	(Eng)	71	74	74	71	290	17220
23	Sam TORRANCE	(Scot)	69	77	75	70	291	12480
	Bob ESTES	(USA)	72	70	76	73	291	12480
	Stephen AMES	(T&T)	68	72	79	72	291	12480
	Peter O'MALLEY	(Aus)	71	71	78	71	291	12480
	Lee JANZEN	(USA)	72	69	80	70	291	12480
28	Scott DUNLAP	(USA)	72	69	80	71	292	10030
	Nick PRICE	(Zim)	66	72	82	72	292	10030
	Shigeki MARUYAMA	(Jpn)	70	73	75	74	292	10030
	Loren ROBERTS	(USA)	66	76	76	74	292	10030
	Ernie ELS	(SA)	72	74	74	72	292	10030
	Sergio GARCIA (AM)	(Sp)	69	75	76	72	292	
33	Mark CALCAVECCHIA	(USA)	69	77	73	74	293	8900
	Santiago LUNA	(Sp)	70	72	80	71	293	8900
	Sven STRÜVER	(Ger)	75	70	80	68	293	8900
36	Patrik SJÖLAND	(Swe)	72	72	77	73	294	8350
	Joakim HAEGGMAN	(Swe)	71	74	78	71	294	8350
	Philip WALTON	(Ire)	68	76	74	76	294	8350
	Naomichi OZAKI	(Jpn)	72	73	76	73	294	8350
	Tom KITE	(USA)	72	69	79	74	294	8350
	Steen TINNING	(Den)	69	76	77	72	294	8350
42	Katsuyoshi TOMORI	(Jpn)	75	71	70	79	295	7581
	David HOWELL	(Eng)	68	77	79	71	295	7581
	David FROST	(SA)	72	73	78	72	295	7581
	Rodger DAVIS	(Aus)	76	70	78	71	295	7581
	David CARTER	(Eng)	71	75	76	73	295	7581
	Nick FALDO	(Eng)	72	73	75	75	295	7581
	Payne STEWART	(USA)	71	71	78	75	295	7581
	Andrew COLTART	(Scot)	68	77	75	75	295	7581
50	Steve STRICKER	(USA)	70	72	80	74	296	6860
	Bill MAYFAIR	(USA)	72	73	77	74	296	6860
	Brandt JOBE	(USA)	70	73	82	71	296	6860
	Larry MIZE	(USA)	70	75	79	72	296	6860
	Frankie MINOZA	(Phil)	69	75	76	76	296	6860
55	Trevor DODDS	(Nam)	73	71	81	72	297	6264
	Eduardo ROMERO	(Arg)	71	70	79	77	297	6264
	Steven JONES	(USA)	73	72	79	73	297	6264
	Justin LEONARD	(USA)	73	73	82	69	297	6264
	Ignacio GARRIDO	(Sp)	71	74	80	72	297	6264
	Ian WOOSNAM	(Wal)	72	74	76	75	297	6264
	Greg CHALMERS	(Aus)	71	75	77	74	297	6264
62	Lee WESTWOOD	(Eng)	71	71	78	78	298	5975
	Carlos Daniel FRANCO	(Para)	71	73	76	78	298	5975
64	Stewart CINK	(USA)	71	73	83	72	299	5800
	Mark BROOKS	(USA)	71	73	75	80	299	5800
	Michael CAMPBELL	(NZ)	73	73	80	73	299	5800
	Fred COUPLES	(USA)	66	74	78	81	299	5800
	Michael LONG	(NZ)	70	74	78	77	299	5800
	Didier DE VOOGHT (AM)	(Bel)	70	76	80	73	299	
69	Andrew CLAPP	(Eng)	72	74	81	73	300	5650
70	Gary EVANS	(Eng)	69	74	84	74	301	5600
71	Bob MAY	(USA)	70	73	85	75	303	5550
72	Andrew MCLARDY	(SA)	72	74	80	78	304	5500
73	Fredrik JACOBSON	(Swe)	67	78	81	79	305	5450
74	Kazuhiko HOSOKAWA	(Jpn)	72	73	81	80	306	5400
75	Robert GILES	(Ire)	72	74	83	78	307	5350
76	Phil MICKELSON	(USA)	71	74	85	78	308	5300
77	Andrew OLDCORN	(Scot)	75	71	84	79	309	5250
78	Dudley HART	(USA)	73	72	85	80	310	5200

Rough time for Phil Mickelson.

Barclays Premier

Barclays Premier is pleased to be associated with the PGA European Tour.

Barclays Premier Central Office, PO Box 122, 2 The Oaks,
Westwood Business Park, Coventry CV4 8YZ. Telephone: (01203) 534642.

Leaney makes it a double

Stephen Leaney held off a fast-finishing
Darren Clarke to take his second
European Tour title of the year

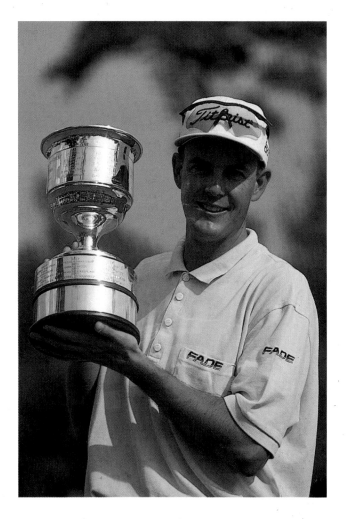

*O*stensibly it was the TNT Dutch Open but for the teams from the BBC, ITN and Sky, not to mention Fleet Street, it was the Rose Show.

The Dutch Open is traditionally held the week after the Open Championship and, for reasons of exhaustion, it sometimes does not get the attention it deserves from the Fourth Estate. This time it was different. Justin Rose was making his professional debut a few days after a truly astonishing performance in the 127th Open at Royal Birkdale.

Playing in his first and last Open as an amateur, Rose, at the age of 17, almost brought the clubhouse down with his unforgettable pitch-in for a birdie at the 18th in a final round of 69. He finished, of course, joint fourth, a position that would have earned him £70,000 had he not been an amateur.

Almost immediately, the boy wonder turned professional, flew to Amsterdam and shot 69 at the Hilversumsche Club to win the pro-am and £625, his first cheque, although he admitted he did not have a bank account. 'It's a nice feeling that I've earned some money by going to work,' Rose said. 'I guess I have to establish myself on the European Tour. That's my objective. At Birkdale I was surprisingly relaxed but here I'm stepping into the unknown. Everything starts now. The Open was fantastic, a week I'll never forget but the slate is wiped clean. I want to get down to business and play well although my expectations aren't too high. The key thing is to make cuts.'

His first shot as a professional in a European Tour event sailed left of the fairway. Then things began to get really bad. On the day that Lee Westwood equalled the course record with a 63, Rose shot 77. 'I felt drained', he said. 'I struggled with my driving and lost my rhythm.' He hooked several drives, promoting the question, was this the Hook of Hampshire, where he lives, or the Hook of Holland? For the record, his first birdie came at the 12th.

In the second round Rose – the previous night he'd retired to his bedroom at 7 pm and was asleep by ten – shot 65 and then had an agonising wait of six hours before discovering that he had missed the cut by one stroke. He finished level par and the guillotine fell at minus one. 'What I've learnt is that the first round is the most important in professional golf. If you

THE COURSE

The 1998 TNT Dutch Open was the 74th edition of the championship and the 19th to be played at Hilversumsche. The club was founded in 1910 and the course, heavily wooded and on undulating ground, is in stark contrast to holland's famous North Sea links. Hilversumsche – the road to the course is lined by showrooms selling Ferraris and Jaguars – is Amsterdam's answer to Sunningdale and indeed, several of the holes are reminiscent of those to be found at the famous Berkshire course. It is not difficult to score well at Hilversumsche provided the ball is kept on the straight and narrow.

don't shoot a low score you've virtually no chance of winning the tournament.' Goodbye England's Rose. He was looking forward to being reunited with his dog Marmaduke, a 'small, white, fluffy thing.'

It sounded more like a description of the moustache of Tiger Woods's caddie, Fluff.

Another who missed the cut was Phil Mickelson who had a 74 after a first round of 68. Mickelson said he had a sleepless night after hearing of the death in a tragic accident in London of Renay Appleby, the wife of the Florida based Australian golfer, Stuart Appleby.

Stephen Leaney was also devastated

Justin Rose (left) in action and cornered by autograph hunters

SHOT OF THE WEEK

Larry Barber, the son of the former American Ryder Cup player Miller Barber, had a hole-in-one with a nine iron at the 125-yard fifth hole in the second round. Barber, from Arizona, had asked for an invitation to play after failing to qualify for the Open at Royal Birkdale. Alas, his ace, which cost him a few drinks in the clubhouse, did not prevent him from missing the cut.

Nick Price (above) was in contention throughout. Brian Davis (left) finished in joint 11th place.

by the news but despite being in what he described as a 'state of shock', the Australian, who had a 66 in the first round, emulated Westwood's feat and equalled the course record with a 63 in the second. It meant that he and Westwood were tied at the top of the leaderboard on 129, 13 under par.

Nick Price was lying third on 133, Jonathan Lomas fourth on 134 with a host of players a stroke further back. While the Rose family returned to Hampshire for a well earned break from the media frenzy, Leaney opened up a two-stroke lead over Westwood, with a 70 to a 72.

The Englishman, who had won seven titles in nine months, paid a heavy price for a six at the 18th where he drove into trees. Apart from the odd shower, the weather was perfect for playing golf and watching it, and Darren Clarke moved up the leaderboard with a 67, five behind Leaney, three behind his stablemate Westwood.

Clarke was in even more inspired form in the final round yet despite producing a 63, Leaney just had enough in reserve to keep the Irishman at bay. In March, Leaney had won the Moroccan Open by eight strokes with a 17 under par aggregate. In Holland he finished at 18 under, won by a stroke from Clarke and received £133,330. 'A very, very close friend lost his wife this week and I have been thinking about that for the last four days.' Leaney said. 'If I'd lost the tournament it would have been no big deal. It

put the game into a different light.'

Leaney has had his own brush with death. Five years ago it was discovered that he had a life-threatening blood clot and he was out of action for seven months after having two ribs removed. The previous season, the 29-year-old from Perth played on the European Challenge Tour and was 11th on the money list with less than £30,000. He did not win but was runner-up four times and that was enough to secure his card for the premier stage.

Paired with Westwood for the second day running, Leaney and the Englishman both scored 67 on the final day. West-

wood was joint third with Price while Clarke's late run – he finished on 267, a stroke behind Leaney – earned him £80,880.

Leaney went to the turn in 33 with three birdies and his only bogey came at the 11th. By contrast, Westwood went out in 36 and then had six threes in seven holes. He came home in 31 but even so Leaney could afford to take a par five at the 18th and retain his lead, which is what he did. 'I always knew I had the game to compete with the best,' Leaney said. 'I'm hoping to go on to bigger things.'

Tim Glover 169

HILVERSUMSCHE GC, HILVERSUM, AMSTERDAM, JULY 23-26, 1998 • PAR 71 • YARDS 6636

Pos	Name	Country	Rnd 1	Rnd 2	Rnd 3	Rnd 4	Total	Prize Money £
1	Stephen LEANEY	(Aus)	66	63	70	67	266	133330
2	Darren CLARKE	(N.Ire)	68	69	67	63	267	88880
3	Lee WESTWOOD	(Eng)	63	66	72	67	268	45035
	Nick PRICE	(Zim)	68	65	69	66	268	45035
5	Costantino ROCCA	(It)	71	65	69	65	270	33880
6	Peter BAKER	(Eng)	70	68	68	65	271	28000
7	Iain PYMAN	(Eng)	73	66	66	68	273	22000
	Ian GARBUTT	(Eng)	68	69	67	69	273	22000
9	Patrik SJÖLAND	(Swe)	67	70	66	71	274	16920
	Mark JAMES	(Eng)	70	69	67	68	274	16920
11	Raphaël JACQUELIN	(Fr)	68	68	70	69	275	12773
	John HUSTON	(USA)	67	69	70	69	275	12773
	Jonathan LOMAS	(Eng)	65	69	71	70	275	12773
	Brian DAVIS	(Eng)	66	72	69	68	275	12773
	Philip WALTON	(Ire)	68	67	70	70	275	12773
	Steen TINNING	(Den)	70	67	69	69	275	12773
17	Peter LONARD	(Aus)	68	67	72	69	276	10160
	Gordon BRAND JNR.	(Scot)	69	70	68	69	276	10160
	Andrew COLTART	(Scot)	71	68	68	69	276	10160
	David GILFORD	(Eng)	71	67	68	70	276	10160
21	Per HAUGSRUD	(Nor)	65	71	71	70	277	8760
	Mark MOULAND	(Wal)	70	67	70	70	277	8760
	Michael LONG	(NZ)	70	70	67	70	277	8760
	Miguel Angel JIMÉNEZ	(Sp)	69	66	69	73	277	8760
	Andrew OLDCORN	(Scot)	69	70	72	66	277	8760
	Paul LAWRIE	(Scot)	67	72	67	71	277	8760
27	Jean VAN DE VELDE	(Fr)	69	69	73	67	278	7680
	Michael CAMPBELL	(NZ)	73	65	70	70	278	7680
	Bernhard LANGER	(Ger)	70	65	72	71	278	7680
30	Marco GORTANA	(It)	67	70	71	71	279	6180
	Pierre FULKE	(Swe)	71	66	73	69	279	6180
	Mats LANNER	(Swe)	69	72	72	66	279	6180
	Robert Jan DERKSEN	(Hol)	70	70	71	68	279	6180
	David HOWELL	(Eng)	71	69	68	71	279	6180
	Greg TURNER	(NZ)	71	69	68	71	279	6180
	Paul MCGINLEY	(Ire)	66	71	71	71	279	6180
	Kalle BRINK	(Swe)	69	70	69	71	279	6180
	Peter MITCHELL	(Eng)	68	71	71	69	279	6180
	Stephen MCALLISTER	(Scot)	68	68	72	71	279	6180
	Jeff REMESY	(Fr)	68	70	71	70	279	6180
	Tom GILLIS	(USA)	71	70	67	71	279	6180
42	Sven STRÜVER	(Ger)	65	70	71	74	280	4960
	Phillip PRICE	(Wal)	69	72	69	70	280	4960
	Richard BOXALL	(Eng)	70	69	69	72	280	4960
45	Scott HENDERSON	(Scot)	71	70	68	72	281	4480
	Peter O'MALLEY	(Aus)	70	71	67	73	281	4480
	Mark ROE	(Eng)	71	68	70	72	281	4480
48	Jamie SPENCE	(Eng)	70	70	72	70	282	4000
	Joakim HAEGGMAN	(Swe)	70	68	72	72	282	4000
	Michele REALE	(It)	72	69	71	70	282	4000
51	Padraig HARRINGTON	(Ire)	69	72	67	75	283	3520
	Katsuyoshi TOMORI	(Jpn)	71	69	71	72	283	3520
	Francisco CEA	(Sp)	70	71	72	70	283	3520
54	Andrew SANDYWELL	(Eng)	72	68	72	72	284	3120
	Mathias GRÖNBERG	(Swe)	70	70	66	78	284	3120
56	Gary EVANS	(Eng)	70	70	71	74	285	2800
	Søren KJELDSEN	(Den)	72	69	71	73	285	2800
58	Seve BALLESTEROS	(Sp)	68	73	71	74	286	2320
	Fredrik HENGE	(Swe)	70	69	74	73	286	2320
	Wayne RILEY	(Aus)	71	70	72	73	286	2320
	Dean ROBERTSON	(Scot)	72	65	73	76	286	2320
	Massimo FLORIOLI	(It)	74	67	70	75	286	2320
	David LYNN	(Eng)	72	69	74	71	286	2320
	Roger WESSELS	(SA)	71	69	75	71	286	2320
65	John BICKERTON	(Eng)	69	71	74	73	287	1600
	Marc FARRY	(Fr)	69	67	77	74	287	1600
67	John HAWKSWORTH	(Eng)	70	70	72	76	288	1198
68	Ross MCFARLANE	(Eng)	69	72	76	72	289	1196

Joint third place for Lee Westwood.

Whole in one.

Parnevik is happy at home

Jesper Parnevik underlined his reputation as Sweden's finest golfer with his second home victory in four years

The Volvo Scandinavian Masters is one of the success stories of tournament golf and Jesper Parnevik's second Masters victory in the space of four years was a fittingly regal way to mark the first staging of a major event at the Kungsängen Club, which was acquired by PGA European Tour Courses plc in 1993.

Kungsängen, appropriately designed by former Swedish number one Anders Forsbrand, means 'King's Meadow' and Parnevik, one of the heroes of Europe's epic Ryder Cup triumph at Valderrama in 1997, is the undisputed monarch of Swedish golf.

His professional entertainer father, Bosse, is an institution in his own right, but Jesper takes charge on the golf course. Six top three finishes helped him end in 12th spot in the 1997 US moneylist with more than $1,217,857 and he arrived back home in his native Stockholm with $1,011,756 already in the bank in 1998 after his breakthrough victory in the Phoenix Open.

Sweden's golf fans, as usual, turned out in force for the event. Nearly 95,000 came through the gates during the week – more than 56,000 over the weekend. The last day attendance of almost 29,000 was just 680 short of the record for the eight-year-old championship, set at Barsebäck near Malmo when Parnevik won in 1995.

Fittingly, 44 Scandinavians were in the starting line-up, 38 of them Swedes – 17 of them survived the halfway cut and five finished in the top ten. It was a veritable Swedish rhapsody from start to finish with the leaderboard looking more like smorgasbord.

PGA European Tour Executive Director Ken Schofield declared: 'This is our future'... and Lars Thonning, managing director of the Masters, announced the prize fund will be up from £800,000 to £1 million in 1999. It is a success story to rank with that of the Open Championship itself so it was fitting that with José Maria Olazábal missing the cut and Colin Montgomerie having to settle for joint 16th place that Parnevik's chief rival for a £133,330 jackpot should be Ryder Cup teammate Darren Clarke, with whom he had fought it out toe-to-toe to share second place behind Justin Leonard at Royal Troon in 1997.

Clarke, second the week before in the TNT Dutch Open, finished runner-up again – three adrift of Parnevik's 11 under par 273 tally – but had family matters on his mind with wife Heather about to give birth to their first child. (Tyrone Benjamin arrived the day after the championship.) But he refused to make excuses after a third round 68 had lifted him from five to only two behind: 'I couldn't get any

THE COURSE

Set amid pine forests and granite outcrops, the Kungsangen course, designed by Anders Forsbrand, incorporates water on nine holes. After opening in 1994 all 18 greens were completely reconstructed over the next two years in addition to major works on trees, bunkers, drains and irrigation systems in line with the policy of PGA European Tour Courses to develop facilities capable of hosting major events.

momentum going and Jesper played really solidly and deserved to win.'

Parnevik professed surprise, however, that he emerged triumphant: 'I felt very tired after my practice round and twice fell back asleep after the alarm went off at 5.30 am on the morning of the first round. I arrived late at the course after stopping to watch a video with my daughter and arrived on the first tee with 15 clubs in the bag, including two putters, and no yardage chart. I just wasn't with it at all and sliced my first tee shot on to the 18th fairway. It was all very unprofessional and after seven holes I was three over par – I expected to be somewhere else at the weekend.'

A spectacular homeward 30, however, earned him a 67 that left him only two behind surprise pacemaker Brian Davis from Enfield, wielding a brand new set of irons he had persuaded the manufacturers to take off the exhibition stand at the Open for his personal use, and 19-year-old

Robert Karlsson splashes out.

Gothenburg amateur Anders Hultman, shortly to take up a golf scholarship at Oklahoma State University.

Hultman had high hopes of doing a

Justin Rose. The Hampshire youngster, who marked his 18th birthday with a battling 71 but added a 75 to miss the cut for the second week running after his marvellous fourth place finish alongside Parnevik in the Open. But the teenage Swede slipped back into the pack. Davis, meanwhile, went on to celebrate his 24th birthday on the final day with a repeat of his 11th place finish a week earlier in Hilversum.

A second round 65, interrupted by an overnight suspension after more than four hours were lost when torrential rain flooded the course minutes after the first matches teed off on day two, swept Parnevik into a lead he was never to relinquish. He admitted: 'To win at Barsebäck was great – to win again is fantastic. It's a great atmosphere but the pressure is tremendous. The Swedish people want you to win and they expect you to win, especially if you are in the lead. I lost a little touch on the greens and had 37 putts

Justin Rose celebrated his 18th birthday during the week but missed the cut.

SHOT OF THE WEEK

Stephen Field (third) and Jean Van de Velde (joint fourth) both holed spectacular birdie chips at the 18th but the shot of the week had to be the 25 feet putt winner Jesper Parnevik, who had struggled all day on the greens, rattled into the hole at express speed for his two at the 12th in the final found after Darren Clarke had holed from similar distance at the 11th to get back to only two behind.

in my final round. It's even harder going out leading a tournament when you don't feel good about your putting – it puts a strain on your whole game. I three-putted twice in the first seven holes and the key was holing from six feet for my birdie four at the ninth and then from 25 feet at the 12th for a two to go three ahead again.'

Clarke, who made three brave back nine birdie threes – two from 20 feet – ended up having to get up and down from a plugged lie in a bunker to save par 'after fun and frolics' at the 17th to keep his nose in front of third placed Stephen Field, who began the week in 181st place in the Volvo Ranking after missing 12 cuts in 14 Tour starts but finished birdie-birdie, chipping in at the last to win over £50,000 and secure his Tour card. Clarke, winner of the Benson and Hedges International Open in May, declared: 'It's my third second place on Tour this year and its more disappointing than satisfying – golf is all about winning.'

Jesper Parnevik and his adoring army of fans would second that.

Gordon Richardson   175

Kungsängen Golf Club, Stockholm, July 30-August 2, 1998 • Par 71 • Yards 6791

Pos	Name	Country	Rnd 1	Rnd 2	Rnd 3	Rnd 4	Total	Prize Money £
1	Jesper PARNEVIK	(Swe)	67	65	71	70	273	133330
2	Darren CLARKE	(N.Ire)	67	70	68	71	276	88880
3	Stephen FIELD	(Eng)	70	68	70	69	277	50070
4	Jean VAN DE VELDE	(Fr)	72	67	70	69	278	36940
	Michael JONZON	(Swe)	69	65	72	72	278	36940
6	José RIVERO	(Sp)	71	73	66	69	279	28000
7	Paolo QUIRICI	(Swi)	72	70	66	72	280	19460
	Per-Ulrik JOHANSSON	(Swe)	69	69	72	70	280	19460
	Mats LANNER	(Swe)	69	69	69	73	280	19460
	Mathias GRÖNBERG	(Swe)	68	69	72	71	280	19460
11	Andrew COLTART	(Scot)	72	70	68	71	281	13072
	Katsuyoshi TOMORI	(Jpn)	69	72	68	72	281	13072
	Mark DAVIS	(Eng)	72	66	72	71	281	13072
	Paul BROADHURST	(Eng)	69	68	71	73	281	13072
	Brian DAVIS	(Eng)	65	72	73	71	281	13072
16	Van PHILLIPS	(Eng)	73	70	69	70	282	9768
	Paul MCGINLEY	(Ire)	73	71	71	67	282	9768
	Colin MONTGOMERIE	(Scot)	70	74	69	69	282	9768
	Greg TURNER	(NZ)	71	73	65	73	282	9768
	Greg CHALMERS	(Aus)	74	70	67	71	282	9768
	Thomas LEVET	(Fr)	71	71	69	71	282	9768
	Pierre FULKE	(Swe)	73	68	73	68	282	9768
	Craig HAINLINE	(USA)	68	72	68	74	282	9768
	Mats HALLBERG	(Swe)	70	67	73	72	282	9768
25	Scott HENDERSON	(Scot)	70	73	69	71	283	7680
	Sam TORRANCE	(Scot)	72	71	70	70	283	7680
	Des SMYTH	(Ire)	71	73	69	70	283	7680
	Henrik NYSTRÖM	(Swe)	72	70	71	70	283	7680
	Rolf MUNTZ	(Hol)	71	70	71	71	283	7680
	Stephen LEANEY	(Aus)	70	71	68	74	283	7680
	Jarmo SANDELIN	(Swe)	68	70	74	71	283	7680
32	Jeff REMESY	(Fr)	72	70	71	71	284	6640
	Ed FRYATT	(Eng)	70	69	71	74	284	6640
34	David LYNN	(Eng)	74	71	71	69	285	6080
	Paul AFFLECK	(Wal)	69	72	74	70	285	6080
	Richard BOXALL	(Eng)	69	72	71	73	285	6080
	Costantino ROCCA	(It)	70	71	70	74	285	6080
	David HOWELL	(Eng)	67	74	69	75	285	6080
39	Olle KARLSSON	(Swe)	71	72	69	74	286	5360
	Søren KJELDSEN	(Den)	73	71	73	69	286	5360
	Kalle BRINK	(Swe)	69	76	66	75	286	5360
	Raphaël JACQUELIN	(Fr)	71	69	72	74	286	5360
43	Steve ALKER	(NZ)	73	70	71	73	287	4480
	Retief GOOSEN	(SA)	69	75	72	71	287	4480
	Sven STRÜVER	(Ger)	72	72	71	72	287	4480
	Ignacio GARRIDO	(Sp)	70	75	70	72	287	4480
	Eamonn DARCY	(Ire)	70	75	71	71	287	4480
	Anssi KANKKONEN	(Fin)	75	70	73	69	287	4480
	Paul EALES	(Eng)	71	74	73	69	287	4480
50	Max ANGLERT	(Swe)	74	70	71	73	288	3520
	Santiago LUNA	(Sp)	74	71	70	73	288	3520
	Mårten OLANDER	(Swe)	70	75	73	70	288	3520
	Dennis EDLUND	(Swe)	71	74	74	69	288	3520
	Thomas GÖGELE	(Ger)	72	69	72	75	288	3520
55	Silvio GRAPPASONNI	(It)	69	74	74	72	289	2800
	Mark ROE	(Eng)	75	69	74	71	289	2800
	Michele REALE	(It)	73	72	72	72	289	2800
	Thomas BJÖRN	(Den)	76	66	71	76	289	2800
59	Domingo HOSPITAL	(Sp)	69	74	73	74	290	2360
	Sandy LYLE	(Scot)	73	72	71	74	290	2360
	Michael LONG	(NZ)	74	71	71	74	290	2360
	Peter LONARD	(Aus)	73	69	73	75	290	2360
	Anders HULTMAN (AM)	(Swe)	65	76	77	72	290	2360
63	Christopher HANELL	(Swe)	68	74	78	71	291	1575
	Ola ELIASSON	(Swe)	71	73	73	74	291	1575
	David CARTER	(Eng)	69	75	74	73	291	1575
	Bradley DREDGE	(Wal)	73	71	71	76	291	1575
	Padraig HARRINGTON	(Ire)	72	70	74	75	291	1575
	Michael CAMPBELL	(NZ)	69	73	78	71	291	1575
	Lian-Wei ZHANG	(Chi)	68	72	72	79	291	1575
70	Anthony WALL	(Eng)	72	71	76	73	292	1191
	David TAPPING	(Eng)	72	73	73	74	292	1191
72	Tom GILLIS	(USA)	73	69	74	77	293	1188
73	Jim PAYNE	(Eng)	73	72	73	76	294	1185
	Patrik SJÖLAND	(Swe)	70	70	72	82	294	1185
75	Fabrice TARNAUD	(Fr)	70	74	76	75	295	1182

Crowds massed on the final day.

IT CAN SIT, WORK LEFT, WORK RIGHT, EVEN BACK UP.
IT COULD BE YOUR NEWEST BEST FRIEND.

THE *NEW* DOUBLE TI, golf's first **DOUBLE COVER, DOUBLE TITANIUM** ball. Our famous high energy, maximum distance titanium core has been fused with a titanium inner cover, allowing the outer cover to have that work it, shot making softness. It may be the **ULTIMATE COMBINATION OF SPIN, DISTANCE & FEEL.** Now if only it could fetch your slippers!

Wilson Staff
TITANIUM

Allan finds the key

Australia's Stephen Allan overcame
a triple bogey in the final round to
capture his first European Tour title

Never judge a book by its cover, so the saying goes. That old adage might conceivably be applied to Australian golfer Stephen Allan.

The 25-year-old from Melbourne possesses the rosy cheeks, twinkling eyes and innocent expression of a church choirboy. Yet underneath that youthful exterior lurks a ruthless streak essential for success on that most gruelling of proving grounds, the European Tour.

Not for nothing is Allan colloquially known on Tour as 'the baby-faced assassin.' At the awe-inspiring setting of the Sporting Club Berlin, he eliminated his nearest challengers with the clinical efficiency and icy calm of a hired hit man. Allan succeeded Ignacio Garrido as German Open champion with an eight under par total of 280 over the Nick Faldo-designed course which attracted unanimous praise from players who tend not to dispense tributes lightly. The Scots – a race always searching for a new golfing hero - must be frustrated that Jock Allan and his wife decided to emigrate from Edinburgh in 1970 and that their offspring, Stephen Douglas, was born in Victoria rather than Leith.

Had that not happened, Stephen might easily be hailed as one of the brightest new stars in the firmament north of Hadrian's Wall. As it is, Allan remains resolutely proud of the Scottish heritage, but adamant that he is a living, breathing Australian and will always remain so.

Before turning professional in 1996, Allan spent several vacations in Scotland, living with relatives and learning the unique feel of links golf. That experience was to stand him in good stead for his sternest of examinations over the 7,082-yard Faldo layout.

The course may be situated 50 miles south-east of Berlin and only 20 miles from the Polish border - in fact, on the site of an old Russian rocket base - but visitors to the Sporting Club might be duped into believing that they are on the Ayrshire or Lancashire coast, and that the sea will be visible over the next sand dune.

Those were the conditions under which the young Australian prevailed. And anyone with an eye for golfing form would not have been in the least surprised to find him entering the winner's enclosure for the first time as a professional.

Allan had demonstrated his capability as early as February, when he finished sec-

THE COURSE

Only three years old, the Nick Faldo course is a tribute to the vision and imagination of its creator. Faldo, who co-designed the 7,082-yard gem deep in the heart of old austere East Germany with Stan Eby, has cunningly employed the sandy texture soil into providing a links course miles from the sea. Wonderfully manicured and a joy for the professionals to play.

Paul Lawrie shared the lead after the first round (right).

ond behind José Maria Olazábal in the Dubai Desert Classic. Only a misjudged three wood at the 72nd hole, which splashed into the greenside lake, deprived him of the chance to ruin the Spaniard's sentimental victory. But the experience served the aggressive Allan well. He was tied seventh in the Peugeot Open de España then just chugged along in a quiet, anonymous way until he reached Germany.

There, Allan drew on the experiences of the recent past and employed them to great effect. Not that he was considered as a potential champion at the halfway stage of a tournament which was initially dominated by another Antipodean, Michael Campbell, and Ryder Cup rookie Garrido. Four players shared the first round lead with five under par rounds of 67. Garrido, showing a resurgence in form after a forlorn spell, was joined by Campbell, Paul Lawrie of Scotland and Frenchman Olivier Edmond at the head of affairs.

New Zealander Campbell then struck

the front, shooting a 70 to carry a two-stroke lead over a clutch of players into the weekend. Allan, after modest scores of 72 and 71, was back in the pack.

All that changed on Saturday. Allan made his move with a 68, as did Garrido, who, clearly revelling in his title defence, also fired a 68 which propelled him into a three-stroke lead over a chasing pack of four players. As the Spaniard was quick to point out: 'Last year I was five clear going into the last round. This year it's only three so it seems I'm in trouble.'

It was an off-the-cuff, flippant remark. Little did he know how prophetic his words would become less than 24 hours later.

After 12 holes Garrido was on course for a successful defence. Eleven under par coasting home, especially when Allan pulled his tee shot at the short 13th into trees, took a lift under penalty, and ended with a triple bogey six.

That dropped Allan to six under – five behind Garrido. Instead of capitulating, as less mentally tough individuals might have done, Allan promptly birdied the 15th and 16th for a final 69. Garrido, meanwhile, dropped four shots to finish with a 74 for 281.

'I was determined not to let one loose shot spoil my tournament', explained Allan. 'I admit I thought I was looking at second place but I didn't allow myself to get down, and then Ignacio let me in.'

Several of his closest

It wasn't very long, but it was of the utmost importance to Stephen Allan. The Australian flew the green at the last and faced a fiendish little pitch and run over swales and hollows. Needing a par to win without facing a play-off, Allan conjured up an exquisite effort off a tight lie to four feet for a title-winning par.

No home title for Bernhard Langer (above). Ignacio Garrido stumbled at the finish (left).

rivals attempted to finish off the job but instead failed. Padraig Harrington bogeyed the last to miss out by one, Mark Roe and Garrido both dropped strokes at the 17th and couldn't force a play-off. They shared second place with Steve Webster, who was unable to birdie the last to take Allan into extra time.

'I knew my game was good enough. It was just a case of getting it all together on the day,' said Allan.

That he did. This was one day when 'the choirboy', rather than the Fat Lady, did all the singing.

Gordon Simpson   181

Sporting Club Berlin, August 6-9, 1998 · Yardage 7082 · Par 72

Pos	Name	Country	Rnd 1	Rnd 2	Rnd 3	Rnd 4	Total	Prize Money £
1	Stephen ALLAN	(Aus)	72	71	68	69	280	116660
2	Steve WEBSTER	(Eng)	69	73	69	70	281	46557
	Mark ROE	(Eng)	71	70	69	71	281	46557
	Ignacio GARRIDO	(Sp)	67	72	68	74	281	46557
	Padraig HARRINGTON	(Ire)	73	69	70	69	281	46557
6	Scott HENDERSON	(Scot)	72	67	73	71	283	24500
7	Paul LAWRIE	(Scot)	67	73	72	72	284	15505
	Michael CAMPBELL	(NZ)	67	70	73	74	284	15505
	Katsuyoshi TOMORI	(Jpn)	72	68	72	72	284	15505
	John WADE	(Aus)	73	70	70	71	284	15505
	Malcolm MACKENZIE	(Eng)	71	75	66	72	284	15505
	Daniel CHOPRA	(Swe)	75	71	67	71	284	15505
13	Miles TUNNICLIFF	(Eng)	73	71	70	71	285	9900
	Jonathan LOMAS	(Eng)	72	73	69	71	285	9900
	Mathew GOGGIN	(Aus)	71	72	70	72	285	9900
	Bernhard LANGER	(Ger)	74	71	67	73	285	9900
	Van PHILLIPS	(Eng)	71	68	74	72	285	9900
	Dennis EDLUND	(Swe)	71	74	69	71	285	9900
	Olivier EDMOND	(Fr)	67	73	70	75	285	9900
20	Sandy LYLE	(Scot)	73	72	71	70	286	8295
	Eamonn DARCY	(Ire)	77	69	68	72	286	8295
22	Sven STRÜVER	(Ger)	71	73	70	73	287	7875
	Jeev Milkha SINGH	(Ind)	75	68	67	77	287	7875
24	Silvio GRAPPASONNI	(It)	70	74	72	72	288	6622
	Olle KARLSSON	(Swe)	70	75	69	74	288	6622
	Paul BROADHURST	(Eng)	72	75	72	69	288	6622
	Paul MCGINLEY	(Ire)	73	73	72	70	288	6622
	Robert KARLSSON	(Swe)	73	72	73	70	288	6622
	Gordon BRAND JNR.	(Scot)	71	70	75	72	288	6622
	Iain PYMAN	(Eng)	73	69	72	74	288	6622
	Derrick COOPER	(Eng)	72	73	69	74	288	6622
	Jamie SPENCE	(Eng)	71	72	75	70	288	6622
	Paul AFFLECK	(Wal)	70	71	71	76	288	6622
	Tobias DIER (AM)	(Ger)	72	69	75	72	288	
34	Craig HAINLINE	(USA)	72	74	70	73	289	5250
	Andrew BEAL	(Eng)	69	72	69	79	289	5250
	Mats HALLBERG	(Swe)	72	73	73	71	289	5250
	Ross MCFARLANE	(Eng)	73	70	73	73	289	5250
	Richard JOHNSON	(Wal)	70	72	74	73	289	5250
	Martin GATES	(Eng)	73	74	70	72	289	5250
40	Paolo QUIRICI	(Swi)	74	71	72	73	290	4410
	Tom GILLIS	(USA)	72	70	73	75	290	4410
	Russell CLAYDON	(Eng)	68	73	73	76	290	4410
	Daren LEE	(Eng)	70	73	72	75	290	4410
	Andrew SANDYWELL	(Eng)	69	76	76	69	290	4410
	Anthony WALL	(Eng)	74	73	69	74	290	4410
46	Rodger DAVIS	(Aus)	73	74	69	75	291	3710
	Gordon J BRAND	(Eng)	75	71	72	73	291	3710
	Ian GARBUTT	(Eng)	72	73	71	75	291	3710
	Wayne RILEY	(Aus)	76	71	73	71	291	3710
50	Raphaël JACQUELIN	(Fr)	76	70	72	74	292	3150
	John MCHENRY	(Ire)	70	75	71	76	292	3150
	Gary EMERSON	(Eng)	70	73	74	75	292	3150
	Anssi KANKKONEN	(Fin)	71	75	73	73	292	3150
54	Sam TORRANCE	(Scot)	75	71	73	74	293	2362
	Michael JONZON	(Swe)	71	73	73	76	293	2362
	Michele REALE	(It)	74	71	74	74	293	2362
	Andrew OLDCORN	(Scot)	74	71	75	73	293	2362
	Jarmo SANDELIN	(Swe)	72	71	74	76	293	2362
	Barry LANE	(Eng)	71	73	72	77	293	2362
	Desvonde BOTES	(SA)	70	74	69	80	293	2362
	Adam HUNTER	(Scot)	73	74	69	77	293	2362
62	Jeff REMESY	(Fr)	76	71	70	77	294	1855
	Andrew CLAPP	(Eng)	72	73	74	75	294	1855
	Brian DAVIS	(Eng)	75	72	71	76	294	1855
	Heinz Peter THÜL	(Ger)	75	70	72	77	294	1855
66	Pedro LINHART	(Sp)	71	72	73	79	295	1045
	Nic HENNING	(SA)	74	73	73	75	295	1045
	Greg OWEN	(Eng)	71	74	73	77	295	1045
	David HIGGINS	(Ire)	77	70	70	78	295	1045
	Emanuele CANONICA	(It)	74	73	76	72	295	1045
	Domingo HOSPITAL	(Sp)	73	72	74	76	295	1045
72	John HAWKSWORTH	(Eng)	73	73	75	75	296	1037
	Greig HUTCHEON	(Scot)	74	73	71	78	296	1037
74	Marc FARRY	(Fr)	74	73	72	78	297	1032
	Bradley DREDGE	(Wal)	72	75	74	76	297	1032
	Kalle BRINK	(Swe)	72	74	75	76	297	1032
77	Jean VAN DE VELDE	(Fr)	71	76	73	78	298	1028
78	Patrick PLATZ	(Ger)	73	74	73	80	300	1026

Halfway leader Michael Campbell.

BOSS
HUGO BOSS

GOLF

HUGO BOSS UK LTD,
TEL. 0171 589 5522

Grönberg is streets ahead

Mathias Grönberg was never headed as he strolled to victory in Ireland

Sweden has not yet produced a golfer with the idol image of Sven Tumba or Björn Borg. These legends were masters of their chosen pursuits, Tumba at ice hockey and Borg at tennis but golf is moving ever closer to producing a player of that calibre. With each passing year the evidence that the Swedish system could soon produce a major champion gets stronger.

Mathias Grönberg was not among the favourites when he arrived at the elegant K Club for the Smurfit European Open but he left Ireland with the richest prize ever offered at an event under the auspices of the European Tour. His ten-shot victory over a field which included the best Europe had to offer was the largest winning margin of the season and his cheque for £208,300 elevated him from 53rd to eighth on the Volvo Ranking.

It was the fourth win of the season by a Swedish player and the 32nd occasion a Swedish name had appeared on a European Tour trophy since Ove Sellberg became the first winner back in 1986. Grönberg is a product of that very successful Swedish system. Before he turned professional at the age of 20 in 1990 he had played for his country at boy, youth and senior grade, won his national boys championship and the British Youths' title and played on the Swedish team which won the World Team Championsip for the Eisenhower Trophy.

It was Jan Blomquist who had the dream that one day Sweden could produce a world beater and with the blessing of the Swedish Federation he set about organising a squad of elite players. He studied the training methods of other sports and applied them to golf. A group of the nation's best toured Europe under his managership and included players like Ove Sellberg, Mats Lanner, Magnus Persson and Anders Forsbrand, the man generally considered the trail blazer with six offcial European Tour titles to his credit.

The results since have been quite stunning. They won the Alfred Dunhill Cup and the World Cup in 1991, Joakim Haegmann become the first Swede to play in the Ryder Cup in 1993 and since then Per-Ulrik Johansson and Jesper Parnevik have played on winning European teams. Furthermore, Parnevik has twice finished runner-up in the Open Championship and in July at Royal Birkdale he finished fourth.

It is a remarkable achievement for a country with such a restricted season, in some places a mere four months. There are now about half a million Swedes playing the game and the Federation has counteracted the effect of several months of snow by establishing winter bases in more southerly parts of Europe where they send the cream of the crop.

Grönberg is conscious of the growing strength of the game in his native land.

Bernhard Langer
(above) and Payne
Stewart (right).

"If golf was an accurate metaphor for business, the bunkers would be bigger and the holes would be smaller."

Business isn't one of the easiest forms of human endeavour.
But it is the one we're best qualified to give you advice on.
See if we can help; get in touch soon.

IF YOU'RE IN BUSINESS, WE'RE IN BUSINESS

Visit any AIB branch   **www.aib.ie**

AIB

Bank

SHOT OF THE WEEK

The 14th is one of the few holes without water. Indeed, it has no bunkers but that does not make it easy. Grönberg, in Saturday's third round, found his second shot in deep rough. He felt he was looking at bogey or even double-bogey but he played a delicate recovery of about nine yards to the green. It had to be perfect to take the contour and the Swede hit the precise spot allowing the ball to roll dead for a par four. He believed it was the most important shot on his way to victory.

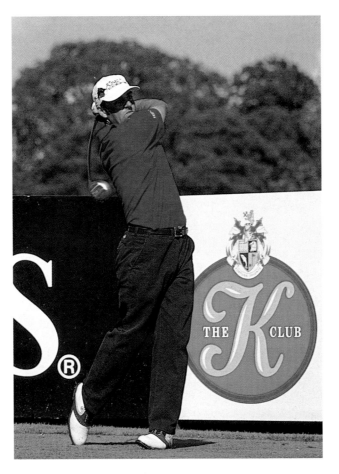

Paul McGinley (above), Darren Clarke (below).

'We have 24 players on the European Tour and about 20 can win if it's their week. There are also many young players not on the Tour who could come out and win,' he said after his victory. He was also aware of the significance of winning the title after Johansson had been champion for the previous two years.

Other Swedes will think now that if Grönberg can win they can too. It was not the Monaco resident's first win, his maiden being three years earlier in the Canon European Masters and the coincidence that each of his

victories carried a five-year exemption was not lost on him. 'I was thinking of going to America but now I don't think I will go. Winning the Smurfit European Open you get a five-year exemption on Tour and I gained that three years ago in Switzerland. My exemption is now prolonged until 2003. This is a great Trophy to win. I think maybe I have played better golf than my Volvo Ranking position but to beat some of the best players in the world by ten shots you have to play really well.'

Among those players were Lee Westwood, the then leader of the Volvo Ranking, who had to retire after only six holes of the final round with a hip injury; Darren Clarke, currently Europe's number two, who had other things on his

Thomas Björn (right) .

mind and did well to finish fourth, and Colin Montgomerie, a spot behind Clarke, who missed the cut.

Clarke's wife had presented him with their first child, Tyrone, two weeks earlier and only five days before the event the people of Ireland and elsewhere were shocked by the terrorist murders of 28 people in a bomb attack on Omagh. Darren's birthplace of Dungannon is just 30 miles from the carnage.

Players, officials and spectators, joined the rest of the country in a poignant silence during play in the third round in remembrance of the fateful day.

Grönberg experienced another interruption in play during the fourth round when a weather warning caused a suspen-

sion but it did not bother him. Nor was he nervous because he used the time to eat some salmon, potatoes and veg. 'I missed breakfast and you need to eat. It was perfect timing. I really enjoyed the last five holes.' It was also the perfect victory for the 28-year-old from Stockholm. He

led after the first day with four under 68, trailed Bernhard Langer and Jose Rivero by a shot at the halfway stage, regained the pole position at ten under after 54 holes and increased his three-stroke lead to ten with a final total of 13 under par.

Colm Smith

THE COURSE

The elegant K Club is one the finest venues on the European Tour. Set in the stud land of County Kildare, the course was designed by Arnold Palmer and on contoured land along the banks of the River Liffey. Water, in fact, is a major feature of the course with only five holes where it is not in evidence. The course measures 7,159 yards with a spectacular finishing hole.

THE K CLUB, DUBLIN, AUGUST 20-23, 1998 · YARDAGE 7159 · PAR 72

Pos	Name	Country	Rnd 1	Rnd 2	Rnd 3	Rnd 4	Total	Prize Money £
1	Mathias GRÖNBERG	(Swe)	68	71	67	69	275	208300
2	Miguel Angel JIMÉNEZ	(Sp)	73	72	71	69	285	108562
	Phillip PRICE	(Wal)	72	74	68	71	285	108562
4	Darren CLARKE	(N.Ire)	69	74	70	73	286	62500
5	Angel CABRERA	(Arg)	72	73	75	67	287	48375
	Craig HAINLINE	(USA)	71	69	69	78	287	48375
7	Jean VAN DE VELDE	(Fr)	78	69	69	72	288	32216
	Paul BROADHURST	(Eng)	72	73	71	72	288	32216
	Bernhard LANGER	(Ger)	73	65	75	75	288	32216
10	Paul LAWRIE	(Scot)	72	72	72	73	289	21187
	José RIVERO	(Sp)	72	66	75	76	289	21187
	David GILFORD	(Eng)	75	74	68	72	289	21187
	Barry LANE	(Eng)	75	69	72	73	289	21187
	Costantino ROCCA	(It)	72	73	72	72	289	21187
	Sam TORRANCE	(Scot)	71	76	70	72	289	21187
16	Peter BAKER	(Eng)	72	76	70	72	290	16512
	Eduardo ROMERO	(Arg)	74	73	76	67	290	16512
	Per HAUGSRUD	(Nor)	72	73	73	72	290	16512
	Santiago LUNA	(Sp)	72	73	76	69	290	16512
20	Roger WESSELS	(SA)	71	71	73	76	291	14625
	José COCERES	(Arg)	74	75	69	73	291	14625
	Paul MCGINLEY	(Ire)	72	72	71	76	291	14625
23	Fabrice TARNAUD	(Fr)	73	74	74	71	292	13125
	John WADE	(Aus)	76	69	76	71	292	13125
	Thomas BJÖRN	(Den)	76	70	69	77	292	13125
	Jarmo SANDELIN	(Swe)	72	77	73	70	292	13125
	Padraig HARRINGTON	(Ire)	71	74	74	73	292	13125
28	Pierre FULKE	(Swe)	78	71	70	74	293	11437
	Greg OWEN	(Eng)	72	75	73	73	293	11437
	Peter HEDBLOM	(Swe)	76	72	72	73	293	11437
	Miles TUNNICLIFF	(Eng)	74	74	72	73	293	11437
32	Francisco CEA	(Sp)	71	75	72	76	294	10000
	Scott HENDERSON	(Scot)	75	73	73	73	294	10000
	Mark JAMES	(Eng)	75	71	73	75	294	10000
	Stephen LEANEY	(Aus)	77	70	72	75	294	10000
	Steen TINNING	(Den)	73	75	73	73	294	10000
37	Ian GARBUTT	(Eng)	74	75	73	73	295	8500
	Richard BOXALL	(Eng)	77	72	73	73	295	8500
	Ian WOOSNAM	(Wal)	73	70	72	80	295	8500
	Ignacio GARRIDO	(Sp)	77	71	72	75	295	8500
	Silvio GRAPPASONNI	(It)	74	75	74	72	295	8500
	Gary NICKLAUS	(USA)	74	66	77	78	295	8500
	José Maria OLAZÁBAL	(Sp)	75	73	75	72	295	8500
44	Mark DAVIS	(Eng)	73	74	74	75	296	7000
	Jim PAYNE	(Eng)	73	72	75	76	296	7000
	Thomas LEVET	(Fr)	73	76	72	75	296	7000
	Paul AFFLECK	(Wal)	77	72	74	73	296	7000
	Wayne WESTNER	(SA)	75	73	74	74	296	7000
49	Jamie SPENCE	(Eng)	75	71	75	76	297	6125
	Paul EALES	(Eng)	74	75	76	72	297	6125
51	Sven STRÜVER	(Ger)	77	71	75	75	298	5625
	Stephen AMES	(T&T)	73	76	76	73	298	5625
53	Dennis EDLUND	(Swe)	76	73	75	75	299	4875
	Kalle BRINK	(Swe)	75	74	75	75	299	4875
	Andrew BEAL	(Eng)	78	70	75	76	299	4875
	Malcolm MACKENZIE	(Eng)	71	77	74	77	299	4875
57	Philip WALTON	(Ire)	76	71	75	78	300	3968
	David CARTER	(Eng)	74	75	77	74	300	3968
	Raphaël JACQUELIN	(Fr)	76	73	76	75	300	3968
	Damian MCGRANE	(Ire)	74	74	76	76	300	3968
61	Roger CHAPMAN	(Eng)	75	71	77	79	302	3500
	David LYNN	(Eng)	76	73	78	75	302	3500
	Des SMYTH	(Ire)	73	75	79	75	302	3500
64	Peter SENIOR	(Aus)	76	73	75	82	306	3187
	Dean ROBERTSON	(Scot)	74	73	77	82	306	3187
66	Søren KJELDSEN	(Den)	75	74	75	83	307	1875

A World Leader in Packaging

The tang of Tavernas de Valldinga,

Spain...

The development of global export markets has created sophisticated demands for packaging which will protect, present and promote a diverse range of products. Fruit and flowers are transported between continents, arriving as fresh as they were picked. Complex electronics need specialised protection for worldwide distribution. Delicate china and glassware must reach distant destinations in perfect condition.

Jefferson Smurfit Group plc has over sixty years' experience in meeting these demands innovatively and cost effectively. Together with its associates, Jefferson Smurfit Group has steadily grown to become the world's largest paper-based packaging organisation and largest recycler of paper, with 400 facilities in over 20 countries throughout Europe, Scandinavia, North and South America, and Asia Pacific.

Smurfit has total control of the packaging manufacturing process, starting with sourcing and sorting waste paper for its own

recycling mills, or producing virgin pulp from its own forests, through to the manufacture of paper and board and the production of a broad range of packaging for diverse markets. Throughout its operations worldwide and across its product range, Smurfit applies its commitment to consistently reliable quality and to environmentally responsible production.

From corrugated board to newsprint; sturdy cases to colourful labels; intricate cartons to specialised sacks, Smurfit is skilled in answering the world's packaging needs.

Prizes in Poznan,

Poland!

JEFFERSON SMURFIT GROUP plc

Worldwide Headquarters:
Clonskeagh, Dublin 4, Ireland.
Phone: (+353 1) 2696622 Fax: (+353 1) 2694481
World Wide Web: htttp://www.smurfit.ie

Smurfit Ireland & UK • Smurfit Continental Europe • Smurfit Latin America • Jefferson Smurfit Corporation USA

Claydon makes the breakthrough

After nine years and six runner-up finishes Russell Claydon finally stood on the winner's rostrum

*I*t looked odds on the BMW International Open producing a Continental European champion for the third year running at Golfclub München Nord-Eichenried, but on a dramatic final afternoon British golfers applied the old one-two.

And for both winner Russell Claydon, who ended 18 under par on 270, and runner-up Jamie Spence, one behind, it was a case of patience being richly rewarded.

At the halfway stage, Thomas Björn, with 1998 victories in the Heineken Classic and Peugeot Open de España already under his belt, seemed poised to follow Swede Robert Karlsson and Frenchman Marc Farry on to the winner's rostrum in Munich after opening rounds of 64, 67 earned him a three-stroke advantage over Germany's Sven Strüver.

After 54 holes Bernhard Langer, in pursuit of an 11th victory on German soil and a first in his native Bavaria to mark his 41st birthday on the Thursday, had emerged as favourite to lift the £141,660 top prize, a second successive 67 hoisting him to the top of the leaderboard alongside Claydon – one ahead of Björn and Thomas Gögele.

With five-time European number one Colin Montgomerie missing back-to-back cuts for the first time since 1991, and Ian Woosnam and newly announced Ryder Cup captain Mark James also among the non-qualifiers, the Continental cause received a further boost.

But the never-say-die spirit of Messrs Claydon, seven shots off the lead at halfway, and Spence, eight adrift, swung the balance.

Claydon was tipped for swift success in the professional ranks after rounding off an impressive amateur career, which included victory in the English Championship and Walker Cup honours, with a brilliant second place to Greg Norman in the 1989 Australian Masters. It was the second time the man with the heavyweight frame, abbreviated swing and three-knuckle grip had achieved distinction alongside the professionals. He was runner-up in the 1988 UAP Under-25s Championship. The pattern continued as he launched his professional career with a tie for second in the 1990 Volvo Open di Firenze, and he was second again in the 1992 Equity and Law Challenge. Claydon subsequently lost out in a play-off to Lee Westwood in the Volvo Scandinavian Masters in 1996 and was twice runner-up in 1997 – to Strüver in the Sun

SHOT OF THE WEEK

Thomas Björn's recovery after a badly pulled second to the 18th in round three. Fearing he might be out of bounds, he played a provisional but he found his first ball behind a tree, contrived to bend his pitch from the rough to within four feet of the flag and made the putt for a birdie four and a 72 that kept him within a stroke of leaders Russell Claydon and Bernhard Langer.

José Maria Olazábal (above). Bernhard Langer (below). Thomas Gögele (right).

Microsystems Dutch Open and to Ignacio Garrido in the Volvo German Open. Was he fed-up and frustrated? Not a bit of it: 'I figured that if I was beating 154 of the 156 starters in a tournament there was nothing to feel negative about. I'd often played really well – like in Holland last year – and it just hadn't happened. Today it did and I am not even one per cent disappointed about winning the week before the Ryder Cup qualifying started. It would be churlish to be picky about weeks after waiting nine years.'

After a spectacular third round 64, in which he holed nothing longer than six feet, Claydon's short game was razor sharp on day four as he single putted eight of the last 11 greens and required

The flat parkland test, with water coming into play on two of the last three holes, had been toughened for the 1998 championship with 14 holes undergoing changes, 12 new bunkers being built and three more reconstructed, five tees re-built and considerable tree planting taking place. Intensive work on the greens produced near perfect putting surfaces.

only 27 putts in all. He birdied four times in a back nine of 32 for a 68.

His first Tour triumph followed three missed cuts on his previous four outings after he had spent eight weeks on the sidelines with a knee injury as the result of a fall, and he was full of praise for the German galleries: 'I was playing with Bernhard Langer and obviously they were rooting for him but they were scrupulously fair and Bernhard's behaviour, as always, was absolutely impeccable.'

As the German dropped two late shots to slip to a 72, Spence nipped in to birdie 15, 16 and 18 for a second successive 66 to snap up second prize of £94,440. 'I can't remember the last time Tottenham beat Arsenal,'

Katsuyoshi Tomori fired a last round 64 to tie for sixth place.

Jamie, an avid supporter of the Gunners mischievously told Russell, an equally fervent fan of north London rivals Spurs.

Spence, too, had had a long wait for a big pay day since shooting 60 en route to his solitary triumph in the 1992 Canon European Masters in Switzerland, managing nothing better than 20th place in his previous 20 Tour events.

Gögele, runner-up in the 1996 Volvo German Open, edged out compatriot Langer (tied with Argentina's Angel Cabrera on 273) for third place on 272 and £53,210.

And halfway hero Björn, after finishing 72,71, had to settle for joint sixth with Britain's Andrew Beal and Derrick Cooper, Spain's Miguel Angel Jiménez and Japan's Katsuyoshi Tomori on 274.

Gordon Richardson   195

GOLFCLUB MÜNCHEN NORD-EICHENRIED, AUGUST 27-30, 1998 • YARDAGE 6914 • PAR 72

Pos	Name	Country	Rnd 1	Rnd 2	Rnd 3	Rnd 4	Total	Prize Money £
1	Russell CLAYDON	(Eng)	66	72	64	68	270	141660
2	Jamie SPENCE	(Eng)	68	71	66	66	271	94440
3	Thomas GÖGELE	(Ger)	65	71	67	69	272	53210
4	Bernhard LANGER	(Ger)	68	67	67	71	273	39250
	Angel CABRERA	(Arg)	69	72	65	67	273	39250
6	Andrew BEAL	(Eng)	68	71	66	69	274	22494
	Miguel Angel JIMÉNEZ	(Sp)	69	71	67	67	274	22494
	Thomas BJÖRN	(Den)	64	67	72	71	274	22494
	Derrick COOPER	(Eng)	71	66	69	68	274	22494
	Katsuyoshi TOMORI	(Jpn)	67	70	73	64	274	22494
11	Pierre FULKE	(Swe)	72	68	70	65	275	15640
12	Domingo HOSPITAL	(Sp)	70	70	68	68	276	14620
13	Paul EALES	(Eng)	68	69	72	68	277	13053
	Peter SENIOR	(Aus)	70	71	71	65	277	13053
	Darren CLARKE	(N.Ire)	68	70	67	72	277	13053
16	Mats LANNER	(Swe)	70	68	72	68	278	11727
	Sam TORRANCE	(Scot)	69	70	72	67	278	11727
18	Steve WEBSTER	(Eng)	69	69	72	70	280	10129
	Jean VAN DE VELDE	(Fr)	69	69	68	74	280	10129
	Costantino ROCCA	(It)	70	71	71	68	280	10129
	José Maria OLAZÁBAL	(Sp)	70	66	73	71	280	10129
	Greg CHALMERS	(Aus)	70	71	66	73	280	10129
	Søren KJELDSEN	(Den)	68	73	71	68	280	10129
24	Santiago LUNA	(Sp)	70	71	69	71	281	9052
	Sven STRÜVER	(Ger)	65	69	74	73	281	9052
26	Olle KARLSSON	(Swe)	72	69	74	67	282	7573
	Raphaël JACQUELIN	(Fr)	73	69	70	70	282	7573
	Roger CHAPMAN	(Eng)	69	72	69	72	282	7573
	Mark ROE	(Eng)	70	70	70	72	282	7573
	Eamonn DARCY	(Ire)	68	71	70	73	282	7573
	Ian GARBUTT	(Eng)	68	73	72	69	282	7573
	Paul LAWRIE	(Scot)	70	69	72	71	282	7573
	Mark MOULAND	(Wal)	69	68	72	73	282	7573
	Bob MAY	(USA)	72	70	69	71	282	7573
	Mats HALLBERG	(Swe)	70	71	70	71	282	7573
36	Brian DAVIS	(Eng)	71	71	70	71	283	6460
37	Gary NICKLAUS	(USA)	69	71	68	76	284	5865
	David HOWELL	(Eng)	69	72	72	71	284	5865
	Fredrik JACOBSON	(Swe)	68	72	73	71	284	5865
	Peter FOWLER	(Aus)	68	74	72	70	284	5865
	Olivier EDMOND	(Fr)	72	70	69	73	284	5865
	Andrew CLAPP	(Eng)	68	72	69	75	284	5865
43	Francisco CEA	(Sp)	70	72	77	66	285	4930
	Paul BROADHURST	(Eng)	70	69	69	77	285	4930
	Robert KARLSSON	(Swe)	72	68	69	76	285	4930
	Eduardo ROMERO	(Arg)	72	68	73	72	285	4930
	Steen TINNING	(Den)	69	72	70	74	285	4930
48	John BICKERTON	(Eng)	70	70	74	72	286	4250
	Andrew OLDCORN	(Scot)	70	67	72	77	286	4250
	Michele REALE	(It)	67	75	71	73	286	4250
51	Michael JONZON	(Swe)	68	74	71	74	287	3655
	Fabrice TARNAUD	(Fr)	73	68	74	72	287	3655
	David LYNN	(Eng)	69	72	71	75	287	3655
	Miles TUNNICLIFF	(Eng)	71	70	70	76	287	3655
55	Diego BORREGO	(Sp)	68	69	75	76	288	2975
	Peter BAKER	(Eng)	69	73	73	73	288	2975
	Greg OWEN	(Eng)	69	70	76	73	288	2975
	Michael LONG	(NZ)	70	72	73	73	288	2975
59	Seve BALLESTEROS	(Sp)	72	66	74	77	289	2592
	Jim PAYNE	(Eng)	69	73	73	74	289	2592
61	Scott HENDERSON	(Scot)	68	73	77	72	290	2380
	David GILFORD	(Eng)	70	71	74	75	290	2380
	Martin GATES	(Eng)	73	69	69	79	290	2380
64	Michael CAMPBELL	(NZ)	71	70	76	74	291	2167
	Richard BOXALL	(Eng)	72	67	77	75	291	2167
66	Stephen FIELD	(Eng)	68	74	77	73	292	1275
67	David TAPPING	(Eng)	68	73	78	78	297	1273

Richard Hills, James McDaid, Mark James, Ken Schofield and Sandy Jones in Ryder Cup Press conference.

Fast greens.

A fast downhiller, breaking sharply from right to left. Every golfer's nightmare. But every driver's dream.

For more information on BMW's advanced braking and suspension systems contact your nearest dealer or www.bmw.com

Freude am Fahren

Strüver is master in the mountains

Sven Strüver captured his third
European title with a play-off
victory in Switzerland

S ven Strüver, who won the Canon European Masters at the first extra hole, has the phlegmatic demeanour of his great hero, Bernhard Langer. At least at the time of the tournament, he also had a beard and, for the first 72 holes, any emotions he might have felt were well and truly under wraps.

All of which added to the mounting tension as he and Sweden's Patrik Sjöland were taken back out to the tee of the 377-yard 18th for the play-off.

After a week in which the weather had been very much a mixture, the sun was out and the Swiss crowd were lapping up the warmth and the heat of the moment. They were packed in the greenside stands and behind the ropes, while the mountaineers among them scaled the starter's chalet and were sitting with their feet dangling from the roof.

Both Strüver and Sjöland bisected the fairway off the tee and now both hit their seconds to nine feet. At this point, John Paramor, the Chief Referee, was called upon to decide who should putt first.

After turning his head one way and then the other five times, Paramor finally opted for Sjöland. The Swede, to his chagrin, pulled the putt fractionally left. Then Strüver seized his opportunity. He had birdied the hole to make the play-off and now, with his 'Langer-type concentration' still intact, he birdied it again for what was

a fourth time in the tournament.

It took rather longer for the result to sink in than for the putt to drop. When it did, this 31-year-old son of a German teaching professional erupted into the widest of smiles and gathered his wife, Stephanie, in his arms. He twirled her round and round by way of celebrating what was arguably the most thrilling of his trio of victories on Tour. It was also worth a cool £133,330, together with a hefty heap of Ryder Cup points, the first on offer for the 1999 instalment of the match.

Though he said it was too soon to start talking about making the European team, Strüver could scarcely have spoken more emphatically – or, for that matter, with more emotion – on the subject: 'Anyone who doesn't want to play in the Ryder Cup shouldn't be a tournament professional.'

Sjöland had been at the summit of the leaderboard at the half-way stage, having attached a 66 to his first round 65 to be eleven under par and a shot ahead of

Though the greens at Crans-sur-Sierre had represented a real problem in 1997, the surfaces were beautifully conditioned for 1998. The newly-redesigned greens on the front half, on the other hand, proved every bit as challenging as their designer, Severiano Ballesteros, would have wished.

Darren Clarke looks like he is playing at home.

Darren Clarke, Strüver and Christophe Bovet. The last-named was the engaging Swiss teaching professional who added an extra dimension to the tournament by raising his game to keep up with Europe's best. Costantino Rocca, the defending champion, was one shot further back.

By Saturday night, Sjöland had a rather stronger foothold on this mountainside championship, having returned a glorious third round 62 to transform his halfway lead into a four-shot affair over Strüver. Yet, by the time he teed off on the Sunday, his lovely putting touch was gone. On top of that, he was no longer bisecting the fairway off the tee, with his drive at the fifth, for example, shooting into the woods on the right.

He stayed in the lead until suddenly, at the 290-yard seventh, Strüver came up with a three wood which looked, for all the world, as if it belonged to the winner. The seventh tee at Crans-sur-Sierre is a mere shelf in the hillside, with the green beyond a valley and a backed by views of the Matterhorn and Mont Blanc. The crowd, having emerged from the woods at the sixth, had only just been prevailed upon to stop gasping at the beauty of it all when they had reason to gasp anew.

Strüver had not only driven the green, but his ball had pulled up six feet to the left of the flag.

Sjöland, whose ball landed short and right, took three to get down for what was a four to a Strüver eagle. Suddenly, the two of them were then level on 20 under par in what was the start of a nail-biter of a closing stretch in which every time Sjöland moved ahead, he would find himself caught.

Darren Clarke pulled up two shots back on 19 under but, for all that he had finished strongly, he was less than impressed.

'So near but so far again on Sunday,' he continued, before going on to acknowledge that the hole which dented his momentum was the 188-yard third. After hitting his six iron into right rough

Gordon Brand Junior (left) and Patrik Sjöland (right).

off the tee, he chipped through the heavily humped putting surface and took three more to get down for a double bogey.

'I tried to get back into the tournament after that but Sven and Patrik were just too strong,' he said, ruefully.

More than once over the week, it had seemed possible that Clarke would overtake his old friend, Lee Westwood, at the top of the Volvo Ranking. In the event, Westwood handed in a closing 68 - a round in which some errant driving was worrying him rather more than a strained hip – and succeeded in clinging to his number one spot. When they left Crans-Sur-Sierre, Westwood had £603,345 to

Clarke's £597,847.

Westwood ended up sharing 12th place with Colin Montgomerie and Sam Torrance, the latter of whom employed two caddies over the week, the back-up having been engaged to keep an eye on Torrance's young son, Daniel. Montgomerie and Torrance were playing alongside each other on the Sunday and it would be fair to say that both were equally disgruntled at the end.

Torrance, who had made no secret of how he was out to play his way into the 1999 Ryder Cup side, was home in an anticlimactic 35 in which he missed a

series of maddening putts.

Montgomerie, for his part, was nothing special going out but, after cramming four birdies and an eagle into his next eight holes, was looking at a homeward 29. Alas, it was not to be. At the 18th on the Saturday, he had hit a second which reared over the spectator stand finishing practically in downtown Crans. On the Sunday, he drove into a bunker and hit his next behind a fairway copse on his way to a second successive six.

Mercifully, the bad memories were going to be buried under a few feet of snow when he returned to Crans for the family Christmas.

Lewine Mair

SHOT OF THE WEEK

Sven Strüver's three wood to six feet at the 290 yards seventh. It was a spectacular shot in the most scenic of settings – and it was the blow which enabled the winner to draw level with Patrik Sjöland for a first time.

CRANS-SUR-SIERRE, CRANS, SWITZERLAND, SEPTEMBER 3-6, 1998 · YARDAGE 6642 · PAR 71

Pos	Name	Country	Rnd 1	Rnd 2	Rnd 3	Rnd 4	Total	Prize Money £
1	Sven STRÜVER	(Ger)	69	63	65	66	263	133330
2	Patrik SJÖLAND	(Swe)	65	66	62	70	263	88880
3	Darren CLARKE	(N.Ire)	64	68	66	67	265	50070
4	Costantino ROCCA	(It)	67	66	67	68	268	40000
5	Alex CEJKA	(Ger)	70	66	67	66	269	30940
	Gordon BRAND JNR.	(Scot)	68	68	66	67	269	30940
7	Jean VAN DE VELDE	(Fr)	67	66	72	65	270	19460
	Miguel Angel JIMÉNEZ	(Sp)	67	69	70	64	270	19460
	Mathias GRÖNBERG	(Swe)	69	68	64	69	270	19460
	Robert KARLSSON	(Swe)	69	69	66	66	270	19460
11	Scott HENDERSON	(Scot)	68	66	68	69	271	14720
12	Lee WESTWOOD	(Eng)	70	68	66	68	272	12960
	Colin MONTGOMERIE	(Scot)	70	66	69	67	272	12960
	Sam TORRANCE	(Scot)	67	68	70	67	272	12960
15	David GILFORD	(Eng)	73	66	67	67	273	11280
	Raphaël JACQUELIN	(Fr)	70	67	68	68	273	11280
	Peter LONARD	(Aus)	70	66	67	70	273	11280
18	Christophe BOVET	(Swi)	68	64	70	72	274	10120
	Silvio GRAPPASONNI	(It)	68	71	65	70	274	10120
20	Eduardo ROMERO	(Arg)	66	71	70	68	275	9000
	Michele REALE	(It)	71	69	70	65	275	9000
	Retief GOOSEN	(SA)	69	70	67	69	275	9000
	Santiago LUNA	(Sp)	69	67	69	70	275	9000
	Pierre FULKE	(Swe)	69	71	67	68	275	9000
	Mats LANNER	(Swe)	70	67	70	68	275	9000
26	Paul EALES	(Eng)	69	67	72	68	276	7800
	Roger CHAPMAN	(Eng)	72	68	69	67	276	7800
	Mats HALLBERG	(Swe)	68	71	70	67	276	7800
	Mark ROE	(Eng)	67	70	67	72	276	7800
30	Fabrice TARNAUD	(Fr)	71	66	68	72	277	6594
	Gary ORR	(Scot)	68	70	68	71	277	6594
	Padraig HARRINGTON	(Ire)	70	69	65	73	277	6594
	Thomas BJÖRN	(Den)	69	70	68	70	277	6594
	Seve BALLESTEROS	(Sp)	70	70	70	67	277	6594
	José RIVERO	(Sp)	68	68	73	68	277	6594
	Jarmo SANDELIN	(Swe)	68	72	66	71	277	6594
37	Angel CABRERA	(Arg)	71	68	70	69	278	5680
	Marc FARRY	(Fr)	72	67	69	70	278	5680
	Richard BOXALL	(Eng)	70	69	66	73	278	5680
	Ivo GINER	(Sp)	71	69	68	70	278	5680
41	Lian-Wei ZHANG	(Chi)	69	70	68	72	279	4880
	Malcolm MACKENZIE	(Eng)	70	69	69	71	279	4880
	Robert COLES	(Eng)	68	71	73	67	279	4880
	Peter SENIOR	(Aus)	72	68	68	71	279	4880
	Francisco CEA	(Sp)	68	72	69	70	279	4880
	Per HAUGSRUD	(Nor)	66	71	70	72	279	4880
47	Gary NICKLAUS	(USA)	70	69	73	68	280	4000
	Phillip PRICE	(Wal)	68	70	71	71	280	4000
	Greg OWEN	(Eng)	70	68	69	73	280	4000
	Jim PAYNE	(Eng)	69	71	71	69	280	4000
	Andrew SHERBORNE	(Eng)	67	69	72	72	280	4000
52	Andrew BEAL	(Eng)	69	70	75	67	281	3120
	José Maria OLAZÁBAL	(Sp)	70	70	69	72	281	3120
	Jamie SPENCE	(Eng)	70	69	70	72	281	3120
	Stephen LEANEY	(Aus)	74	66	72	69	281	3120
	Stephen SCAHILL	(NZ)	71	68	71	71	281	3120
	Jonathan LOMAS	(Eng)	69	71	71	70	281	3120
58	Howard CLARK	(Eng)	70	69	71	72	282	2560
59	Bradley DREDGE	(Wal)	71	67	72	73	283	2440
	Roger WESSELS	(SA)	68	72	70	73	283	2440
61	Katsuyoshi TOMORI	(Jpn)	69	68	73	74	284	2200
	Gary EVANS	(Eng)	70	69	70	75	284	2200
	Mark MOULAND	(Wal)	70	70	75	69	284	2200
	Mike CUNNING	(USA)	71	66	73	74	284	2200
65	Andrew CLAPP	(Eng)	73	67	73	72	285	2000
66	Jeev Milkha SINGH	(Ind)	71	69	75	73	288	1199
	Barry LANE	(Eng)	72	68	74	74	288	1199
68	Anthony WALL	(Eng)	71	68	72	82	293	1196

A chalet doubles as a grandstand.

Canon

IT'S PLAYED FOR THIS, BUT IT'S WON WITH THIS

POTENTIAL.
IT'S THERE TO
BE REALISED

Canon is proud to be an Official Sponsor of the PGA European Tour.
http://sport.europe.canon.com

Montgomerie makes the right call

A telephone call to his former coach,

Bill Ferguson, put Colin Montgomerie

back on line

There was a buzz in the air, a curious hum, an electricity which sent shivers down the spine. Colin Montgomerie was promising good things, Darren Clarke was charging towards the top of the European leaderboard while Sam Torrance and Ian Woosnam were determined to feature in the Ryder Cup selection.

The sky was leaden, wind fresh and the sun occasionally poked through clouds. There was also a smell of deep water, the kind you get in these parts, blown from the trout lakes that cut into the 18th hole at the Marriott Forest of

THE COURSE

Colin Montgomerie wasn't the only winner at the Forest of Arden. The decision by Marriott Hotels to pump £750,000 into new holes and drainage during the last year, clearly paid dividends. Heavy rain Saturday night and Sunday morning offered a tough test. 'I didn't think we would play. All credit to the greenstaff. The money spent made it playable. The drainage is remarkable and I like the greens on the new holes. They were the best,' said Montgomerie. The fourth green was re-designed and enlarged to 750 square metres with two new fairway bunkers and a water hazard positioned to the left of the green. The 14th green was enlarged by 250 metres and a new fairway bunker placed on the left. 1000 African Marigolds were added to shape the Forest of Arden sign by the 18th tee, and 3000 trees were planted throughout the winter months and all 50 bunkers were cleared and refilled with 400 tonnes of new sand. 'I like the course. It suits me. It's set up well. The rough is very penal – a pity it's not like that more often – it demands every club in your bag,' said Darren Clarke, first day leader.

Jarmo Sandelin
lets fly.

Arden. It was a potent cocktail that offered one of the best British Masters ever.

In the end, there was no doubt who many golfers wanted to have a One 2 One with. Their doctor. Medical or swing. Clarke drank Night Nurse and coughed and spluttered his way through four rounds. Thomas Björn and Paul McGinley had already left the Forest of Arden – both discovering life was a pain in the neck. Björn winged off to Denmark for treatment, while McGinley pulled a muscle during round one, where he finished a painful day on three over 75. Argentinian Eduardo Romero also searched for creams and massages to soothe a painful backache. While poor Ian Garbutt had left even earlier after twisting his ankle running under a tree trying to shelter from heavy rain on the Wednesday.

Then there was Lee Westwood. He arrived suffering from a hip complaint, fearing serious trouble – until golf-loving Harley Street specialist Antoni Jakubowski turned on his television. The Canadian, a top chiropractor and consultant to Formula One drivers, witnessed how Westwood was walking.

He believed his trouble was much deeper rooted in his spine. Jakubowski contacted Westwood's manager, Andrew 'Chubby' Chandler, and suggested a series of X-rays at a local Midland hospital.

His theory proved correct. The pictures showed lower back problems which could have had serious consequences for the golfer's season and possibly his future. 'We've caught everything just in time,' said Jakubowski. Westwood, who went into the tournament as Europe's top

SHOT OF THE WEEK

Ian Woosnam's second shot on the 511-yard par five 17th during the second round. After finding water on the 16th and finishing with a double-bogey, he decided to 'go for it'. A driver and fairway wood got to the edge of the green and a wedge to three feet. He nearly birdied the 18th but the confidence gained took him on a run of four birdies – six overall on the back nine - and a score of 28.

earner, said, 'I was just so relieved that it could be treated without need for surgery.'

Montgomerie was in pain also, arriving after missing two successive cuts, although he did feel he was coming out of his 'little spell'. He had the Press Corps in laughter when asked who he would like to have a One 2 One with: 'James Bond, although only fictional – he is a role model for anyone who aspires to travelling the world in fast cars and planes – I'd ask him how he manages to keep so cool in such ridiculously dangerous situations.'

But he revealed using a gadget that

would have witnessed 'Q' leaping with delight. He took delivery of a Laser Aimer, invented by American short-game guru Dave Peltz, to assist his putting. The intention is to determine whether or not the player is aiming the putter head in the right direction. 'I use it in my hotel bedroom – when there's no soccer on television,' he said. He added: 'Dave has tested 1500 of the world's best professionals and only two were aiming correctly, Lee Janzen and Howard Twitty. I was about three inches out on a putt of 21 feet but which, I was told, was not too bad. But it's a scary thought that to hole a putt I had to push it. I actually had to do something wrong to hole the putt.'

Fittingly, it was the use of a good old-fashioned telephone that had changed Montgomerie's season. But more of that later.

As streams of people filtered over the course, Clarke's giant shadow loomed large over the opening round where his five under-par 67 again put him in a position to win. The burly Ulsterman had arrived in the heart of England having played 64 rounds and won £597,847 – yet was still deeply dissatisfied with his golf. Clarke had eight top ten-finishes in 17 events and one victory. So it wasn't just his head swimming from 'flu and body rattling like a moneybox after taking a medicine cabinet of tablets. 'All I can do is put myself in a position to win, unfortunately I haven't made the most of it on previous Sundays,' he said.

Swiss Paolo Quirici finished one shot behind, with Sam Torrance and Andrew Sherbourne, Robert Lee and Carl Suneson forming the underguard, two behind.

A chip shot that failed to drop brought Eduardo Romero to his knees.

Suneson and Clarke shared the lead after round two, but the day belonged to Welshman Ian Woosnam.

When Tiger Woods won the 1997 Masters, he had a first round in which he was out in 40 and back in 30. Woosnam's two halves in the second round had a far more interesting ring. Out in 38 and back in 28 for a 66 that left him three shots off the halfway lead. He had been six over par for the tournament after a double-bogey at the 16th, his seventh hole. 'It got so bad I was ready to use the sponsor's phone and contact my pilot ready for a swift take-off home,' said the jet-owning golfer. 'I can't remember ever hitting 28 before.' Even more remarkable because he practised his putting standing barefoot on a snooker table in his Jersey home. He took down the overhead lights and explained: 'It's a true surface. If you knock them straight down there, then you know you are hitting the ball just where you are aiming. But I hit everything right so I realised I must be turning my right hand when under pressure.'

Any hopes Justin Rose held of making a smooth transition to the professional ranks sadly crashed, despite a second round 70 and he missed his sixth successive cut.

Without a hint that he was about to make his move, the powerful figure of Montgomerie suddenly produced a reminder of his awesome talent at the end of round three. An amazing 31 players were separated by only four shots, with Quirici being the surprise leader. In that log-jam was Montgomerie, playing down all thoughts that a sixth Volvo Ranking triumph was his goal.

A round of 70, however, made him a menacing figure. When Montgomerie left the US PGA in Seattle the first thing he did arriving at the airport was to send an SOS to his former coach Bill Ferguson. The pair shocked golf four years earlier when Montgomerie decided to sever their successful relationship. Now he wanted him back to help him overcome a 'mini crisis'.

Ferguson reckoned it would take 2000 shots to fully restore Montgomerie's natural game and reduce his odd shot to the left. If the use of his first 70 was to good effect, then the last day's 69 was devastat-ing. The 35-year-old Scot emerged through the Forest of Arden to prove himself something of a Robin Hood.

No one knows his way through the dark woods, towering trees and thick undergrowth like him – he had won once and been second on three other visits.

When Quirici drifted away, Pierre Fulke and Romero made charges, but Montgomerie steadily took over, finally putting the £125,000 winner's cheque beyond dispute when holing from 20 feet on the 17th to go two shots clear. He dropped one on the last, but the winning line was crossed.

Smiling, enjoying the minute, he wanted a swift One 2 One with Ferguson. 'I could not have done it without him,' he said. He added: 'I have entered all the final tournaments of the year.' Then with a smile. 'Read into that what you will.' He remained upbeat about the rest of the year. The man who has been European number one for five years was now number three. He added: 'Number three doesn't like being number three.'

Autumn was going to be interesting.

Tony Stenson

Marriott Forest of Arden, Coventry, September 10-13, 1998 · Par 72 · Yards 7106

Pos	Name	Country	Rnd 1	Rnd 2	Rnd 3	Rnd 4	Total	Prize Money £
1	Colin MONTGOMERIE	(Scot)	70	72	70	69	281	125000
2	Pierre FULKE	(Swe)	71	72	72	67	282	65130
	Eduardo ROMERO	(Arg)	70	69	75	68	282	65130
4	Ignacio GARRIDO	(Sp)	70	73	71	69	283	31840
	Andrew OLDCORN	(Scot)	71	73	71	68	283	31840
	Paolo QUIRICI	(Swi)	68	73	70	72	283	31840
7	Greg OWEN	(Eng)	70	71	73	70	284	22500
8	Russell CLAYDON	(Eng)	72	73	68	72	285	16072
	John BICKERTON	(Eng)	70	75	73	67	285	16072
	Sam TORRANCE	(Scot)	69	72	71	73	285	16072
	Daniel CHOPRA	(Swe)	71	72	69	73	285	16072
12	Anssi KANKKONEN	(Fin)	71	69	76	70	286	11118
	Marc FARRY	(Fr)	73	72	67	74	286	11118
	Mark ROE	(Eng)	72	69	71	74	286	11118
	Søren KJELDSEN	(Den)	72	71	72	71	286	11118
	Lee WESTWOOD	(Eng)	73	70	73	70	286	11118
	Ian WOOSNAM	(Wal)	75	66	73	72	286	11118
	Greg CHALMERS	(Aus)	72	73	74	67	286	11118
	Sergio GARCIA (AM)	(Sp)	71	73	69	73	286	
19	Mats LANNER	(Swe)	71	73	73	70	287	8220
	Craig HAINLINE	(USA)	72	71	70	74	287	8220
	Carl SUNESON	(Sp)	69	69	75	74	287	8220
	Michael CAMPBELL	(NZ)	71	69	76	71	287	8220
	Darren CLARKE	(N.Ire)	67	71	74	75	287	8220
	Miguel Angel JIMÉNEZ	(Sp)	70	75	72	70	287	8220
	Peter O'MALLEY	(Aus)	73	71	72	71	287	8220
	Paul BROADHURST	(Eng)	79	65	74	69	287	8220
	Costantino ROCCA	(It)	71	72	71	73	287	8220
	Olle KARLSSON	(Swe)	75	67	71	74	287	8220
29	Robert COLES	(Eng)	73	72	76	67	288	6450
	Santiago LUNA	(Sp)	70	73	73	72	288	6450
	Robert LEE	(Eng)	69	74	73	72	288	6450
	Peter MITCHELL	(Eng)	75	70	73	70	288	6450
	Ross DRUMMOND	(Scot)	72	72	69	75	288	6450
	Michael LONG	(NZ)	75	69	73	71	288	6450
35	Carl MASON	(Eng)	72	73	68	76	289	5625
	Greig HUTCHEON	(Scot)	72	70	71	76	289	5625
	Mathias GRÖNBERG	(Swe)	75	70	75	69	289	5625
	Knud STORGAARD	(Den)	75	69	75	70	289	5625
39	Jonathan LOMAS	(Eng)	72	72	74	72	290	5025
	Per HAUGSRUD	(Nor)	72	72	72	74	290	5025
	Diego BORREGO	(Sp)	72	70	73	75	290	5025
	José COCERES	(Arg)	74	70	71	75	290	5025
	Trevor IMMELMAN (AM)	(SA)	71	71	76	72	290	
43	Mark MOULAND	(Wal)	72	71	72	76	291	4350
	Andrew BEAL	(Eng)	71	71	74	75	291	4350
	Richard BOXALL	(Eng)	73	70	71	77	291	4350
	Andrew COLTART	(Scot)	72	70	72	77	291	4350
	Roger CHAPMAN	(Eng)	76	69	71	75	291	4350
48	Angel CABRERA	(Arg)	73	69	71	79	292	3450
	Roger WESSELS	(SA)	72	70	73	77	292	3450
	Thomas LEVET	(Fr)	76	69	73	74	292	3450
	Gary ORR	(Scot)	71	73	73	75	292	3450
	Massimo FLORIOLI	(It)	75	70	75	72	292	3450
	Van PHILLIPS	(Eng)	73	72	73	74	292	3450
	Iain PYMAN	(Eng)	76	69	76	71	292	3450

Pos	Name	Country	Rnd 1	Rnd 2	Rnd 3	Rnd 4	Total	Prize Money
55	Steven RICHARDSON	(Eng)	74	70	73	76	293	2512
	Stephen ALLAN	(Aus)	71	72	80	70	293	2512
	Gary EVANS	(Eng)	74	71	75	73	293	2512
	Tony JOHNSTONE	(Zim)	73	72	76	72	293	2512
	Stephen LEANEY	(Aus)	74	69	74	76	293	2512
	Peter BAKER	(Eng)	72	73	71	77	293	2512
61	David HOWELL	(Eng)	72	73	73	76	294	2025
	Sven STRÜVER	(Ger)	71	73	76	74	294	2025
	Per-Ulrik JOHANSSON	(Swe)	72	71	74	77	294	2025
	Silvio GRAPPASONNI	(It)	71	72	77	74	294	2025
	Carl WATTS	(Eng)	71	74	71	78	294	2025
66	Jim PAYNE	(Eng)	74	71	73	77	295	1124
	Peter SENIOR	(Aus)	71	74	74	76	295	1124
68	Barry LANE	(Eng)	73	72	77	74	296	1121
69	Jarmo SANDELIN	(Swe)	70	69	76	82	297	1119
70	Stuart CAGE	(Eng)	75	68	83	73	299	1117

Per-Ulrik Johansson.

Jiménez stays cool when the chips are down

Miguel Angel Jiménez held off
a star-studded field
in a dramatic finale

W hen five of the world's top ten players converge late in a long season to contest a European Tour title it is safe to assume each of them has a special motive for being there.

Their reasons were diverse and compelling and produced one of the best all-star casts of the year outside a major championship as they assembled in the elegant surrounding of the Saint-Nom-la-Bretèche Club close to Versailles for the Trophée Lancôme.

David Duval, currently second in the world rankings, admitted that he was putting his toe in European waters and clearly aware of the need to broaden his international reputation. Mark O'Meara, ranked third and the reigning Open and Masters champion, more simply was back to defend the title he won a year earlier.

Colin Montgomerie and Lee Westwood were heavily involved in the race to win the Volvo Ranking title, and newly-wed Fred Couples was making a tentative but sure-footed return after a traumatic season during which his father died and he was plagued by back problems.

For good measure, add in the tower-

ing presence of Nick Faldo to the cast list, back in Europe for the declared purpose of picking up early Ryder Cup points, and the stage was set for one of the most thrilling confrontations of the year.

While it is true to suggest that most of them came away from the French event with sound reasons to be cheerful, the ultimate prize was denied them as Miguel Angel Jiménez ignored all their reputations and captured the trophy in dramatic style.

The consolation for O'Meara and Duval was that they remained in contention for all four rounds and both had a realistic chance of victory that somehow

eluded them at the last moment.

The persistence of their challenge heightened the value of the courtly Miguel Angel's achievement. Respected as an able second-in-command – as he proved as vice-captain in the 1997 Ryder Cup match – this dignified man quietly held centre stage and refused to yield even when the pressures bore down on him. It was without question the most important victory of his career.

Montgomerie left town still trailing Westwood in the Volvo Ranking pursuit despite a joint 11th place finish in which he broke par in all but one round, while Westwood never found his customary aggressive stride but was to prove only a week later that the aberration had no lasting effect on him.

Faldo came away with a new-found spring in his stride and the proof that months of hard work to regain his best form had begun to show signs of paying off as he produced a last round 65 which included an impressive opening run of three successive birdies to finish in sixth place. It was his best performance of the year and he was clearly pleased with the result and explained: 'I needed to test myself under pressure to see how the swing would respond and this will breed the confidence I need.'

And Couples, whose new bride stayed home to look after the children from her first marriage, at least discovered that he has regained the competitive fitness and edge and needs only a greater measure of accuracy with his putter to move back among the winners after he finished in ninth position.

THE COURSE

Set in rolling country-side on lush parkland that at times makes the fairways slow running. Several greens are perched into the terrain in such a manner that an approach shot with too much spin can roll off and into difficult hollows. The finishing hole – a downhill par three – is rare for a course of such stature but works effectively because of the pond which menaces the right edge of the green and the left hand bunkers which narrow the target area. Many titles have been lost here over the years.

Success, of course, takes many forms and for Anthony Wall the greatest achievement of his week was to ensure his livelihood for the next season by winning enough money to retain his European Tour privileges.

He found himself in the distinguished company of Duval and O'Meara on the final day but showed no signs of stage-fright as he matched the US Masters champion's 69 to finish in

Colin Montgomerie plays spot the player.

seventh place, but more importantly acquire the £22,000 that assured him a place on the 1999 European Tour.

There were other footnotes to be found in the margin of such a great event, not least of which was the welcome news that Jesper Parnevik had rejoined the European Tour and would be eligible to earn Ryder Cup points. Though still playing on the US Tour, he

SHOT OF THE WEEK

Miguel Angel Jiménez was under acute pressure when his tee shot finished left of the final green and perilously close to the grandstand. He had endured a roller coaster performance and at that moment had five birdies, one eagle but six bogeys on his card. There was a nagging fear that the outcome might still be decided by his reaction to the obvious consequences of his next shot because he knew that if he dropped a stroke he would find himself surrounded by an all-star cast in a play-off that included O'Meara, Duval, Sandelin and Greg Turner. He coaxed the wedge shot onto the green then watched as the ball ran into the hole for a birdie two and a brilliant victory.

has been able to make the European commitment because of the inclusion of three new world championships among the 11 contests a player must attend to retain his card.

Jarmo Sandelin survived a rules query and had to wait overnight before learning whether he could continue in the tournament. The problem began when his ball appeared to move on the green as he was about to putt in the third round.

He agreed that it did move but that he did not ground his club which meant there was no penalty. Only after Chief Referee John Paramour had questioned playing companions Lee

Last round 69 ensured Anthony Wall his player's card for 1999.

Westwood and Patrik Sjöland as well as the caddies was it decided to allow Sandelin to carry on. And he celebrated his relief by scoring a superlative last round 63.

The most bizarre moment of the week came when an elderly French lady found a golf ball near the 18th green and kindly handed it over to a young boy as a souvenir. What she did not know was that it was still in play and belonged to Colin Montgomerie. He was allowed to put down a replacement then chipped on to the green and holed from 20 yards for his par. Nice one.

Michael McDonnell   213

Saint-Nom-La-Bretèche, September 17-20 , 1998 • Par 71 • Yards 6903

Pos	Name	Country	Rnd 1	Rnd 2	Rnd 3	Rnd 4	Total	Prize Money £
1	Miguel Angel JIMÉNEZ	(Sp)	67	70	67	69	273	133330
2	Greg TURNER	(NZ)	67	71	68	69	275	53207
	Jarmo SANDELIN	(Swe)	68	74	70	63	275	53207
	Mark O'MEARA	(USA)	70	67	69	69	275	53207
	David DUVAL	(USA)	69	72	67	67	275	53207
6	Nick FALDO	(Eng)	70	71	70	65	276	28000
7	Anthony WALL	(Eng)	71	70	67	69	277	22000
	Peter O'MALLEY	(Aus)	68	72	68	69	277	22000
9	Fred COUPLES	(USA)	70	68	70	70	278	16920
	Per-Ulrik JOHANSSON	(Swe)	74	68	68	68	278	16920
11	Sam TORRANCE	(Scot)	70	73	72	64	279	13400
	Gordon BRAND JNR.	(Scot)	68	72	69	70	279	13400
	Alex CEJKA	(Ger)	69	69	74	67	279	13400
	Colin MONTGOMERIE	(Scot)	69	68	69	73	279	13400
15	Roger WESSELS	(SA)	73	70	68	69	280	11280
	Peter LONARD	(Aus)	71	70	68	71	280	11280
	Silvio GRAPPASONNI	(It)	74	69	69	68	280	11280
18	Fredrik JACOBSON	(Swe)	72	70	72	67	281	9280
	Mats HALLBERG	(Swe)	70	70	73	68	281	9280
	Greg CHALMERS	(Aus)	72	70	68	71	281	9280
	José COCERES	(Arg)	70	70	71	70	281	9280
	Thomas LEVET	(Fr)	72	69	69	71	281	9280
	Thomas BJORN	(Den)	74	69	67	71	281	9280
	Barry LANE	(Eng)	73	69	70	69	281	9280
	Paul BROADHURST	(Eng)	69	71	69	72	281	9280
	Sergio GARCIA (AM)	(Sp)	69	68	73	71	281	
26	Olivier EDMOND	(Fr)	74	69	71	68	282	7680
	David GILFORD	(Eng)	72	69	74	67	282	7680
	Peter MITCHELL	(Eng)	69	69	72	72	282	7680
	Paul MCGINLEY	(Ire)	71	69	70	72	282	7680
	Marc PENDARIES	(Fr)	72	69	70	71	282	7680
31	Greg OWEN	(Eng)	74	70	70	69	283	6840
	Katsuyoshi TOMORI	(Jpn)	69	70	71	73	283	6840
33	Bob MAY	(USA)	69	75	69	71	284	6080
	Patrik SJÖLAND	(Swe)	71	71	72	70	284	6080
	Nicolas VANHOOTEGEM	(Bel)	70	72	70	72	284	6080
	Brad FAXON	(USA)	73	69	73	69	284	6080
	Olle KARLSSON	(Swe)	73	71	68	72	284	6080
	Stephen ALLAN	(Aus)	67	73	71	73	284	6080
	Philip WALTON	(Ire)	73	71	73	67	284	6080
40	Howard CLARK	(Eng)	71	72	72	70	285	4960
	Gary EVANS	(Eng)	71	69	77	68	285	4960
	Michael CAMPBELL	(NZ)	69	72	76	68	285	4960
	Carl SUNESON	(Sp)	72	72	70	71	285	4960
	Mark JAMES	(Eng)	70	68	76	71	285	4960
	Steven RICHARDSON	(Eng)	70	70	71	74	285	4960
	Gary ORR	(Scot)	72	69	68	76	285	4960
47	Iain PYMAN	(Eng)	72	69	70	75	286	4080
	Jesper PARNEVIK	(Swe)	73	70	70	73	286	4080
	Derrick COOPER	(Eng)	67	72	72	75	286	4080
	Paolo QUIRICI	(Swi)	73	71	70	72	286	4080
51	Eamonn DARCY	(Ire)	67	71	74	75	287	3440
	Michael LONG	(NZ)	75	63	78	71	287	3440
	José RIVERO	(Sp)	69	73	71	74	287	3440
	Angel CABRERA	(Arg)	70	69	72	76	287	3440
55	Mark MOULAND	(Wal)	71	71	74	72	288	2960
	Fabrice TARNAUD	(Fr)	73	71	71	73	288	2960
57	Rolf MUNTZ	(Hol)	73	70	71	75	289	2216
	Andrew COLTART	(Scot)	71	69	73	76	289	2216
	Retief GOOSEN	(SA)	70	73	73	73	289	2216
	Ivo GINER	(Sp)	74	69	77	69	289	2216
	Paul LAWRIE	(Scot)	72	72	72	73	289	2216
	Mathias GRÖNBERG	(Swe)	69	72	76	72	289	2216
	Marc FARRY	(Fr)	68	74	72	75	289	2216
	Brian DAVIS	(Eng)	70	73	77	69	289	2216
	Robert COLES	(Eng)	72	71	74	72	289	2216
	Rodger DAVIS	(Aus)	72	70	76	71	289	2216
67	Raymond RUSSELL	(Scot)	71	72	73	74	290	1196
	Mats LANNER	(Swe)	71	73	78	68	290	1196
	Jim PAYNE	(Eng)	71	69	76	74	290	1196
70	Andrew SHERBORNE	(Eng)	76	68	74	73	291	1192
71	Lee WESTWOOD	(Eng)	70	72	73	77	292	1188
	Seve BALLESTEROS	(Sp)	69	73	75	75	292	1188
	Michael JONZON	(Swe)	73	70	78	71	292	1188

Leading US money-winner David Duval.

**"ONCE YOU UNDERSTAND
THE BASIC SWING,
IT'S JUST A MATTER OF ADAPTING IT
TO DIFFERENT SITUATIONS."**

DAVID LEADBETTER.

His gift as a communicator and his adaptability make David Leadbetter one of golf's most sought-after teachers. His student list includes many of the world's top players because, instead of shaping the golfer to fit the game, he shapes the game to fit the golfer. "When I first see someone," he says, "I have a vision of how I'd like to see that person play. Everything I do works toward that." Just how highly the world's best golfers value Leadbetter's advice can be judged by the gift he received in appreciation from an Open winner: a specially-inscribed Rolex Day-Date. David Leadbetter can trace many parallels between his Rolex and the ideal golf swing. "It's reliable. It's efficient. It's good-looking. And it does the business every time."

ROLEX
of Geneva

Day-Date.
Officially Certified Swiss Chronometer.
For information on the Rolex range write to:
Rolex UK, 3 Stratford Place, London W1N 0ER
or telephone 0171- 629 5071.

Montgomerie in ascendancy

Victory in Germany put Colin Montgomerie

back in a familiar place

on the Volvo Ranking

A fter a frustrating summer, Colin Montgomerie underlined once again he has the skill and fortitude to win under the greatest of pressure and in the process regained pole position in the race to top the Volvo Ranking for an unprecedented sixth successive year.

There is no greater test of nerve than coming to the last hole needing a par or birdie to win. Twice this season Montgomerie's nerve has been examined and found not to be wanting. He needed a birdie four at the last to win the Volvo PGA Championship, and got up and down from 100 yards to win the title. At Gut Lärchenhof he had to work just as hard to win the Linde German Masters, holing a six foot putt for a par and a one shot victory over US PGA champion Vijay Singh and Swede Robert Karlssson.

In the process Montgomerie leapfrogged long-time Volvo Ranking leader Lee Westwood, and Darren Clarke, to occupy a position he has made his own over the past five seasons. But more importantly the win marked a remarkable turnaround of fortunes. Only a month earlier Montgomerie suffered the frustration of missing two consecutive cuts for the first time since 1991. That, and a disappointing US PGA Championship, prompted him to make a phone call to coach Bill Ferguson, reuniting them after an 18-month split. Since then Montgomerie had hit more balls on the practice range than he had ever struck in his life in an effort to eliminate a hook that had plagued him over the past few months. When they started working together again Montgomerie told Ferguson he hoped to win two tournaments by the end of the year. He did better than that, winning two tournaments in three weeks.

The 18th at Gut Lärchenhof contains all the difficulties that course-designer Jack Nicklaus could muster with water running all the way down the left and widening towards the green. The headwind on the final Sunday merely added to the problems that had to be overcome.

Montgomerie made no mistake, hit-

THE COURSE

Designed by Jack Nicklaus, Gut Lärchenhof is a spectacular oasis in the middle of an arable desert in the region around Dusseldorf and Frankfurt, an area known as Germany's golfing 'heart'. Opened two years ago, it is a typical Nicklaus layout with plenty of opportunities to tuck the holes into the corners of the greens. The course features some lovely par threes, notably the 16th with water to the right, but the two key holes are undoubtedly the ninth and 18th, both par fours which are played around a lake.

ting his tee shot to the left side of the fairway and then a four iron to the safe right-hand side of the green. Two putts later he was champion. 'Mastering the 18th at Cologne with water all the way down the left proved I've got the new swing more or less under control,' he said. 'The occasional tweak in that direction is still a danger but I'm almost there.'

Putting lessons from Dave Pelz also helped to elevate Montgomerie back to the number one spot in Europe. 'I had to make a really tough putt to win the Volvo PGA at Wentworth and one from six feet here after leaving the first putt short – that's as much about courage as skill and it's very satisfying when you do it.'

Montgomerie threw down the gauntlet to his Volvo Ranking rivals Westwood and Clarke when he opened with a blistering 65,

seven under par, to share the first round lead with Singh and former Walker Cup amateur Van Phillips. Westwood responded superbly to record a 66 while Clarke shot a 69.

Singh moved into the lead at the halfway stage by shooting a 67 despite bemoaning a succession of squandered opportunities after squeezing four birdies into his first six holes. But it was Padraig Harrington and Steve Webster who stole the show in the second round, shooting 64 and 65 respectively to move within a shot of the lead alongside Westwood, Montgomerie, Karlsson and another Swede, Jarmo Sandelin. Westwood's round included a string of missed birdie chances, six from inside three yards, but he showed his mettle to

A steady week for Jim Payne.

finish eagle, par, birdie for a 67.

Saturday is traditionally moving day and sure enough it was Montgomerie who broke free from the pack by posting a 66 for a 17 under par total of 199, taking a one-shot lead into the final round ahead of Harrington with Webster and Singh a further shot back.

With only two holes left of the third round Singh appeared to be in command but a surprising end to the round cost him dear. The Fijian was leading by one standing on the 17th tee but he missed the green and then proceeded to miss the ball completely with his chip, the club sliding straight under the ball. A double bogey six was followed by a bogey at the last when he drove into the lake and in the space of two holes he had slipped two behind Montgomerie.

Australian veteran Rodger Davis, the oldest player in the field at 47, found himself just three shots off the lead after pick-

Colin Montgomerie's tee shot on the last hole at Gut Lärchenhof was as important a drive as he has had to make since the 18th at Valderamma in the last match of the Ryder Cup twelve months earlier. On this occasion he needed a par to win but was faced with a tee shot straight into the wind with a lake running down the left side of the fairway. Montgomerie hit the ideal drive to the left of the fairway from where he was able to hit a four iron to the safe side of the green and two putt for victory.

Nick Faldo (left) drives while Vijay Singh (right) ponders.

ing up nine birdies on his way to a course-record 63, his lowest score for five years.

But Montgomerie was determined to hold onto his overnight lead and although Karlsson threatened to spoil the party when he birdied the 12th and then

pitched in for an eagle on the 13th to go to 21 under par and lead by one, Montgomerie rose to the challenge by birdieing the long 13th and 15th to edge back in front. The Swede went on to shoot a 65 while Singh fought back with two birdies in the last three holes for a

steely 66 to share second place.

By winning the £166,660 first prize Montgomerie claimed his 17th European Tour title and significantly, returned to the top of the Volvo Ranking for the first time since July.

Roddy Williams   219

GUT LÄRCHENHOF, COLOGNE, SEPTEMBER 24-27, 1998 · YARDAGE 7014 · PAR 72

Pos	Name	Country	Rnd 1	Rnd 2	Rnd 3	Rnd 4	Total	Prize Money £
1	Colin MONTGOMERIE	(Scot)	65	68	66	67	266	166660
2	Robert KARLSSON	(Swe)	68	65	69	65	267	86850
	Vijay SINGH	(Fij)	65	67	69	66	267	86850
4	Steve WEBSTER	(Eng)	68	65	68	67	268	50000
5	Per-Ulrik JOHANSSON	(Swe)	68	67	67	67	269	42400
6	Lee WESTWOOD	(Eng)	66	67	72	66	271	32500
	Paul MCGINLEY	(Ire)	69	68	67	67	271	32500
8	Jarmo SANDELIN	(Swe)	66	67	74	65	272	22433
	Jean VAN DE VELDE	(Fr)	67	67	70	68	272	22433
	Padraig HARRINGTON	(Ire)	69	64	67	72	272	22433
11	Gary NICKLAUS	(USA)	70	71	67	65	273	16735
	Raymond RUSSELL	(Scot)	67	68	68	70	273	16735
	Marc FARRY	(Fr)	68	68	67	70	273	16735
	Retief GOOSEN	(SA)	68	67	67	71	273	16735
15	Gordon BRAND JNR.	(Scot)	67	70	72	65	274	13266
	Klas ERIKSSON	(Swe)	69	71	67	67	274	13266
	Bernhard LANGER	(Ger)	69	69	68	68	274	13266
	Michael LONG	(NZ)	71	65	68	70	274	13266
	Peter O'MALLEY	(Aus)	68	69	65	72	274	13266
	Rodger DAVIS	(Aus)	70	69	63	72	274	13266
21	Peter MITCHELL	(Eng)	70	68	70	67	275	10800
	Miles TUNNICLIFF	(Eng)	68	67	73	67	275	10800
	Jim PAYNE	(Eng)	69	66	71	69	275	10800
	Darren CLARKE	(N.Ire)	69	70	67	69	275	10800
	Greg TURNER	(NZ)	68	71	67	69	275	10800
	José Maria OLAZÁBAL	(Sp)	69	66	70	70	275	10800
	Iain PYMAN	(Eng)	68	67	69	71	275	10800
28	Stephen ALLAN	(Aus)	70	68	69	69	276	8511
	Scott HENDERSON	(Scot)	71	71	65	69	276	8511
	Fabrice TARNAUD	(Fr)	72	70	67	67	276	8511
	Steven RICHARDSON	(Eng)	69	72	69	66	276	8511
	Brad FAXON	(USA)	68	72	68	68	276	8511
	Anthony WALL	(Eng)	70	68	70	68	276	8511
	Ignacio GARRIDO	(Sp)	69	70	70	67	276	8511
	Santiago LUNA	(Sp)	68	66	71	71	276	8511
	Costantino ROCCA	(It)	70	68	66	72	276	8511
37	Clinton WHITELAW	(SA)	68	70	70	69	277	7100
	Ian GARBUTT	(Eng)	66	71	69	71	277	7100
	Richard BOXALL	(Eng)	66	70	69	72	277	7100
	Sven STRÜVER	(Ger)	66	70	68	73	277	7100
41	Richard GREEN	(Aus)	74	68	67	69	278	6200
	Nick FALDO	(Eng)	71	69	70	68	278	6200
	Paul BROADHURST	(Eng)	68	71	71	68	278	6200
	Mark JAMES	(Eng)	69	68	70	71	278	6200
	Per HAUGSRUD	(Nor)	67	70	69	72	278	6200
46	Thomas GÖGELE	(Ger)	70	68	71	70	279	5500
	Van PHILLIPS	(Eng)	65	70	70	74	279	5500
48	Paul EALES	(Eng)	69	70	70	71	280	4600
	David CARTER	(Eng)	68	70	71	71	280	4600
	David GILFORD	(Eng)	73	68	69	70	280	4600
	Seve BALLESTEROS	(Sp)	72	69	69	70	280	4600
	Miguel Angel JIMÉNEZ	(Sp)	72	68	72	68	280	4600
	Mathias GRÖNBERG	(Swe)	71	68	68	73	280	4600
	Carl SUNESON	(Sp)	68	67	71	74	280	4600
55	Domingo HOSPITAL	(Sp)	71	71	70	69	281	3350
	Heinz Peter THÜL	(Ger)	71	71	68	71	281	3350
	Silvio GRAPPASONNI	(It)	68	71	71	71	281	3350
	Derrick COOPER	(Eng)	71	70	70	70	281	3350
	José RIVERO	(Sp)	69	73	70	69	281	3350
	Gary EVANS	(Eng)	70	67	71	73	281	3350
61	Sam TORRANCE	(Scot)	71	71	69	72	283	2750
	Russell CLAYDON	(Eng)	74	68	70	71	283	2750
	Michael JONZON	(Swe)	73	68	71	71	283	2750
	Patrik SJÖLAND	(Swe)	73	68	73	69	283	2750
65	Daniel CHOPRA	(Swe)	67	72	71	74	284	1832
	Roger CHAPMAN	(Eng)	68	74	71	71	284	1832
	Phillip PRICE	(Wal)	69	73	73	69	284	1832
68	Felix LUBENAU	(Ger)	75	67	72	71	285	1496
69	Peter BAKER	(Eng)	70	72	71	73	286	1494
70	Fredrik JACOBSON	(Swe)	72	70	69	76	287	1491
	Dennis EDLUND	(Swe)	72	69	71	75	287	1491
72	Dean ROBERTSON	(Scot)	73	67	73	75	288	1488
73	Jamie SPENCE	(Eng)	71	70	77	71	289	1486

Steve Webster.

Westwood takes up the challenge

Victory in Belgium for Lee Westwood

ensured the battle for the 1998 Volvo

Ranking title would go to the wire

*L*ee Westwood, by his own admission, was stuck in a rut. By mid-August, the easy-going Englishman from Worksop had achieved his goals – a magnificent maiden victory in America, three tournament wins on the European Tour, including back-to-back successes at Hamburg and Hanbury Manor. The majors, something of a disappointment, were over for another year.

So, as his 1998 campaign moved into the 'Autumn Swing', Westwood suddenly realised that he was inexplicably lacking in the drive which propelled him to those outstanding triumphs on both sides of the Atlantic.

The breaks, he complained, were going against him. A nagging hip injury didn't help either. For the first time in a phenomenally successful season, Westwood felt at odds with himself and his game. He was abnormally impatient; not at all his usual affable self.

All that changed when Colin Montgomerie won the Linde German Masters to overhaul Westwood at the top of the Volvo Ranking by a matter of £111,926, then promptly withdrew from the Belgacom Open to keep his powder dry for the final end-of-season push.

The young Ryder Cup hero did some

quick mental arithmetic. Win the Belgacom Open and the gap at the the top of the Volvo Ranking would be trimmed to £45,266. It didn't require Albert Einstein to deduce from those sums that if Westwood won the Volvo Masters then, irrespective of what Montgomerie did, he would claim the coveted title of European number one for the first time.

By the following Sunday, the son of a maths teacher had totted up another £66,660 to his burgeoning earnings, and the stage had been set for a thrilling finale to another titanic struggle to top the Volvo Ranking.

'I needed motivating,' explained Westwood, as his fourth European Tour trophy of a wonderful year sat glistening in front of him in the Media Centre at Royal Zoute. 'I gave myself a good talking to. Basically, I needed a kick up the backside. I started feeling sorry for myself, which is a pathetic attitude. If you're in a

THE COURSE

Nick Faldo described Royal Zoute as a 'hidden gem'. Lee Westwood claimed the venue is one of the best on the European Tour. The unanimous vote from all the players is that the 6,907-yard, par 71 course is welcome back on the rota any time. Immaculately conditioned, green and lush despite being so close to the sea, Royal Zoute proved a wonderful test.

Nick Faldo lost a little balance after an opening 65.

lull, you're in a lull and you have to play your way through it.'

As a result, the Lee Westwood who rode into town for the Belgacom Open, eyes narrowed and trigger-finger itching like that of a Wild West gunslinger, was a golfer reborn. His zest for the game – and the struggle to win the Volvo Ranking – had been rekindled and, in racing parlance, he was always travelling like the winner from the 'off'.

Not that he had things all his own way. Far from it. Sweden's Fredrik Jacobson began the tournament over the superb Royal Zoute course in danger of losing his card. He was ranked 124 and calculated he needed to finish no worse than eighth to retain his status among the elite for 1999.

For Jacobson, as well as Westwood, the Belgacom Open proved to be a case of getting the job done.

Three players, Robert Karlsson, Greg Turner and Van Phillips, led the way after the first round with seven under par 64s, just a stroke ahead of some notable players including three-time Open and Masters champion Nick Faldo.

Westwood carded a 67 and added a 68 on a second day in which Jacobson (65, 67) swept into the lead on ten under par. The highlight of that day, however, was a course record 62 by England's Greg Owen, who sheepishly revealed later that he had packed his suitcase in preparation for missing the cut.

Fredrik Jacobson (top) and New Zealand's Greg Turner (above) were both in at the finish.

Not even a matter for debate – Lee Westwood's glorious pitching wedge for an eagle two at the 384-yard tenth hole in the final round. At the time, he was trailing leaders Greg Turner and Fredrik Jacobson by two strokes. With that one shot, as the ball landed beyond the flag and sucked back into the hole, Westwood was level and on his way to another title.

Owen trimmed two strokes off the old record and eventually tied for 21st, helping his upwardly mobile move from 144th to 89th in the Volvo Ranking in the space of six weeks.

At the 'business end' of the tournament, Westwood had moved into overdrive with a third round 67 which carried him within a stroke of the 54-hole lead held by Jacobson (69) and Turner (67).

Faldo, by now, was out of contention, but the player widely tipped to succeed him in terms of major championship glory, had his game and temperament under control.

The critical shot in the final round came at the tenth, where Westwood holed a pitching wedge from 116 yards to leap into a tie for the lead at 14 under par. He then birdied the 12th and 16th to close with a 66 and a 16 under par aggregate of 268.

Jacobson, meanwhile, displayed considerable mental courage, holing from 12 feet at the 15th and 17th to shoot 67 and tie Westwood on 268.

Somehow, though, you sensed it was Westwood's day. Sure enough, he trundled in a birdie putt from 25 feet at the first extra hole; Jacobson couldn't match it, and the contest was over.

Westwood looked ahead to Montecastillo, refreshed and ready for a scrap to the bitter end. Jacobson collected £44,440 and secured the right to play on the European Tour for another season. For both men, a week to savour.

Gordon Simpson   225

Royal Zoute, Belgium, October 1-4, 1998 · Yardage 6907 · Par 71

Pos	Name	Country	Rnd 1	Rnd 2	Rnd 3	Rnd 4	Total	Prize Money £
1	Lee WESTWOOD	(Eng)	67	68	67	66	268	66660
2	Fredrik JACOBSON	(Swe)	65	67	69	67	268	44440
3	Robert KARLSSON	(Swe)	64	72	68	66	270	22520
	Greg TURNER	(NZ)	64	70	67	69	270	22520
5	Jarmo SANDELIN	(Swe)	70	67	66	69	272	15470
	Peter MITCHELL	(Eng)	70	68	66	68	272	15470
7	Alex CEJKA	(Ger)	69	71	67	66	273	10306
	Michael JONZON	(Swe)	70	67	69	67	273	10306
	Mark MOULAND	(Wal)	71	71	67	64	273	10306
10	Paul AFFLECK	(Wal)	70	70	69	65	274	6617
	Peter O'MALLEY	(Aus)	69	67	69	69	274	6617
	Joakim HAEGGMAN	(Swe)	70	68	69	67	274	6617
	Paolo QUIRICI	(Swi)	67	71	66	70	274	6617
	Anthony WALL	(Eng)	69	68	67	70	274	6617
	Rolf MUNTZ	(Hol)	66	67	73	68	274	6617
	Gordon BRAND JNR.	(Scot)	71	68	68	67	274	6617
17	Dean ROBERTSON	(Scot)	71	68	69	67	275	5080
	Mark JAMES	(Eng)	68	72	67	68	275	5080
	Jean VAN DE VELDE	(Fr)	69	72	67	67	275	5080
	José RIVERO	(Sp)	67	71	70	67	275	5080
21	Padraig HARRINGTON	(Ire)	74	68	67	67	276	4320
	Sven STRÜVER	(Ger)	67	69	67	73	276	4320
	Raymond RUSSELL	(Scot)	70	69	69	68	276	4320
	Per-Ulrik JOHANSSON	(Swe)	69	67	71	69	276	4320
	Greg OWEN	(Eng)	74	62	71	69	276	4320
	Gary EVANS	(Eng)	71	69	68	68	276	4320
	Robert Jan DERKSEN	(Hol)	68	70	69	69	276	4320
28	Olle KARLSSON	(Swe)	70	69	72	66	277	3780
	Adam HUNTER	(Scot)	69	70	70	68	277	3780
30	Nick FALDO	(Eng)	65	72	72	69	278	3430
	Daniel CHOPRA	(Swe)	71	69	70	68	278	3430
	Van PHILLIPS	(Eng)	64	72	70	72	278	3430
	Andrew BEAL	(Eng)	66	71	72	69	278	3430
34	Peter BAKER	(Eng)	68	70	69	72	279	3040
	José Maria OLAZÁBAL	(Sp)	68	71	74	66	279	3040
	Carl SUNESON	(Sp)	69	70	72	68	279	3040
	Ross DRUMMOND	(Scot)	68	71	70	70	279	3040
	Stephen BENNETT	(Eng)	68	71	71	69	279	3040
39	Tom GILLIS	(USA)	67	74	67	72	280	2720
	Howard CLARK	(Eng)	71	71	69	69	280	2720
	Pedro LINHART	(Sp)	71	70	71	68	280	2720
42	Wayne RILEY	(Aus)	68	70	69	74	281	2480
	David HOWELL	(Eng)	71	69	74	67	281	2480
	Philip WALTON	(Ire)	73	69	68	71	281	2480
45	Fredrik HENGE	(Swe)	69	73	69	71	282	2120
	Richard BOXALL	(Eng)	68	74	69	71	282	2120
	Roger CHAPMAN	(Eng)	70	68	73	71	282	2120
	Chris VAN DER VELDE	(Hol)	70	71	69	72	282	2120
	Steve ALKER	(NZ)	70	72	71	69	282	2120
	Marc FARRY	(Fr)	72	70	70	70	282	2120
51	Andrew SHERBORNE	(Eng)	66	71	73	73	283	1720
	Ivo GINER	(Sp)	70	70	73	70	283	1720
	Ignacio GARRIDO	(Sp)	73	67	71	72	283	1720
	Olivier EDMOND	(Fr)	68	72	75	68	283	1720
55	Nicolas VANHOOTEGEM	(Bel)	71	70	70	73	284	1400
	Derrick COOPER	(Eng)	72	70	71	71	284	1400
	Brian DAVIS	(Eng)	70	71	72	71	284	1400
	Klas ERIKSSON	(Swe)	73	69	74	68	284	1400
59	Francisco CEA	(Sp)	69	72	78	66	285	1180
	Rodger DAVIS	(Aus)	70	72	71	72	285	1180
	Sam TORRANCE	(Scot)	70	71	70	74	285	1180
	Stephen SCAHILL	(NZ)	71	70	71	73	285	1180
63	Malcolm MACKENZIE	(Eng)	69	71	72	74	286	1060
	Jim PAYNE	(Eng)	69	73	72	72	286	1060
65	Didier DE VOOGHT	(Bel)	70	72	74	72	288	1000
66	Phil GOLDING	(Eng)	72	70	73	74	289	600
67	Joakim RASK	(Swe)	70	70	73	77	290	598

Jarmo Sandelin on his way to a tie for fifth place.

ESCADA
SPORT

It's all the same for South Africa

South Africa fielded the same team

that won last year and staged

a memorable repeat

With 40mph winds howling through the Auld Grey Toun, you needed a pretty strong grip to hold on to the Alfred Dunhill Cup, and South Africa, fielding the same squad of skipper David Frost, Retief Goosen and Ernie Els, showed themselves once again the men for all seasons as they retained the title with a 3-0 win over Spain in the final.

What seasons they were at St. Andrews. From the most perfect autumn

Thursday could offer, a great-to-be-alive day with birdies and eagles to match, through rain-lashed Friday when no one broke 70, and a bright-and-breezy Saturday when favourites USA, champions South Africa and second seeds Australia, as expected, won their groups and Spain's sudden-death victory destroyed tartan dreams of a home victory, to a hold-on-to-your hats Sunday that provided the week's high drama.

Goosen was the hero of the week,

coming from behind to post his tenth consecutive triumph in the competition as South Africa eclipsed Spain in a final far closer than the 3-0 scoreline suggested, but by then the spectators had already been captivated by a plethora of outstanding matches involving the finest golfers in the world.

The American team of John Daly, Mark O'Meara and Tiger Woods were deserving of the title of tournament favourites. After all Daly had won the Open Championship at St. Andrews in 1995, and he adores this special place. O'Meara arrived as the Masters and Open champion of 1998; and the inspirational Woods is a player whose peers exclaim has driven all in golf to reach for new heights.

Drawing the biggest galleries of the week, Daly's smash-and-grab golf was as intoxicating as the braw Scottish air. Four

wins from four, three eagles, lashing the ball incredible distances, on to the green at the ninth (356 yards), 12th (316) and 18th (354) – and those who were there to see it will never forget an awesome blow at the Road Hole, just 77 yards short of the putting surface and bang in the middle of the narrowest part of the fairway, or the

Spanish duo of José Maria Olazábal (left), Miguel Angel Jiménez (right).

miraculous parachute shot that baled him out against Per-Ulrik Johansson from behind the Road Bunker.

It may have been disrespectful to the

staid Old Lady of St Andrews but this was a man happy in his work on a course where he had been Open champion, and didn't the spectators have fun. Hard to believe that this was the same golfer who had missed his six previous cuts and at a lowly 126th in the world rankings, required a special invitation to show off

THE COURSE

St Andrews has never been in better condition, said top scorer Retief Goosen. No score under 66 all week (and none better than 71 on Sunday) meant the real victress was the Old Course herself, but, as always, there were those moments at which to marvel, those shots to savour, that make watching golf on this the most historic of courses nothing short of enthralling.

his extraordinary skills.

By defeating Lee Westwood, Nobuo Serizawa, Johansson and Miguel Angel Jiménez, Daly was boosting his Alfred Dunhill Cup record to eight wins out of nine and ironically turned out to be the only undefeated American. Ironic because he was three over par for his 72 holes to Tiger's 14 under. Sadly, for Woods, two pulled putts from six feet and four feet on the last two greens in his semi-final encounter with Spain's Santiago Luna turned the tournament pear-shaped for the Americans, none of whom had lost a match until then.

A cumulative 18 under par for four matches, O'Meara's men were out while the South Africans, at six over par for five with Goosen top point-scorer despite never having beaten 71, were marching to the beat of champions. Figures, however, can always camouflage the cut and thrust of golf, and the medal matchplay variety employed at the Alfred Dunhill Cup has brought moments of high theatre with the 17th and 18th, such pivotal holes.

The week had started with the pro-am result any sponsor would die for – victory for the Duke of York and an invitation to the seven-handicap Prince from winning pro O'Meara to give him in a call in Orlando 'and we'll fix up a fourball with Tiger and Payne Stewart.' It continued on a high on day one with Frenchman Thomas Levet holing-in-one with an eight-iron at the 178-yard eighth. Misery, though for the pride

SHOT OF THE WEEK

Close between John Daly's parachute shot to three feet on the Road Hole that saved the day after two miscues against Per-Ulrik Johansson and a similar effort from Santiago Luna that stunned Tiger Woods into submission. On degree of difficulty and perfection of execution (bearing in mind the two previous shots), the vote goes to Daly – by the margin of a golf ball cover.

Santiago Luna (above) and Lee Westwood (top).

of Britain, Lee Westwood and Colin Montgomerie, beaten in their opening matches, a sign of things to come.

Day two and the heavens fell in, though Nick Price eagled the tenth with a 128-yard eight iron second. Less cheerful were New Zealander Michael Long, who ran up a nine at the usually innocuous ninth, and Andrew Coltart, whose six iron over the wall at the Road Hole meant a seven to Darren Clarke's three that snatched defeat from the jaws of victory. Coltart, three up on the 17th tee, would have won 3 and 2 in matchplay. Instead, it's victory for Clarke by 73-75. The magic of the Dunhill.

Day three, and farewell to the Scots thanks to a 'fat' sand wedge from Jiménez that just clears the Swilcan Burn and rolls up stone dead at the first extra hole. The Spaniard says sorry, but Montgomerie is heartbroken. 'We wanted to get through for all the wonderful Scottish support we've received this week,' he said.

With South Africa too strong for Australia and Luna and Olazábal putting on their Sunday best to turf out the USA, it's Spain v South Africa, a war of attrition in ferocious conditions that turn the course into a par 75, according to Els. 'That's what made Retief's 72 so fantastic,' says Els.

'Now I'm looking forward to next year and trying to beat Greg Norman's record of 11 straight wins,' said a jubilant Goosen. So are we, and who will stop South Africa becoming the first country to win the Alfred Dunhill Cup three times in succession? Certainly not the weatherman.

Jeremy Chapman 231

OLD COURSE, ST. ANDREWS, 8TH - 11TH OCTOBER 1998 • YARDAGE 7,094 • PAR 72

Final

SOUTH AFRICA	3	0	SPAIN
Retief Goosen	72	73	Santiago Luna
David Frost	76	78	Miguel Angel Jiménez
Ernie Els	75	77	José Maria Olazábal

Semi-Final

SPAIN	2	1	USA
Miguel Angel Jiménez	75	73	John Daly
Santiago Luna	71	72	Tiger Woods
José Maria Olazábal	72	76	Mark O'Meara

Semi-Final

SOUTH AFRICA	2	1	AUSTRALIA
David Frost	72	78	Craig Parry
Retief Goosen	71	74	Stuart Appleby
Ernie Els	73	72	Steve Elkington

Group One

DAY 1

SWEDEN beat JAPAN 3-0
Patrik Sjöland (69) beat Hiroyuki Fujita (77)
Mathias Grönberg (78) beat Nobuo Serizawa (79)
Per-Ulrik Johansson (71) beat Katsuma Miyamoto (76)

USA beat ENGLAND 3-0
John Daly (70) beat Lee Westwood (73)
Tiger Woods (66) beat David Carter (74)
Mark O'Meara (67) beat Peter Baker (74)

DAY 2

USA beat JAPAN 3-0
John Daly (77) beat Nobuo Serizawa (80)
Tiger Woods (70) beat Katsumasa Miyamoto (77)
Mark O'Meara (70) beat Hiroyuki Fujita (75)

SWEDEN beat ENGLAND 3-0
Mathias Grönberg (72)* beat Lee Westwood (72)
*at 1st extra hole
Per-Ulrik Johansson (70) beat David Carter (73)
Patrik Sjöland (70) beat Peter Baker (73)

DAY 3

USA beat SWEDEN 2-0
John Daly (71) beat Per-Ulrik Johansson (72)
Tiger Woods (66) beat Mathias Grönberg (73)
Mark O'Meara (68) Patrik Sjöland (68) (no play-off)

ENGLAND beat JAPAN 3-0
Lee Westwood (70) beat Katsumasa Miyamoto (71)
Peter Baker (71) beat Hiroyuki Fujita (73)
David Carter (69) beat Nobuo Serizawa (75)

Group Two

DAY 1

SCOTLAND beat CHINA 2-1
Gary Orr (75) beat Wu Xiang-Bing (76)
Andrew Coltart (73) beat Cheng Jun (78)
Colin Montgomerie (73) lost to Zhang Lian-Wei (72)

SPAIN beat IRELAND 2-1
Santiago Luna (71) lost to Darren Clarke (71)*
at 4th extra hole
Miguel Angel Jiménez (70) beat Paul McGinley (72)
José Maria Olazábal (73) beat Padraig Harrington (75)

DAY 2

SPAIN beat CHINA 2-1
José Maria Olazábal (78) lost to Wu Xiang-Bing (77)
Miguel Angel Jiménez (76) beat Zhang Lian-Wei (83)
Santiago Luna (80) beat Cheng Jun (81)

SCOTLAND beat IRELAND 2-1
Andrew Coltart (75) lost to Darren Clarke (73)
Gary Orr (77) beat Padraig Harrington (78)
Colin Montgomerie (72) beat Paul McGinley (78)

DAY 3

SPAIN beat SCOTLAND 2-1
José Maria Olazábal (68) beat Gary Orr (71)
Miguel Angel Jiménez (70)* beat Colin Montgomerie (70) * at 1st extra hole
Santiagao Luna (74) lost to Andrew Coltart (73)

IRELAND beat CHINA 3-0
Darren Clarke (71) beat Zhang Lian-Wei (73)
Paul McGinley (74) beat Cheng Jun (78)
Padraig Harrington (71) beat Wu Ziang-Bing (74)

Group Three

DAY 1

NEW ZEALAND lost to KOREA 1-2
Michael Long (76) lost to Shin Yong-Jin (75)
Frank Nobilo (75) lost to Kang Wook-Soon (71)
Greg Turner (70) beat Kim Jong-Duck (73)

AUSTRALIA beat ARGENTINA 1-2
Stuart Appleby (66) beat José Coceres (77)
Craig Parry (70) beat Angel Cabrera (75)
Steve Elkington (70)* beat Eduardo Romero (70)
* at 1st extra hole

DAY 2

NEW ZEALAND beat ARGENTINA 2-1
Greg Turner (75) beat Eduardo Romero (DQ – did not complete round)
Frank Nobilo (71) beat Angel Cabrera (77)
Michael Long (81) lost to José Coceres (75)

AUSTRALIA beat KOREA 3-0
Craig Parry (75)* beat Shin Yong-Jin (75)
* at 1st extra hole
Stuart Appleby (73) beat Kang Wook-Soon (77)
Steve Elkington (72) beat Kim Jong-Duck (77)

DAY 3

ARGENTINA beat KOREA 2-1
Eduardo Romero (72) lost to Shin Yong-Jin (72)*
at 1st extra hole
Angel Cabrera (72) beat Kim Jong-Duck (73)
José Coceres (71) beat Kang Wook-Soon (72)

AUSTRALIA lost to NEW ZEALAND 1-2
Craig Parry (70) beat Michael Long (71)
Stuart Appleby (73) lost to Greg Turner (72)
Steve Elkington (74) lost to Frank Nobilo (72)

Group Four

DAY 1

SOUTH AFRICA beat FRANCE 3-0
Retief Goosen (72) beat Olivier Edmond (73)
David Frost (70) beat Thomas Levet (75)
Ernie Els (69) beat Jean Van de Velde (72)

ZIMBABWE beat GERMANY 3-0
Tony Johnstone (69) beat Sven Strüver (76)
Nick Price (72) beat Thomas Gögele (73)
Mark McNulty (73) beat Alex Cejka (75)

DAY 2

ZIMBABWE lost to FRANCE 1-2
Mark McNulty (81) lost to Jean Van de Velde (71)
Tony Johnstone (79) lost to Thomas Levet (77)
Nick Price (70) beat Olivier Edmond (78)

SOUTH AFRICA lost to GERMANY 1-2
David Frost (78) lost to Thomas Gögele (78)*
2nd extra hole
Retief Goosen (76) beat Alex Cejka (77)
Ernie Els (76) lost to Sven Strüver (76)*
at 1st extra hole

DAY 3

GERMANY beat FRANCE 2-1
Thomas Gögele (69) beat Thomas Levet (72)
Alex Cejka (75) lost to Jean Van de Velde (72)
Sven Strüver (68) beat Olivier Edmond (70)

ZIMBABWE lost to SOUTH AFRICA 1-2
Tony Johnstone (77) lost to Ernie Els (71)
Nick Price (69) beat David Frost (71)
Mark McNulty (76) lost to Retief Goosen (71)

Prize Money

Country	Team £	Player £	Total £
Winners			
S AFRICA (6)	300,000	100,000	300,000
Runners-Up			
SPAIN (4)	150,000	50,000	150,000
Losing Semi-Finalists			
USA (1)	95,000	31,666	
AUSTRALIA (2)	95,000	31,666	190,000

Country	Team £	Player £	Total £
Group One			
USA (1)			
SWEDEN (8)	45,000	15,000	
ENGLAND	25,500	8,500	
JAPAN	19,500	6,500	90,000
Group Two			
SPAIN (4)			
SCOTLAND (5)	45,000	15,000	
IRELAND	25,500	8,500	
CHINA	19,500	6,500	90,000

Country	Team £	Player £	Total £
Group Three			
SOUTH AFRICA (6)			
GERMANY	45,000	15,000	
ZIMBABWE(3)	25,500	8,500	
FRANCE	19,500	6,500	90,000
Group Four			
AUSTRALIA (2)			
NEW ZEALAND (7)	45,000	15,000	
ARGENTINA	25,500	8,500	
KOREA	19,500	6,500	90,000

* Number in parentheses indicates seeds

ALFRED DUNHILL

LONDON

THE FACETED WATCH

SPONSOR OF THE ALFRED DUNHILL CUP, OLD COURSE, ST. ANDREWS
7TH-10TH OCTOBER 1999

O'Meara crowns a glorious year

Mark O'Meara took another title
after a wonderful final
with Tiger Woods

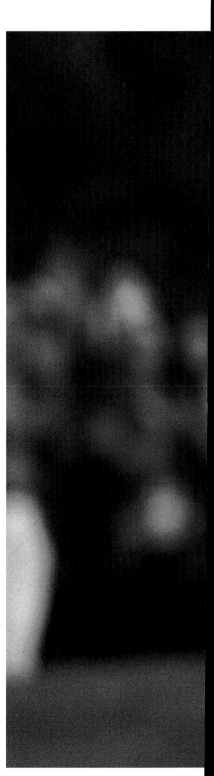

They came in their thousands to watch a Tiger hunt in the leafy Surrey woods. But it was not until the very last hole of the very last match of an enthralling Cisco World Match-Play Championship that Tiger Woods – the world's number one and most charismatic golfer – was finally snared by his best friend Mark O'Meara. 'He has been taking the cash out of my pocket all year and now he has done it again,' joked 22-year-old Woods ruefully after seeing the 41-year-old O'Meara become the oldest ever winner in the 35-year history of Wentworth's famous autumn classic.

For O'Meara, who also became only the third American to win the title in the past 20 years (following Corey Pavin in 1993 and Bill Rogers in 1979), the coruscatingly dramatic one hole victory was the third leg of a unique treble – he having already won the Masters Tournament and the Open Championship.

'I could never even have dreamed at the start of this year that I would be sitting here reflecting on winning two Majors and fourth place in another, as well as beating the world's best player to win this prestigious title,' admitted O'Meara, who finished a remarkable 26 under par for his 12 rounds in the championship.

The previous time that Woods and his 'big brother' O'Meara had met on the golf course was for 30 dollars in a fun match in Florida. Woods won that one, but the canny O'Meara then talked his young protégé into a putting contest and promptly won his money back.

This time there was considerably more cash at stake, with the winner netting £170,000 and the runner-up taking home £90,000 – but from the start it was clear that the contest was more about pride and prestige than just financial gain.

Woods began as if he wanted to get it over in a hurry, going four up in the first six holes and when O'Meara struck an imperious second shot to less than three feet at the 11th and asked: 'You'd give me that at home wouldn't you?', Tiger shook his head. O'Meara, having holed it, pointedly measured the distance with his putter.

Woods went four up again at the 16th but a wild slice from the fairway at 17

THE COURSE

The players, sponsors, organisers and fans were united in their praise for Wentworth Course Superintendent Chris Kennedy, West Course head greenkeeper Graham Matheson and their staff, for rescuing the event from potential disaster. After a very wet summer three inches of rain fell in the last six days of September. A heavy downpour two days before the event was followed by an inch of rain on the Friday night. A team of 40 laboured from 6.00 am pumping out bunkers and fairways and repairing greens to allow play to begin at 11 am. New champion Mark O'Meara summed up everyone's feelings saying: 'How they managed to get the course back into magnificent condition was a near miracle.'

caused a concession and allowed O'Meara to lunch a little more comfortably at three down.

The sun-kissed afternoon round was pure sporting theatre for the enthralled gallery as both players peppered the flags with brilliant approach shots. The 12th proved pivotal, however, with O'Meara 'ripping' a two iron shot 218 yards, with the ball hitting the stick to finish just 18 inches away for a vital eagle. Woods was never to lead again, although he looked sure to win the 16th only to three putt after O'Meara sunk a remarkable 20 footer.

A half at the 17th when Woods holed bravely from ten feet made sure the match went to the last, but as the tension was screwed almost to breaking point it was the older man who held his nerve to hole

from 15 feet from the front fringe to prevent Woods taking it into sudden-death.

Having clearly won the hearts of the Wentworth fans with his courageous battle to win the title at his first attempt, Woods underlined his own feelings declaring: 'The ebb and flow of match-play is a beautiful thing. Over 36 holes so much can happen. It was a game I will always cherish, even though I lost.'

O'Meara's eloquence in victory matched the elegance of his swing as he replied: 'Tiger hits shots I could never hit. He has more imagination and he is more powerful. But I'd like to think that what I have picked up over the years is a bit of wisdom and a lot of patience.'

The final proved a fitting climax to a week that encompassed all four seasons and produced a host of sporting memories. There was the unexpected delight of late-late substitute Ian Woosnam rediscovering his putting magic to outgun his Ryder Cup team mate Darren Clarke – only to see it desert him just when he needed it most to clinch a famous win over Woods, three putting at the 36th and then losing at the first play-off hole.

Ian Woosnam is the centre of attention (above). Competitors and officials line up with Mark McCormack (front centre), founder of the World Match-Play Championship (right). Tiger Woods and Mark O'Meara in the Wentworth dusk (left).

Tiger Woods is flat out.

There was the stunning first round display of defending champion Vijay Singh, equalling Tony Jacklin's record of an outward 29. He looked set for a record breaking winning margin against Patrik Sjöland (one hole first round winner over Steve Stricker) only for the brave young Swede to make it a slightly more respectable 7 and 6.

Just a day later the biter was bit even harder, as O'Meara, who had ended Colin Montgomerie's hopes of a memorable Wentworth double (to go along with his Volvo PGA triumph) destroyed Singh with eight birdies in the first ten holes on his way to inflicting a

SHOT OF THE WEEK

Until the last afternoon, the prime candidate for shot of the week was Lee Westwood's 236-yard three wood to 20 feet for eagle at the 12th, in his second round win over Ernie Els. That was bettered, however, at that same par five hole, right in the heat of the final battle. Mark O'Meara, behind for the third time, drilled a laser-like two iron 218 yards, that hit the flag stick and settled just two feet away for a crucial eagle. 'I just ripped it right at it. That probably has to rank as one of my shots of the year.' he declared.

record 11 and 10 defeat.

There was the hope that Britain's brightest young discovery, Lee Westwood, a triumphant 21 under par after convincing victories over Stuart Appleby and three times champion Ernie Els, might go all the way. Then he ran into Woods in Saturday's rain-delayed semifinals and saw a three hole lead after seven, turn into a 5 and 4 defeat, as Tiger warmed to the magic of Wentworth match-play.

A truly world-class field produced record scores for record-breaking crowds with an epic final to match the very best. Yes, Tiger's a wonderful thing all right – but sometimes even a Tiger has to bow to his Big Brother.

John Whitbread

WENTWORTH CLUB (WEST COURSE), SURREY, OCTOBER 15-18, 1998 · YARDAGE 7006 · PAR 72

First Round

		Prize money
Patrik Sjöland (Swe) beat Steve Stricker (USA) (8)	1 hole	£30,000
Colin Montgomerie (Scot) (5) beat Thomas Björn (Den)	4 & 3	£30,000
Lee Westwood (Eng) (6) beat Stuart Appleby (Aus)	8 & 7	£30,000
Ian Woosnam (Wal) beat Darren Clarke (N.Ire) (7)	4 & 3	£30,000

Second Round

		Prize money
*Vijay Singh (Fij) (1) beat Patrik Sjöland	7 & 6	£40,000
*Mark O'Meara (USA) (4) beat Colin Montgomerie	5 & 4	£40,000
Lee Westwood beat *Ernie Els (SA) (3)	2 & 1	£40,000
*Tiger Woods (USA) (2) beat Ian Woosnam	at 37th	£40,000

Semi-Finals

Mark O'Meara beat Vijay Singh	11 & 10	—
Tiger Woods beat Lee Westwood	5 & 4	—

Final

		Prize money
Mark O'Meara beat	1 hole	£170,000
Tiger Woods		£90,000

*seeded into the second round

Colin Montgomerie (above), Mark O'Meara (top).

Swedish blend is strongest

Jarmo Sandelin and Olle Karlsson
were the perfect match in Bordeaux

Olle Karlsson expected to spend two weeks before the Volvo Masters practising in his native Sweden. Instead he came in at short notice to win the Open Novotel Perrier in Bordeaux with partner Jarmo Sandelin by three shots.

Sandelin had been due to play first with Alex Cejka and then with Thomas Gögele but both men dropped out. It all led to Karlsson receiving a call from the European Tour office on the Saturday before the tournament began and the 29-year-old Swede joked: 'I think I was ninth

reserve and last man in but I was delighted to play.'

Karlsson did not just play. He proved the strong man of the partnership, especially on the final day when he shot a five-under-par 66, including a real pressure birdie at the 443 yard final hole to ensure

THE COURSE

The Médoc golf course has generous fairways but with heather and gorse in abundance to catch the wayward shot. The greens are tightly bunkered and water comes into play at eight holes, especially at the short fifth and eighth. When a strong wind is blowing in from the nearby Atlantic the course is a more than difficult par 71.

Seve Ballesteros teamed up with Miguel Angel Jiménez.

SHOT OF THE WEEK

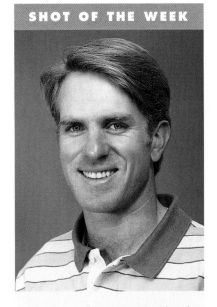

Frenchman Christian Cévaër played the shot of the week on the opening day when, playing a blind shot, he holed out from 80 yards with his sand-wedge for an eagle three at the 556-yard second. 'It's a pity I couldn't see it,' said Christian later. 'I heard the crowd clapping, so I knew it was close and then someone told me it took one bounce and went in.'

Amateur pairing of Sergio Garcia and Trevor Immelman

victory for his team.

The two Swedes had arrived on the 18th tee on the last day, just one shot ahead of Richard Boxall and Derrick Cooper, well aware that they both needed par fours to take the £70,000 first prize. Both hit the fairway with good drives and Sandelin, playing first, struck an eight iron some 20 feet from the flag. Karlsson, 150 yards from the green, also hit an eight iron to within two feet for a certain birdie.

Victory was assured but to add icing to the cake, Sandelin, suitably inspired by his partner's superb shot, rolled in his putt for a birdie three before watching Karlsson sink his. Sandelin shot a one under par 70 and the Swedes finished with a 90 holes aggregate of 329, 26 under.

They had been joint fifth with a 62 after the first day four-ball, joint third with a 63 after the second day foursomes and led by four shots after a third day green-somes round of 63 which took them to 20 under.

On the final day they did not start well in the aggregate singles with Sandelin one over at the turn and Karlsson one under. They began to improve as they turned for home but Severiano Ballesteros and Miguel Angel Jiménez, playing three

GOLF DU MÉDOC, BORDEAUX, FRANCE, OCTOBER 15-18, 1998 · YARDAGE 6909 · PAR 71

Pos	Names	Rnd 1	Rnd 2	Rnd 3	Rnd 4	Total	Prize Money		Pos	Names	Rnd 1	Rnd 2	Rnd 3	Rnd 4	Total	Prize Money
							£ each			M MACKENZIE / A SHERBORNE	64	71	68	141	344	3375
									18	G ORR / A HUNTER	62	70	69	144	345	2900
1	J SANDELIN / O KARLSSON	62	68	63	136	329	35000		19	T LEVET / B TEILLERIA	68	70	67	141	346	2750
2	R BOXALL / D COOPER	65	69	65	133	332	25000			J ROBSON / F JACOBSON	64	72	72	138	346	2750
3	S BALLESTEROS / M A JIMÉNEZ	64	69	67	134	334	17500		21	C POTTIER / M PENDARIES	67	74	68	138	347	2550
4	J REMESY / R JAQUELIN	61	68	68	138	335	12500			R CHAPMAN / M MOULAND	66	69	69	143	347	2550
5	J LOMAS / S BOTTOMLEY	66	67	71	133	337	7750		23	P LAWRIE / S HENDERSON	69	72	69	138	348	2400
	P BAKER / P BROADHURST	67	68	64	138	337	7750		24	D HOWELL / W RILEY	66	74	67	142	349	2200
7	M LANNER / P HEDBLOM	65	70	70	133	338	5500			D CARTER / I PYMAN	63	74	71	141	349	2200
	S GARCIA (A) / T IMMELMAN (A)	64	70	66	138	338	—			N JOAKIMIDES /C CÉVAER	60	73	65	151	349	2200
9	J RIVERO / S LUNA	60	66	71	142	339	4750		27	B DAVIS / V PHILLIPS	67	74	73	137	351	2000
10	P MITCHELL / J SPENCE	67	71	66	137	341	4375		28	D BORREGO / F ORTIZ	66	68	72	147	353	1900
	R McFARLANE / D J RUSSELL	63	67	70	141	341	4375		29	J M OLAZÁBAL / D HOSPITAL	67	71	73	143	354	1800
12	D EDLUND / K ERIKSSON	61	72	73	136	342	4000		30	MI JONZON / A FORSBRAND	67	75	69	144	355	1650
13	O DAVID (A) / D MONTESI (A)	62	70	68	143	343				S CAGE / R RUSSELL	66	74	71	144	355	1650
14	J PAYNE / P PRICE	63	73	64	138	344	3375		32	C RAVETTO (A) / G HAVRET (A)	69	73	72	144	358	—
	P EDMOND/O EDMOND	65	72	69	138	344	3375		33	S BRANGER (A) / N BLACTOT (A)	64	77	72	155	368	—
	I GARRIDO/C SUNESON	62	69	72	141	344	3375		34	M ROE / M FARRY	66	71	W/D			1500

holes ahead, caught them at 22 under when Ballesteros birdied the long 14th and Jiménez had an eagle three. But the Spaniards could make no further impression and, with Ballesteros three-putting the last green, they fell back to third place at 21 under.

So it was left to Boxall and Cooper, twice winners of the Sunningdale Foursomes and second in this tournament two years ago, to make the biggest challenge. These two close friends had finished the third day on 14 under but on day four, with both men in outstanding form, they had moved up to 21 under after 14 holes.

Cooper then birdied the 15th and Boxall the last to finish on 23 under before the Swedes, with the Englishmen watching them on TV, made their grandstand finish.

Earlier in the tournament, Frenchmen Nicolas Joakimides and Christian Cévaër had shared the first day lead with Spaniards José Rivero and Santiago Luna after both had shot 11-under par 60s.

Richard Boxall and Derrick Cooper (standing) had to settle for second place.

Joakimides and Cévaër fell back on the second day but Rivero and Luna kept up the pace with a best of the day 66 in the foursomes to take a three shot lead on another French pair, Jeff Remesy and Raphaël Jacquelin.

The Spaniards had lost in a play-off to Michael Jonzon and Anders Forsbrand last year and were hoping to go one better. But on the third day, as Sandelin and Karlsson surged into the lead, Rivero and Luna, with level par 71 in the greensomes, fell back to joint second place with Remesy and Jacquelin.

With two singles rounds to be played on the last day, ten pairs were in reasonable sight of the leaders but, despite Sandelin being only level par until the final hole, Karlsson, with four birdies on the back nine, made sure that a Swedish pair won for the second successive year.

As Karlsson, clutching the trophy, remarked: 'Jarmo and I had never played together before and we both did our own thing. We never interfered with each other's game and everything just clicked. It was great fun and I want to come back.'

John Oakley

Clarke the master as Montgomerie reigns

Darren Clarke put aside a series
of near misses with an emphatic
victory at Montecastillo

*T*hey will forever be known on the European Tour as 'The Monty Years'. And, just as some were preparing end of an era scripts, Colin Montgomerie showed that they aren't over yet.

In 1993 Montgomerie arrived at the season-ending Volvo Masters at Valderrama knowing he had to win the tournament even to have a chance of winning the Volvo Ranking for the first time. He did and he did.

In 1994, thanks to victories in the Spanish, English and German Opens, the Volvo Masters was just a lap of honour for him. In 1995 he had to play the last nine holes on arguably the toughest course in Europe in one under par to make it a hat-trick and deny Sam Torrance. Thanks to a putt of four feet on the final green, he did.

In 1996, still at Valderrama, Ian Woosnam, despite four high-class wins during the year, was powerless to prevent the Scot equalling Peter Oosterhuis's record of four successive Vardon Trophy triumphs.

Then, in 1997, with the scene switching to Montecastillo, near Jerez, Montgomerie, to make it five, had to hold off Bernhard Langer and Darren Clarke. He did.

'The competition is increasing all the time,' he commented then. 'For that reason each time I've won the Ranking has been more satisfying than the last. My greatest asset is that I have an incredible desire and ambition to succeed. It's kept me going throughout my career. It has never wilted at all.'

Now he arrived back at the same course with that desire and ambition still intact and still on top – but with Lee Westwood and Clarke again breathing down his neck. The scene was set for another thrilling climax to a thrilling season, one which had once more taken the Tour's members around the world and given them unprecedented opportunities and incentives.

Westwood, just as Langer had been a year earlier, was some £45,000 behind Montgomerie. If he won the tournament – and he was the defending champion – he would be the new number one. If he was second Montgomerie would have to match him, if he was third Montgomerie had to be 11th and if he was fourth

A tale of three bunkers: Ernie Els (above left), Nick Faldo (centre), Robert Karlsson (above right). Andrew Coltart (right). Winner Darren Clarke celebrates (opposite).

Montgomerie would need only 44th spot. He ruled that one out of his mind.

Clarke, just as he had been 12 months before, needed nothing less than victory and even that would be no good if Montgomerie was eighth or Westwood second.

At the end of the first day – played in heavenly weather, such a contrast from the storms that had forced the abandonment of the final round in 1997 – nobody could do better than 67, five under. Of the six who managed that score, interest focused on the fact that one of them was Clarke, armed with a new driver, new irons and a five wood that served him so well. Montgomerie and Westwood produced 70s for only a share of 18th place, but the Ulsterman's brilliant birdie at the last (see 'Shot of the Week') took him alongside Gordon Brand Junior, 1995 winner Alex Cejka, Jarmo Sandelin and Australians Peter O'Malley and Greg Chalmers.

Patrik Sjöland (above left), Nick Faldo with coach Chip Koehlke (above), Ian Woosnam with coach
Bill Ferguson (above right). Indian putter trick from José Maria Olazálal (below). Lee Westwood (opposite page).

Like the stars they are, Montgomerie and West-wood responded. The latter, fighting off a rib muscle injury, shot 68 to move into third place, but the former trumped that with a 67 and was second, three behind the new leader Peter Lonard, whose 66 gave him a halfway total of 134, ten under. Clarke stumbled to a 73 and at six adrift had left himself a mountain to climb.

The following day, after the sun burned off early morning fog, the battle heated up even more. With Lonard this time struggling to a 76 – it contained an eight on the long 12th – Westwood seized the chance to go into the joint lead with O'Malley, while a matching closing birdie from Mont-gomerie kept him only one behind and Clarke's 68 brought him just three back.

So with 18 holes to go all things remained possible and, entirely fittingly, the battle for the Volvo Ranking was being fought out on the leaderboard.

Montgomerie liked the fact that he was now playing just ahead of Westwood rather than just behind him. 'It's different

this time – he can watch my birdies go in,' said the Scot, his competitive juices really flowing.

But Clarke was playing ahead of them

both and while they couldn't see what he was doing they certainly got to hear about it. Four birdies in the first five holes were followed by an eagle putt from ten feet on the 517-yard ninth for an outward 30 and then he holed from 20 feet for yet another birdie at the short 11th.

He had charged three clear of the field, but Mont-gomerie had covered such a possibility by going out in 34 himself to be in joint second place and his main concern remained Westwood. The scoreboards showed that with a front nine 36 West-wood had fallen one behind Montgomerie and four behind Clarke. He needed to get going, but instead he went – big time.

The 172-yard 14th had seen a hole-in-one from Bernhard Langer the day before, but now it saw a quadruple bogey seven, with Westwood twice having to return to the tee after pulling five irons unplayable. In five horrible min-utes a season's endeavour to be number one had all come unstuck.

Montgomerie got word of this on the

THE COURSE

Jack Nicklaus designed Montecastillo, a course that looks down on the Spanish city of Jerez, famous the world over for its sherry and brandy bodegas. There are few more inviting tees than the 16th, perched 200 feet above the fairway, while the bunkers glisten white with the same crushed marble that is used at Augusta National, home of the Masters. But what impressed Europe's stars most was the conditioning of the course on their return after all the weather problems in 1997. The greens were considered among the quickest of the season.

16th and his focus was now entirely on ensuring he did not drop to ninth to let Clarke in. There was never a moment's danger and third place completed a quite remarkable 'six of the best' triumph, one that brought him record earnings of £993,077.

Clarke, meanwhile, could not be faulted. He was caught by Andrew Coltart but while the Thornhill player three-putted the 17th Clarke delivered the *coup de grâce* with a wedge to seven feet on the last and a birdie putt that enabled him to equal the course record of 63 – and win the £166,000 first prize by two.

Peter O'Malley had his moment in the sun.

SHOT OF THE WEEK

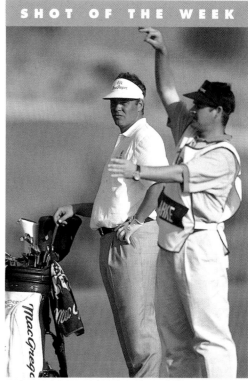

Every Tour player will tell you that you can't win a tournament in the first round, but you can lose it. So when Darren Clarke hit his drive into a fairway bunker on the 18th on day one there was the potential for calamity. The flag was tight by the lake and many would have been tempted to ignore it, aim elsewhere and accept the penalty for being in sand in the first place. But Clarke did not want his day's work to end in a whimper. From 170 yards he flew a six iron over the water and saw the ball nestle down six feet from the flag. After holing the putt for a birdie – and before going on to win the title in such sparkling style – he said: 'Maybe I was aiming six feet right rather than left, but that was a proper shot. One of the ten best I've hit this year.'

Finally, he had done what he had threatened to do so often during the year. And while it wasn't enough to unseat Montgomerie, the victory took him above Westwood and served notice that in 1999 both could bring 'The Monty Years' chapter in the Tour's history to a close. But there again, when you've won six, why not seven… or eight…?

Mark Garrod

Montecastillo, Jerez, Spain, October 29-November 1, 1998 · Yardage 7058 · Par 72

Pos	Name	Country	Rnd 1	Rnd 2	Rnd 3	Rnd 4	Total	Prize Money £		Name	Country	Rnd 1	Rnd 2	Rnd 3	Rnd 4	Total	Prize Money £
										Roger WESSELS	(SA)	71	71	72	72	286	9000
									34	Massimo FLORIOLI	(It)	74	73	69	71	287	8100
1	Darren CLARKE	(N.Ire)	67	73	68	63	271	166000	35	Paolo QUIRICI	(Swi)	72	74	73	69	288	7800
2	Andrew COLTART	(Scot)	69	73	65	66	273	110000	36	Mark ROE	(Eng)	73	69	75	72	289	6900
3	Colin MONTGOMERIE	(Scot)	70	67	69	68	274	63000		Jamie SPENCE	(Eng)	69	74	72	74	289	6900
4	Peter O'MALLEY	(Aus)	67	71	67	70	275	46500		Mark MCNULTY	(Zim)	73	70	74	72	289	6900
	Peter BAKER	(Eng)	69	72	67	67	275	46500		Costantino ROCCA	(It)	71	75	72	71	289	6900
6	Bernhard LANGER	(Ger)	72	69	67	68	276	35500		Nick FALDO	(Eng)	71	73	70	75	289	6900
7	José Maria OLAZABAL	(Sp)	68	70	70	70	278	30000	41	Ian GARBUTT	(Eng)	72	73	68	77	290	5300
8	Craig HAINLINE	(USA)	73	70	67	69	279	21125		David GILFORD	(Eng)	69	73	75	73	290	5300
	Robert ALLENBY	(Aus)	69	73	70	67	279	21125		Phillip PRICE	(Wal)	71	72	74	73	290	5300
	Sam TORRANCE	(Scot)	72	69	69	69	279	21125		Ian WOOSNAM	(Wal)	74	71	74	71	290	5300
	Ernie ELS	(SA)	70	71	68	70	279	21125		Stephen ALLAN	(Aus)	74	72	73	71	290	5300
12	Alex CEJKA	(Ger)	67	73	69	71	280	15575		Russell CLAYDON	(Eng)	72	71	75	72	290	5300
	Stephen LEANEY	(Aus)	71	70	68	71	280	15575		Seve BALLESTEROS	(Sp)	72	72	71	75	290	5300
	Lee WESTWOOD	(Eng)	70	68	67	75	280	15575		Thomas BJORN	(Den)	72	67	75	76	290	5300
	Peter LONARD	(Aus)	68	66	75	71	280	15575	49	Gary ORR	(Scot)	69	75	72	75	291	4120
16	Padraig HARRINGTON	(Ire)	70	69	70	72	281	13900		Per-Ulrik JOHANSSON	(Swe)	71	75	73	72	291	4120
	Mathias GRÖNBERG	(Swe)	73	67	68	73	281	13900		Retief GOOSEN	(SA)	75	68	79	69	291	4120
	Miguel Angel JIMÉNEZ	(Sp)	71	72	69	69	281	13900		Patrik SJÖLAND	(Swe)	72	72	73	74	291	4120
19	Paul MCGINLEY	(Ire)	68	72	69	73	282	12500		David HOWELL	(Eng)	72	71	72	76	291	4120
	Greg CHALMERS	(Aus)	67	75	70	70	282	12500	54	Paul BROADHURST	(Eng)	72	75	71	74	292	3750
	Katsuyoshi TOMORI	(Jpn)	72	71	70	69	282	12500		Sven STRÜVER	(Ger)	72	71	71	78	292	3750
	Gordon BRAND JNR.	(Scot)	67	74	68	73	282	12500	56	Mats HALLBERG	(Swe)	73	72	73	76	294	3500
23	Jarmo SANDELIN	(Swe)	67	71	73	72	283	11500		Thomas GÖGELE	(Ger)	72	74	69	79	294	3500
24	Jean VAN DE VELDE	(Fr)	75	69	68	72	284	10950		Mats LANNER	(Swe)	77	72	69	76	294	3500
	Santiago LUNA	(Sp)	69	72	72	71	284	10950	59	Olle KARLSSON	(Swe)	75	75	74	71	295	3300
26	Angel CABRERA	(Arg)	70	69	74	72	285	10200	60	Pierre FULKE	(Swe)	69	74	75	78	296	3200
	Greg TURNER	(NZ)	73	72	68	72	285	10200	61	Mike HARWOOD	(Aus)	74	74	73	77	298	3050
	Robert KARLSSON	(Swe)	72	77	68	68	285	10200		Tony JOHNSTONE	(Zim)	72	72	74	80	298	3050
29	Steve WEBSTER	(Eng)	70	75	67	74	286	9000	63	Ignacio GARRIDO	(Sp)	72	76	73	78	299	2900
	Van PHILLIPS	(Eng)	73	71	71	71	286	9000	64	David CARTER	(Eng)	77	76	69	78	300	2800
	Peter MITCHELL	(Eng)	72	70	68	76	286	9000	65	Jun CHENG	(Chi)	73	70	84	85	312	2700
	Eduardo ROMERO	(Arg)	75	73	69	69	286	9000	66	Mark JAMES	(Eng)	73	75	69	RETD	217	2600

The season's winners receive their traditional award of Hugo Boss cashmere jackets.

VOLVO

OLVO SUPPORTS GOLF

Volvo is the principal sponsor of the European Tour with title sponsorships of the Volvo PGA Championship, Volvo Scandinavian Masters and Volvo Masters. In the Far East, on the Asian PGA Tour, we have our flagship event, the Volvo China Open, supported by the Volvo Masters of Malaysia and the Volvo Asian Matchplay.

e Volvo S80 – superior safety and a quite incredible driving expe-
nce. In a spacious and quiet interior. Unique safety solutions are
ndard. In a side impact, the IC inflatable safety curtain provides
d and neck protection for all passengers. And the front seats with
WHIPS system help to prevent whiplash injuries.

The in-line five or six cylinder engine (from 140 to 272 bhp) deve-
lops ample low-rev power – for relaxed driving. The advanced chassis
with multi-link suspension provides outstanding ride comfort and
total control.

Volvo S80, the world's most exciting safe choice.

O'Meara flowers as Rose blooms

Mark O'Meara was the dominant figure in the 1998 major championship but Justin Rose grabbed the headlines

Every so often, the game of golf summons up a moment which lingers in the consciousness for ever; a sublime, visceral image which even the passing of time cannot diminish.

Delve into the data chips buried deep in the memory banks of the mind and press 'click' on 1970, as an elated Jack Nicklaus hurled his putter skywards, almost decapitating Doug Sanders, after winning a play-off for the Open at St Andrews.

Press 'click' again on 1984 to re-live the sheer exhilaration on the dark features of Severiano Ballesteros, punching the air triumphantly as he clinched the claret jug.

Remember the moment Sandy Lyle sank to his knees at Royal St George's, believing – wrongly – that a misjudged chip at the last had cost him the Open. Recall how a lachrymose Nick Faldo uncharacteristically broke down after a courageous fight back at Muirfield in 1992.

Add to those defining, unforgettable golfing moments Royal Birkdale 1998, and a 17-year-old amateur by the name of

Justin Peter Rose, from the village of Hook in Hampshire. The teenager with the ready smile and an articulacy beyond his tender years, melted the hearts of the British public with a remarkable performance for one so young.

He was a headline writer's ultimate dream. The tabloid press was transformed into a horticultural sideshow with massive slabs of bold type proclaiming 'Rose

Blooms', 'Rose Blossoms' and 'Hello, England's Rose'.

Britain loves its sporting heroes. If they are tall, slim, well-groomed, unfailingly courteous and do not speak in soccer-style clichés, then so much the better.

Teenage girls swooned at his 'cuteness'. Their mothers probably wished their daughters would bring him home for a cup of tea. And through it all, Rose simply kept smiling and chatting amiably to the galleries as he strode into the history books.

Let the record show that Mark O'Meara won the 127th Open. Let the record also show that Justin Rose (Am) finished tied for fourth on 282, two over par and only two strokes behind the eventual champion.

It was a breathtaking feat, given that the 1998 Open was played in some of the coldest, wettest and windiest conditions in recent times. None of those handicaps had the slightest debilitating effect on the young man from Hampshire.

Rose had begun the Open in relative obscurity. He ended the Championship

255

with the cloak of anonymity discarded for ever. He was a celebrity; a superstar-in-waiting, and the Press and public clamoured for a piece of him.

Two things happened to send Rose hurtling into the limelight. The first came on Friday, as the Lancashire coast was battered by high winds and squally showers.

Rose was imperturbable as he shot a four under par 66, the joint lowest round by an amateur in the Open. In the circumstances, it was a Herculean effort and in the time it took to pick a safe route around Birkdale, the Englishman had achieved hero status.

The second thing – and the moment which will remain etched in the mind *à la* Nicklaus, Ballesteros, Lyle or Faldo – came as the Birkdale clock nudged 6pm on Sunday evening.

Rose was three over par. He knew he could not win but his competitive instinct told him not to quit. At the 72nd hole, he missed the fairway and hacked out of the rough with a five iron.

His caddie, Stuart Bradley, says it's 47 yards to the hole, with bunkers guarding the approach. There is a collective holding of breath in the hushed gallery as, almost magnetically, the ball is sucked towards and into the cup.

In the nearby media centre, where the denouement was being watched by the world's Press, the effect raised the hairs on the back of necks as the noise from thousands of hoarse throats shook the structure to its foundations.

It was an electrifying, spine-tingling moment as a slightly bewildered and disbelieving Rose spread his arms wide, one clutching his doffed baseball cap, the other gripping his trusty sand-wedge, eyes closed and head raised to the skies as if giving thanks for some form of divine intervention.

That birdie three enabled the teenager to claim a share of fourth place with Jim

Furyk, Jesper Parnevik and Scotland's Raymond Russell who had seemed in danger of losing his European Tour card, but reclaimed it by virtue of a tenacious closing 66.

World number one Tiger Woods, the first round leader with a 65, also finished strongly with a 66 for 281, just a solitary stroke outside the play-off which involved O'Meara and fellow American Brian Watts.

Watts, based in Japan because he was unable to win his card in America, led after two and three rounds by shooting 68, 69 and 73. O'Meara, after scores of 72, 68 and 72 was lurking in the background and ready to pounce.

Fred Couples tests the water at Augusta.

Once again, the final hole proved to be a cauldron of excitement. O'Meara, with another 68, was safely in the clubhouse on level par. Watts, in a greenside bunker in two, planted his left foot in the sand and bent his right foot outside the sand before exploding to within tap-in range. In the space of half an hour, the gallery had witnessed two exquisite, almost miraculous strokes on that hole.

O'Meara won the four-hole play-off in one under par figures to the one over of Watts. The claret jug was his to cradle, just moments after Rose pocketed the amateur silver medal.

There can be little doubt that 1998 will rank as O'Meara's *Annus Mirabilis*. As one golf writer impishly put it, the

American's record in the majors was akin to waiting for a bus – you wait 17 years for one to come along then all of a sudden two arrive at once!

That was the case for the 41-year-old from Windermere, Florida, who joined the US PGA Tour in 1981 but failed to make an impact in the majors until the second week of April 1998.

For more than a year, O'Meara's principal claim to fame – in the eyes of the media at any rate – was that he happened to be Tiger Woods's closest friend and as such received constant interrogation about the life and times of the defending Masters champion.

That changed in the space of 14 weeks as O'Meara not only lifted the Open title but succeeded Woods at Augusta National, where he triumphed in a pulsating climax among the heavenly scents of the dogwood and azaleas.

From a European standpoint, though, the Masters proved that Darren Clarke, making his debut at Augusta National, is a potent force in the global game. He tied for eighth alongside Woods, Colin Montgomerie and Justin Leonard on 285, three under par.

The big Ulsterman was assisted by two eagles on Saturday – at the 13th and 15th. Montgomerie, ironically, claimed his highest major finish of the year in the major he feels he has the least chance of winning.

He missed the cut at the Open – the fifth such failure in eight years – and tied for 18th in the US Open and for 44th in the US PGA, where he was only one stroke off the pace at halfway. But more of that later.

The real excitement at Augusta was reserved for the unlikely, predatory figure of Jack Nicklaus, 58 years young, creeping stealthily up the leaderboard. The Golden Bear ultimately closed with a 68 to tie for sixth – a remarkable achievement for a legend with a bad hip, but one that still did

Champion
Mark O'Meara,
Darren Clarke,
Tiger Woods and
Jack Nicklaus
at the Masters.

David Duval (above left) and Payne Stewart (above right) at the US Open. An emotional Lee Janzen (below) took the honours.

not surprise those who have followed his career.

By Sunday afternoon, the oldest adage in major championship golf, and one well known to Nicklaus, had again come to pass. The back nine holes at Augusta National can be savage or inspirational, depending on the practitioner, but it is, more often than not, where the Masters is won or lost.

On this occasion it lifted O'Meara to previously unattained heights as he birdied the closing two holes to elbow aside the long-time likely winner, Fred Couples, and up-and-coming newcomer David Duval. O'Meara's final 67 earned him the green jacket with a nine under par total of 279.

If Darren Clarke displayed his maturity at Augusta, then his close friend Lee Westwood also rubber-stamped his qualities as a major champion in waiting.

Possibly, the young Ryder Cup player from Worksop was inadvertently undone in his major titles assaults by winning twice in the weeks leading up to 'the big ones'.

Prior to the Masters, Westwood made his breakthrough on the PGA Tour, cruising to a magnificent victory in the Freeport-McDermott Classic in New Orleans.

Five days before the Open at Royal Birkdale, he also collected the Standard Life Loch Lomond. Naturally, Westwood was ebullient in both instances about his chances of back-to-back victories, but in reality the mental strain of winning appeared to deprive the Englishman of his razor-sharp cutting edge.

It was a different story, however, at the US Open in San Francisco. Westwood arrived at the Olympic Club 'refreshed' from a non-win-

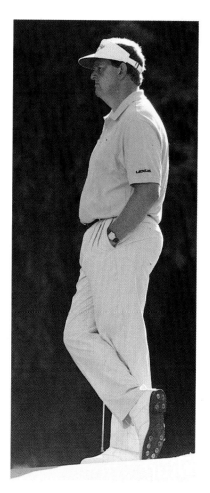

Nick Faldo (left) and Colin Montgomerie (right) suffered disappointment at the USPGA, as Vijay Singh gets his hands on the trophy (centre).

ning performance in New York. He then proceeded to tie for seventh – the highest finish by a European in a tournament notorious for its degree of difficulty.

Westwood shot 141 over the weekend – better than anyone above him in the final order – to share seventh with Duval and Jeff Maggert.

Montgomerie, after a depressing 77 on Saturday, bounced back with a 69 on Sunday to tie for 18th with José Maria Olazábal, who had not been able to build on an opening 68.

In the event, Lee Janzen carried off his second US Open title, following victory at Baltusrol in 1993. On that occasion, Payne Stewart looked the probable winner, but Janzen proved to be his nemesis. History was to repeat itself at The Olympic Club five years on.

Janzen shot a closing 68 to Stewart's 74 to complete the biggest final round comeback for 25 years and the third biggest in the history of the event. Yet it

didn't seem possible when Janzen bogeyed the second and third holes on Sunday to trail Stewart by seven shots.

However when a gust of wind blew his ball from a tree at the fifth – as he was making his way back to the tee to play another – Dame Fortune was on Janzen's side as he went on to win by the minimum margin.

Also by his side was a veteran Englishman by the name of Dave Musgrove, who had caddied for Sandy Lyle as he captured his two major titles. It turned out to be a good year in the majors for the European bag carriers.

In the final major in 1998, at Sahalee in Seattle, it was the turn of Scotland's Dave Renwick to pocket his winning percentage from Vijay Singh's triumphant march to victory in the US PGA Championship.

Once again, this major proved to be frustrating to another Scot – Montgomerie – who opened with 70 and 67 to move

within a stroke of the Fijian (whose name means 'Victory' in Hindu) – at halfway.

Sadly, his game disintegrated – prompting an urgent telephone call to his former coach, Bill Ferguson – and rounds of 77 and 74 left him tied for 44th.

Westwood missed the cut for the first time in an American major, leaving Swede Per-Ulrik Johansson, with a final 68, as leading European player, at joint 23rd.

Former winners Nick Price and Steve Elkington both threatened Singh, as did O'Meara – seeking to emulate Ben Hogan's three majors in a season 45 years earlier – and Steve Stricker.

None of them managed to catch Singh on Sunday afternoon. His rounds of 70, 66, 67 and 68 for 271 edged him home by two from Stricker. It was quite a performance from the man who cut his teeth on the European Tour, and another indication that the global fascination of golf continues to increase.

Gordon Simpson

Bennett dominates

Five victories and record prize-money
made Warren Bennett the man to beat
on the 1998 European Challenge Tour

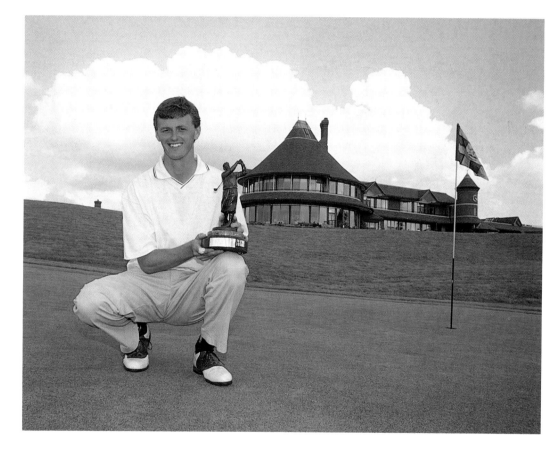

The European Challenge Tour celebrated its tenth birthday in 1998 while enjoying good health and growing stronger with each passing week. In those ten years several players have made their mark, but no one has quite dominated as Warren Bennett has in the past year.

The former England international proved he was the man for all seasons by rewriting the record books, setting new marks which will take some beating. Five victories, over £81,000 in winnings, £30,000 more than the previous best set by Michele Reale of Italy only a year earlier, and a stroke average of 69.51. Impressive figures and no mistake. A glance through other statistics show that of the 19 tournaments he played, he missed only one cut and recorded 12 top ten finishes. What's more, in a six-week period from early July until mid-August, he packed in four victories and a second place in as widely differing venues as Slovenia, France, Switzerland, England and Russia, and was a collective 86 under par for 20 rounds.

None of this would have been possible without two key ingredients, sound health and a good caddie. The Watford-based 27-year-old might have achieved these successes and his Tour card much earlier if he hadn't been dogged by a recurring neck injury since he turned professional in 1994. Although he won his first Challenge Tour title in 1995, it wasn't until late 1997 that he underlined his potential with a nine-shot victory in Bilbao. That week he was injury-free. A winter of gym work brought him out for 1998 fitter and determined to succeed. 'I just wanted to sort out my health, then the golf would take care of itself,' he said.

Two top ten finishes in Africa set the ball rolling but he had to wait until late May in France before securing the first of his five wins. It was just prior to the Challenge de France that Warren's brother Jason took over as full-time caddie which has given Team Bennett a more professional approach. 'Having Jason on my bag has been a big help.' Warren added. 'We discussed it last Christmas and we both thought it was a good idea. It makes me feel so much better because he is good for

261

CHALLENGE TOUR RANKINGS

				£
1	Warren BENNETT	(Eng)	(19)	81052
2	Per NYMAN	(Swe)	(22)	37196
3	Massimo SCARPA	(It)	(17)	35523
4	Roger WINCHESTER	(Eng)	(22)	33796
5	Ricardo GONZALEZ	(Arg)	(16)	33159
6	John BICKERTON	(Eng)	(14)	30205
7	John MELLOR	(Eng)	(21)	30015
8	Fredrik LINDGREN	(Swe)	(21)	28864
9	John SENDEN	(Aus)	(10)	28769
10	Soren HANSEN	(Den)	(21)	27984
11	Max ANGLERT	(Swe)	(20)	27522
12	Jorge BERENDT	(Arg)	(17)	27194
13	Christopher HANELL	(Swe)	(23)	26884
14	Stephen GALLACHER	(Scot	(22)	26673
15	Daren LEE	(Eng)	(16)	26133
16	Kevin CARISSIMI	(USA)	(24)	24890
17	Scott WATSON	(Eng)	(20)	23627
18	Jose Manuel LARA	(Sp)	(15)	22343
19	Marc PENDARIES	(Fr)	(23)	22109
20	Marcello SANTI	(It)	(25)	21729
21	Thomas NIELSEN	(Nor)	(20)	21673
22	Jeremy ROBINSON	(Eng)	(21)	21567
23	David R JONES	(Eng)	(22)	18764
24	Mikael LUNDBERG	(Swe)	(19)	18732
25	Gary EMERSON	(Eng)	(10)	18213
26	Mårten OLANDER	(Swe)	(17)	18007
27	Raimo SJÖBERG	(Swe)	(17)	17524
28	Robert LEE	(Eng)	(15)	15985
29	David PARK	(Wal)	(22)	15467
30	Morten BACKHAUSEN	(Den)	(23)	15174
31	Markus BRIER	(Aut)	(19)	14764
32	Francisco VALERA	(Sp)	(15)	14162
33	Fredrik LARSSON	(Swe)	(15)	13859
34	Christian CEVAER	(Fr)	(16)	13754
35	Anders HANSEN	(Den)	(21)	13750
36	Euan LITTLE	(Scot	(17)	13131
37	Henrik BJORNSTAD	(Nor)	(18)	12735
38	Alvaro SALTO	(Sp)	(12)	12599
39	José CARRILES	(Sp)	(14)	12591
40	Pauli HUGHES	(Fin)	(20)	12242
41	Johan RYSTRÖM	(Swe)	(13)	12057
42	Magnus PERSSON	(Swe)	(12)	12053
43	Antoine LEBOUC	(Fr)	(22)	11480
44	Jesus Maria ARRUTI	(Sp)	(16)	10727
45	Benoit TELLERIA	(Fr)	(20)	10627
46	Elliot BOULT	(NZ)	(14)	10586
47	Frédéric CUPILLARD	(Fr)	(18)	10460
48	Brian NELSON	(USA)	(9)	10292
49	Pehr MAGNEBRANT	(Swe)	(11)	9389
50	Stephen SCAHILL	(NZ)	(12)	9225

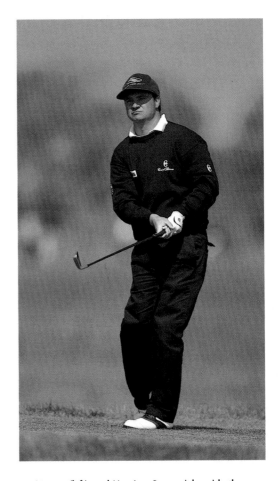

Per Nyman (left), and Massimo Scarpa (above) both earned their cards for the European Tour for 1999.

me both on and off the course. I couldn't have asked for more this season. It has been beyond my expectations. I didn't think I would win five events, that's a lot anywhere, even in the amateur game. At the start of the season I just wanted to get my card and this has given me a lot of confidence going into 1999.'

Bennett made sure of finishing as ranking leader well before the end of the season yet he didn't change his approach. He wanted to win every time he teed it up and even in the AXA Grand Final in Portugal he almost did it again, being beaten at the fourth extra hole of a sudden-death play-off by Jorge Berendt of Argentina, who will play alongside Bennett on the European Tour in 1999.

Looking at the latest 15 graduates from the Challenge Tour, five are English, four come from Sweden, two from Argentina, and one each from Italy, Denmark, Australia and Scotland.

Per Nyman of Sweden got closest to Bennett by finishing second on the rankings, a remarkable performance considering he didn't manage a victory.

Nevertheless, two second places, two thirds and two fourth places brought their own rewards. John Bickerton, Max Anglert, Christopher Hanell and Daren Lee also failed to mount the winner's rostrum but owed their promotion to consistency.

Italy's Massimo Scarpa, with two victories on the Challenge Tour is back on the main Tour after losing his card through injury in 1997. Two Englishmen, Roger Winchester and John Mellor, and a Scot, Stephen Gallacher, together with Fredrik Lindgren from Sweden will also be making welcome returns to the premier level. John Senden from Australia who has won twice in only ten outings, Ricardo Gonzalez from Argentina, winner of the Kenya Open and Soren Hansen from Denmark winner of the Navision Open will play on the European Tour next year for the very first time.

How many of these will emerge as winners in the higher level remains to be seen. But Bennett has the class and ability to emulate the likes of former Challenge Tour graduates Costantino Rocca, Thomas Björn and Ignacio Garrido providing he stays fighting fit.

David Hamilton

On the tee – the future stars of European golf

What have Costantino Rocca, Thomas Björn and Ignacio Garrido got in common apart from being winners on the European Tour and members of the victorious 1997 Ryder Cup team at Valderrama? They all graduated from the tough, character-building, talent-testing, greatly respected European Challenge Tour.

There are more like them on the way, and the facts to prove it are in the 1999 **European Challenge Tour Guide.**

Hundreds of would-be champions put their ambitions to the test on the Challenge Tour. It demands skill, determination, dedication and the ability to often handle bitter disappointment on the way to success.

All of this was shown in 1998 by England's Warren Bennett whose comeback after a frustrating previous season produced a remarkable story. He won five titles to become the runaway No. 1 on European Challenge Tour Rankings.

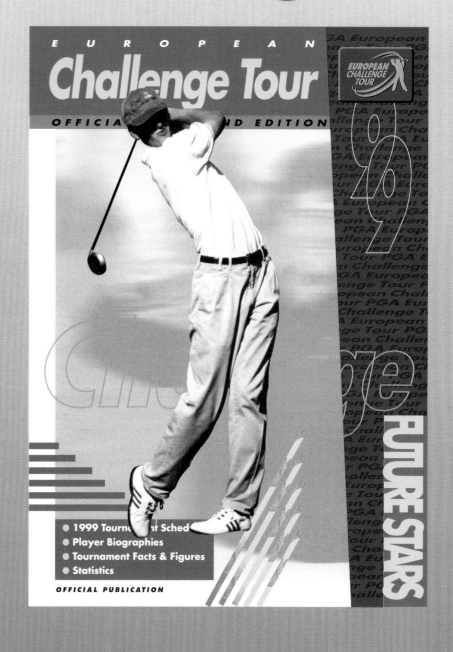

And that, along with his closest 14 challengers, earned him promotion to the 1999 European Tour and the chance to bid for Ryder Cup fame.

How he did it, the history of the Challenge Tour, biographies of its up-and-coming players, tournament records, statistics, everything worth knowing about this proving ground for future stars is covered by the 1999 Challenge Tour Guide.

It amounts to a staggering story of endeavour.

Ordering a copy of the 1999 **European Challenge Tour Guide** is simple.

Send a cheque for £12.50 (which includes postage and packaging), made payable to the PGA European Tour, to Frances Jennings, Communications Division, European Tour, Wentworth Drive, Virginia Water, Surrey GU25 4LX, or telephone 01344 842881 with credit card details.

Incentive and opportunity raise the standard

The European Seniors Tour

was even more competitive in 1998

When Christy O'Connor Junior summoned all his vast tournament experience to shoot a last round 65 at Edinburgh's formidable Dalmahoy layout, he couldn't believe that his 12 under par 276 aggregage was not good enough to win the Golden Charter Scottish Seniors Open. The jovial Irishman had given his best in only his second European Senior Tour event after turning 50, but had to settle for a share of fourth place.

The former Ryder Cup star was three shots adrift of home winner David Huish and was prompted to comment: 'The scoring on a tough golf course out there was incredible. It matches what you would expect on the main European Tour.'

He was referring to the fact that 39 of the 56 qualifiers were below par. Indeed, it wasn't the first time in 1998 that the Tour's top golfers had littered a scoreboard with red figures. It happened with sufficient regularity to be solid testimony to the high quality of golf being paraded by these sea-soned professionals around Europe's golf arenas.

But playing statistics were only part of another highly successful summer for Managing Director Andy Stubbs, his fellow administrators and players. To the framework of 19 ranking tournaments was added a prize fund of more than £2 million and a glowing clutch of personal success stories. Added together, it took the Tour to a new level of maturity with the 'embryonic' tag, so familiar in recent years, finally jettisoned. In Churchillian terms 1998 was perhaps the end of the beginning. Now there is sufficient scope and opportunity for talented professionals and amateurs alike to carve out a lucrative late career, not to mention a comfortable pension around some of Europe' s best golf watering holes.

None is achieving that better than Tommy Horton who for the third successive summer topped the European Seniors Tour Money List with three victories and a haul of £127,656 to collect the John Jacobs Trophy for the fourth time in six years.

Appropriately, he opened the campaign as he ended the previous season - with a victory. This time in the new El Bosque Senior Open in Spain and by a

264

nine-shot record margin. In June the Royal Jersey professional produced one of his trademark late charges, carding a closing 67 to snatch the De Vere Hotels Classic at Belton Woods by just one stroke from local favourite Ian Richardson.

Horton's third win was achieved at the prestigious PGA National Course at the Belfry where he had a two-shot margin over Italian Renato Campagnoli and Jim Rhodes. But he was to miss out on his one remaining ambition yet again at the Senior British Open at Royal Portrush. This time Horton's former Ryder Cup col-

double rocketed Huggett to the top of the rankings. He eventually finished second behind Horton and his final £102,382 made him only the second senior to top £100,000 in a year.

Although beaten at Wentworth, Coles was successful in an earlier play-off against Ireland's David Jones for the Philips PFA Classic at Meon Valley. It was his 42nd title worldwide. One of the sweetest swingers in golf was still getting results at the age of 63. It was both fitting and timely that Coles should be presented with a Lifetime Achievement Award by Lladro at the Seniors Tour Awards dinner

Seniors Open. And nobody enjoyed it more than Verwey who held off the late, twin challenge from Maurice Bembridge and – who else? – Tommy Horton for a two-shot success. Bembridge had already collected his second Seniors title, edging out South Staffs club professional Jim Rhodes in yet another play-off for the Swedish Seniors at Fagelbro.

Two other former Ryder Cup players made winner's speeches. Brian Waites became the first Tour man to break 200 for 54 holes, his 195 giving him the Elf Seniors Open in France by four shots. And Malcolm Gregson held on to take

Tommy Horton receives his Trophy from John Jacobs at the Tournament of Champions at The Buckinghamshire.

league Brian Huggett, revitalised with a new putter after 28 years, took the Tour's flagship title, beating Ulsterman Eddie Polland in a play-off.

It was a back-to-back success for the Welshman who, a week earlier had sparked his best run of form for two years with another extra time win in the Schroder Senior Masters at Wentworth. Polland was again on the receiving end in the shoot-out alongside Neil Coles. The

at Wentworth.

Another double winner was South Africa's former Senior British Open winner Bobby Verwey. Having turned to the long handled putter he swept his way to victory in the Lawrence Batley Seniors, beating Spain's consistent Antonio Garrido in a play-off.

After a three-week break the Tour moved to the luxury resort of Bad Ragaz for the Credit Suisse Private Banking

the Is Molas Seniors Open in Sardinia by a couple of strokes after Horton, once more, had raced out of the bunch with a 66 for second spot.

John Morgan took a break from collecting qualifying dollars on the US Senior Tour to bid for the Senior British Open. He finished in the bunch but made his visit the more memorable by winning the following week's West of Ireland title, his seventh in Europe, at East Clare.

Six first time winners combined to ensure the Tour's bigger cheques continued to be spread around. Three of them qualified at the previous year's Tour School, American Bob Lendzion (winner of the Beko Classic in Turkey), Ireland's American-based Joe McDermott (AIB Irish Open) and Australian Bob Shearer (Jersey Senior Open).

Northern Ireland's Paul Leonard finally found the winning formula with a resounding seven-shot margin in the Efteling European Trophy and Canadian grandfather Bill Hardwick celebrated Father's Day in style with two strokes to spare in the Ryder Seniors Classic.

One of the most heart-warming stories came right at the climax of a wonderful season. John Garner, whose only win on the European Tour had come in 1972, finally savoured that glorious winning feeling 26 years on by capturing the Tour's grand finale, the Tournament of Champions at The Buckinghamshire. It was a triumph over the elements by the former Ryder Cup player, who defied the rain and wind and a courageous challenge from the tenacious Polland to win his first Seniors title by a shot in the weather-shortened event.

Ultimately, the Tournament of Champions lived up to its billing as the highlight of the inceasingly competitive schedule, but memories of the 1998 sea-

SENIORS MONEY LIST

				£
1	Tommy HORTON	(Eng)	(18)	127656
2	Brian HUGGETT	(Wal)	(12)	102382
3	Eddie POLLAND	(N.Ire)	(19)	92145
4	David JONES	(N.Ire)	(17)	74133
5	Noel RATCLIFFE	(Aus)	(19)	69528
6	Jim RHODES	(Eng)	(19)	64021
7	Bobby VERWEY	(SA)	(18)	62595
8	Neil COLES	(Eng)	(13)	58663
* 9	Denis O'SULLIVAN	(Ire)	(16)	54990
10	Brian WAITES	(Eng)	(19)	54515
11	Antonio GARRIDO	(Sp)	(18)	54271
* 12	Bob LENDZION	(USA)	(16)	54165
13	Malcolm GREGSON	(Eng)	(17)	54023
14	Maurice BEMBRIDGE	(Eng)	(19)	53414
15	John GARNER	(Eng)	(17)	48134
16	David HUISH	(Scot)	(14)	45271
17	Paul LEONARD	(N. Ir)	(19)	44976
18	Bill HARDWICK	(Can)	(19)	43640
19	Bill BRASK	(USA)	(11)	43621
20	Terry GALE	(Aus)	(13)	43495
21	John FOURIE	(SA)	(19)	42025
22	Renato CAMPAGNOLI	(It)	(14)	40784
* 23	Barry SANDRY	(Eng)	(18)	38622
24	David CREAMER	(Eng)	(19)	37686
* 25	Joe MCDERMOTT	(Ire)	(17)	36689
26	Liam HIGGINS	(Ire)	(18)	36074
* 27	Michael SLATER	(Eng)	(19)	35340
28	Norman WOOD	(Scot)	(19)	32522
29	Ian RICHARDSON	(Eng)	(19)	28429
30	Alberto CROCE	(It)	(16)	27272
31	David OAKLEY	(USA)	(12)	26492
32	Bob SHEARER	(Aus)	(11)	26014
33	John MORGAN	(Eng)	(4)	25906
34	Craig DEFOY	(Wal)	(16)	24986
* 35	Jay DOLAN III	(USA)	(18)	23932
36	Peter TOWNSEND	(Eng)	(18)	23579
37	Tony JACKLIN	(Eng)	(9)	21306
38	J.R. DELICH	(USA)	(18)	20770
39	Snell LANCASTER	(USA)	(16)	19215
40	Arnold O'CONNOR	(Ire)	(16)	18649
41	Hugh INGGS	(SA)	(17)	18273
* 42	José CABO	(Sp)	(12)	18062
43	Doug DALZIEL	(USA)	(13)	16714
* 44	Geoff PARSLOW	(Aus)	(18)	16008
45	Iain CLARK	(Scot)	(6)	14363
46	Gordon PARKHILL	(N.Ire)	(16)	13820
47	Bob MENNE	(USA)	(14)	13352
48	Christy O'CONNOR JNR	(Ire)	(3)	12285
49	John HUDSON	(Eng)	(18)	10861
50	TR JONES	(USA)	(16)	10810

* Denotes 1997 Seniors Qualifying School Graduate
\# Denotes Affiliate Member

Photographs:
John Garner winner of the Tournament of Champions (left), and Brian Huggett, winner of the Senior British Open.

son are not entirely focused on winners.

Ulsterman Polland demonstrated his competitive edge for most of the schedule but had the frustration of finishing second three times, one of them in his first bid for big prize of the Senior British Open on his home soil. Polland's long-hitting fellow countryman David Jones was also a familiar sight in many a leading bunch. But he had to settle for two runners-up spots in six top-five finishes.

Perhaps the most encouraging story from last summer for anyone with an interest in the potential and wider agenda of the European Seniors Tour was that featuring Cork businessman Denis O'Sullivan. A former Irish amateur champion, he shunned an invitation to captain his national team in order to become a senior professional.

After qualifying at the Tour School, O'Sullivan's immense competitive talent emerged to the extent of earning him ninth place in the Money List with £54,990 in his rookie season. Into the bargain he picked up three second place cheques and, in the distinguished company at the Senior British Open, played well enough for a share of fifth. He said: 'This has been a wonderful new experience for me. I know now that I can win. I just love playing on the Seniors Tour.' A sentiment now shared by many.

Bryan Potter

He's done it again — three years in a row as No.1 Senior

Who? Tommy Horton, of course, top of the European Seniors Tour Money List and winner of the John Jacobs Trophy for a third consecutive year. How did he do it? The 1999 **European Seniors Tour Guide** tells all.

Biographies, records, statistics, everything worth knowing about the increasingly popular, fast growing Seniors Tour is packed into its 250-page **official guide**.

How many Tour titles did Tommy win in 1998? (three actually). Who was the runaway winner of most Super Senior prizes? (Neil Coles). Which two prestigious tournaments did former Ryder Cup captain Brian Huggett win on the way to finishing second in the Money List? (Senior British Open and Schroder Senior Masters). Where and when will the enduring talents of Europe's finest over-50 golfers challenge for £3 million prize money in 1999 to greet the new millennium? The **guide** has the answers and thousands more facts to make it a fascinating work of reference for all Seniors Tour enthusiasts.

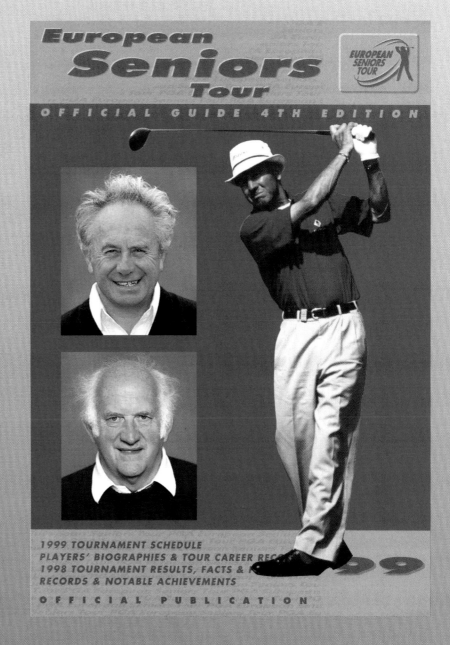

Ordering a copy of the 1999 European Tour Seniors Guide is simple.

Send a cheque for £12.50 (which includes postage and packaging), made payable to the PGA European Tour, to Frances Jennings, Communications Division, European Tour, Wentworth Drive, Virginia Water, Surrey GU25 4LX, or telephone 01344 842881 with credit card details.

Canon Shot of the Year

Miguel Angel Jiménez,

18th hole, Saint-Nom-La-Bretèche,

Trophée Lancôme

Miguel Angel Jiménez went into the final round of the Trophée Lancôme with a two stroke lead over a field which included Masters and Open champion, Mark O'Meara and US Tour leading money-winner, David Duval.

In the final round, Sweden's Jarmo Sandelin closed with a 63 to set an early clubhouse target of 275, nine under par. He was joined by New Zealand's Greg Turner, O'Meara and then Duval.

Jiménez arrived on the 18th tee needing a par three on the 209-yard finisher to take the title and the first prize of £133,330. Taking care to avoid the water on the right he missed the green on the left, the ball finishing under the grandstand. From here he had to go to the dropping zone, from where O'Meara had failed to get up and down minutes earlier.

Following his drop, Jiménez faced a daunting chip over a ridge onto a green that sloped away from him. If he left the ball short then he would face a downhill, right to left putt for his par. If he overhit the shot the ball could run off the green into the water. To add to the difficulties, the ball was sitting down in the two-inch semi-rough but Jiménez made perfect contact, sending the ball just over the ridge towards the hole. The line and speed were exactly right and the ball ran straight into the middle of the cup for a birdie and a two-stroke victory margin which propelled him to the top of the Ryder Cup points table.

It was Jiménez's second title of the year and the fourth European Tour win of his career. The new champion said: 'This win is very special because it's the first time my wife was here to see it. It's also important for the Ryder Cup. It was nice to be Seve's vice-captain but it would be nicer to be on the team next time.'

The shot was a worthy winner of the 1998 Canon Shot of the Year as it was executed to perfection at a crucial moment under extreme pressure and in circumstances made all the more enthralling by the strength of the field.

New horizons beckon

The opening of PGA Golf de Catalunya and the final

preparation of the Marquess course at Woburn demonstrate

the forward momentum of PGA European Tour Courses

*L*arge crowds flocked to the Kungsängen Golf Club, near Stockholm, in August to witness home hero Jesper Parnevik capture his second Volvo Scandinavian Masters title within the space of four years. Kungsängen translates to King's Meadow and Parnevik emerged as the king of Swedish golf after four days of intense competition.

While Parnevik became the first Swedish player to win two Scandinavian Masters, the tournament marked another stage in the growth of PGA European Tour Courses Plc. Following the strategy of owning and managing courses as venues for tournaments on the European Tour, Kungsängen joined an exclusive list of courses within PGA European Tour Courses' portfolio that have staged European Tour events.

PGA European Tour

Courses is uniquely placed for the ownership, development and management of golf courses that can host professional tournaments under the auspices of the PGA European Tour. The aim of the Company is to expand and develop golf facilities throughout Europe that not only provide a championship test for professionals but also offer outstanding amenities for the visiting golfer.

This philosophy is implemented at four flagship courses, Kungsängen, Quinta do Lago in Portugal, Woburn Golf and Country Club in England and PGA Golf de Catalunya in Spain.

The last named course, lying 45 minutes north east of Barcelona in the La Selva region, close to Girona, is the newest facility to be opened for play. Designed by Angel Gallardo and Neil Coles, two men with illustrious playing careers on the European Tour and with equally illustrious credentials as golf course architects. Between them they have created a very special golfers' haven on land dense with cork, oak and pine trees with the mountains of Montseny to the west and vistas of the Pyrenees to the north. Overall the course measures 7,200 yards from the back tees.

Gallardo, who is Vice-chairman of the PGA European Tour Board of Directors, first set eyes on the land ten years ago when he was approached by the Royal Automobile Club of Catalunya to assess its feasibil-

PGA European Tour Courses PLC

ity as a golf course. 'When I first visited the site,' says Gallardo, 'the sheer size of the land was staggering. It was dense with vegetation and it was difficult to visualise anything. I spoke to Neil Coles and we eventually arrived at our preferred clubhouse position and were able to route the holes to return to the clubhouse. Before the course was finished I had already played each hole in my mind, analysed each drive and approach shot, how the greens should slope, the reward for a good shot and the penalty for a bad one.'

resorts in Europe. It has full clubhouse facilities, bars and restaurants, a driving range, putting greens and a golf academy.

One of the most famous names in British golf is that of Woburn Golf and Country Club which has hosted 12 British Masters tournaments and, in 1999, will stage its ninth Weetabix British Women's Open. The Duke's and Duchess courses are well established and they will be joined shortly by the Marquess course thereby making Woburn one of the few 54-hole venues in England. The Marquess

'Now with the creation of the Marquess course, so named after Lord Tavistock who first brought golf to Woburn, I can sit back and say "I told you so", for without doubt the magnificent course being constructed is destined to become one of the finest, not just in Europe, but anywhere.'

The policy of expansion and development that underlines PGA European Tour Courses' approach has been further emphasised in 1998 and the Company is well situated for the future. Ken Schofield,

GA GOLF DE ATALUNYA

Quinta do Lago

The Marquess Course at Woburn (left). Opposite page, Angel Gallardo and Neil Coles (near left) survey the work in progress at PGA Golf de Catalunya (left centre). Jesper Parnevik at Kungsängen Golf Club, near Stockholm, (far left).

Neil Coles, MBE, who is Chairman of the PGA European Tour Board of Directors and whose playing career stretches back over 40 years,. concurs with Gallardo. 'The site is very attractive with mature cork, oak trees, firs and heathers and the undulating terrain offered some interesting hole options. We designed the course with a number of elevated tee positions which provide some spectacular views. With most courses you have to create spectator mounding, the setting of this course gave us all the viewing locations that are needed for a major tournament.'

PGA Golf de Catalunya is destined to take its place as one of the finest golf

course has been designed by Peter Alliss and European Golf Design and will become the home of a European Tour event when it is ready for play.

The Marquess measures 7,300 yards and the undulating fairways thread their way through magnificent pines, chestnuts and oaks. The greenside bunkers place the premium on accuracy and the rolling greens provide a variety of pin positions.

BBC television commentator Alex Hay, former Club Professional and then Managing Director of Woburn says: 'For the last 12 years I have believed that this Estate hid what could surely be one of golf's finest gems.'

Executive Director of the PGA European Tour, summarises: 'The development of European Tour Courses signifies not only our desire to enter the 21st Century with a strong portfolio of courses, but also to design and refine our own courses for Tour competition. This will support our policy to provide the best possible courses for play on the European Tour, the European Seniors Tour and the European Challenge Tour. PGA Golf de Catalunya is a case in point; the newest course in the portfolio, designed by Neil Coles and Angel Gallardo, and set on undulating land. We feel confident it will challenge the best players in the world.'

271

Golfer of the Month Awards 1998

Thomas Björn (left)
JANUARY

José Maria Olazábal (right)
FEBRUARY

Ernie Els
MARCH

Thomas Levet
APRIL

Colin Montgomerie (top)
MAY AND SEPTEMBER

Sam Torrance (left below)
JUNE

David Carter
JULY

Mathias Grönberg (right below)
AUGUST

Darren Clarke
OCTOBER

There is also a Golfer of the Year Award. The winner in 1998 was

Lee Westwood.

Nine new winners in 1998

Tiger Woods
JOHNNIE WALKER CLASSIC

Andrew Coltart
QATAR MASTERS

Thomas Levet
CANNES OPEN

Stephen Leaney
**MOROCCAN OPEN and
TNT DUTCH OPEN**

Patrik Sjöland
ITALIAN OPEN

David Carter
MURPHY'S IRISH OPEN

Stephen Allan
GERMAN OPEN

Russell Claydon
BMW INTERNATIONAL OPEN

Olle Karlsson
OPEN NOVOTEL PERRIER
(with Jarmo Sandelin)

273

History and tradition maintained

The World Cup of Golf continues
to play a major role in the global
development of the game

The World Cup of Golf, which, in the year 2000, will become part of the World Golf Championships, was first launched as the Canada Cup in 1953. It has a proud tradition of being hosted by no fewer than 22 different countries, following the first visit to New Zealand where in 1998 it was played at the magnificent Gulf Harbour complex in Auckland, and in 1999 will unfold at The Mines Resort and Golf Club, Kuala Lumpur, Malaysia.

Malaysia's latest showcase, the magnificent Mines Resort City, sprawling over 1,000 acres with over 5 million sq. ft built-up area of development, is a masterpiece crafted from the world's largest open cast tin mine. The Mines Resort City is just a ten minute drive from the city of Kuala Lumpur and set in the fastest growth area of the Southern

**Nick Faldo and David Carter
steered England to victory
in New Zealand.**

Burch Riber with Dato Lee Kim (above left). Paul McGinley and Padraig Harrington triumphed in 1977 (above right).
David Carter (below) celebrates England's victory.

Corridor with a population of one million from Putrajaya, Seri Kembangan, Balakong, Cheras. Sg Besi, Bangi and Serdang. The Mines Resort City is within close proximity of the future developments of the new Kuala Lumpur International Airport (KLIA) at Sepang, the Administrative Capital of Malaysia at Putrajaya, the National Sports Complex and the Commonwealth Games Village at Bukit Jalil, the Selangor Turf Club and Technology Park Malaysia.

The course, designed by leading golf architect, Robert Trent Jones Junior, will have been opened five years when the event takes place in Malaysia on November 18-21, and then, renamed the World Cup Team, it will move on to the United States (2000), South Africa (2001) and Japan (2002).

Ken Schofield, Executive Director of the European Tour, said: 'During the early stages of the planning process for the World Golf Championships, the International Federation of PGA Tours knew it would be important to have a significant team competition as part of the series. The players have always enjoyed competing in the World Cup of Golf, and we anticipate a very similar reaction when we introduce our team event in 2000. The International Golf Association and the World Cup of Golf have played an important role in the development of golf world-wide during the past five decades, and we are grateful for the world-wide exposure the event has brought to golf.

The World Cup of Golf has a wonderful history of tradition, and in the last ten years the European Tour has been directly involved with the competition. During that time Burch Riber, as Executive Director of the IGA, has seen that the tradition has been continued and in addition David Ciclitira, Chairman and Chief Executive of the Parallel Media Group, has successfully and innovatively promoted the event.'

The World Cup of Golf took a huge step forward when, in 1995, it went to the People's Republic of China, so becoming the first major international golfing event to be held in mainland China, since when it has been played at Erinvale Golf Club in Cape Town, where South Africa was suc-

cessful, at Kiawah Island in the United States where Ireland (Padraig Harrington and Paul McGinley) triumphed and Colin Montgomerie won the individual prize, and in Auckland, New Zealand.

The Gulf Harbour development, only a short drive out of Auckland, is one of the most spectacular in the South Pacific Region with marina, luxury hotel, conference centre and residential facilities. The golf course, with all its exciting views, and compared favourably to the famous American course, Pebble Beach, where the US Open Championship has been staged, provided the competition with another outstanding venue.

It was at Gulf Harbour that England gained its first World Cup title when the partnership of Nick Faldo and David Carter triumphed by two shots over Italy, represented by Costantino Rocca and Massimo Florioli, with the Scottish pairing of Colin Montgomerie and Andrew Coltart taking joint third place.

The World Cup of Golf is a two-man team event featuring the top golfing nations and in recent times a notable record was established when the Americans Fred Couples and David Love III became the first partnership in the history of the event to win four years in succession. This historic moment was sealed at Mission Hills, on the outskirts of Shenzhen, in 1995 when the United States won by 14 shots, as they had done in Puerto Rico in 1994.

Mitchell Platts   275

The dream becomes a reality

The plans of the International
Federation of PGA Tours
are now implemented for 1999

The year of 1999 will be remembered for taking golf out of the 20th Century and into the 21st with the advent of the World Golf Championships.

All of which would startle King James II of Scotland who, more than 500 years ago, saw his archers deeply engrossed in 'putting the ball' when they should have been sharpening their arrows to deal with the English invaders. He determined to put them, and the obsessive game of golf, out of bounds, and a ban was entered upon the Parliamentary statute books in 1457 in order to break the hold that golf had on his fighting men. In fact King James should be credited with having been able to gaze into the future. Clearly he saw ahead to the time when the game with the hole in it would become an obsession and an addictive influence on future generations.

This addiction became global when, soon after the successful introduction of the Open Championship in 1860, Britain's adventurous young men took their golf games with them to far-flung parts of the world where new golf clubs were being formed such as the St Andrew's Club of Yonkers on Hudson.

The turn of the last century saw golf enjoying its first golden era with the game being dominated by three individuals known collectively as The Great Triumvirate – John Henry Taylor, a West countryman, Harry Vardon, a Channel Islander, and James Braid, a Scot. In 21 years of the Open Championship they totalled 16 wins between them. The game had never known such giants.

On the fairways the globalisation of the game made significant strides in 1921 when Jock Hutchison, albeit a Scottish immigrant American, won the Open Championship at St Andrews, long since recognised as the home of golf, and the famous claret jug crossed the Atlantic for the first time.

America's golfers were on the march.

Walter Hagen and Bobby Jones were followed by Gene Sarazen and Sam Snead,

Byron Nelson and Ben Hogan, Arnold Palmer and Jack Nicklaus, Lee Trevino and Tom Watson. They challenged the world and as the popularity of the game spread to every corner, the world chal- lenged them. Britain's Henry Cotton and Tony Jacklin, South Africa's Bobby Locke and Gary Player, Australia's Peter Thomson, New Zealand's Bob Charles and Argentina's Roberto de Vicenzo all picked up the gauntlet thrown down by the Americans.

Then, spurred by the deeds of these great champions, came a new wave of players. Spain's Severiano Ballesteros and

The Great Triumvirate: Taylor and Braid watch Vardon (above left). Bobby Jones at St Andrews in 1927 (above). Walter Hagen (near right), Gene Sarazen (far right).

277

Gary Player (left), Bob Charles (above) and Roberto de Vicenzo (right), all picked up the guantlet thrown down by the Americans. (Below), Kosaku Shimada, Executive Director of the PGA Tour of Japan, Arnold Mentz, Commissioner of the Southern Africa PGA Tour, Ken Schofield, Executive Director of the European Tour, Tim Finchem, the Commissioner of the US PGA Tour, and Arthur Sanderson, Executive Director of the PGA Tours of Australasia, declare: 'This is no time to dream about the future; it's time to build it.'

José Maria Olazábal; Britain's Nick Faldo, Ian Woosnam, and Sandy Lyle; Germany's Bernhard Langer, Australia's Greg Norman and Steve Elkington followed quickly by Britain's Darren Clarke, Colin Montgomerie and Lee Westwood, Denmark's Thomas Bjorn, a host of Swedish golfers, Italy's Costantino Rocca, Fiji's Vijay Singh, and from America David Duval and Tiger Woods.

Their dedication to the practice range, technical excellence and sheer desire to succeed has elevated the game to new heights and the Tours responded to this global warming of golf by forming the International Federation of PGA Tours.

The Federation was formed in March, 1996. Tim Finchem, the Commissioner of the PGA Tour, would later pay tribute to Greg Norman, and others, for bringing to the agenda the theme of a World Tour, but the Federation wanted much more. The Tours were determined that the game, based from those early days on integrity, should progress in an orderly manner. In other words this was no time to dream about the future; it was time to build it.

That future was shaped in a series of meetings, and confirmed to all when at the 1998 Open Championship, Ken Schofield, Executive Director of the European Tour, Arnold Mentz, Commissioner of the Southern Africa PGA Tour, Arthur Sanderson, Executive Director of the PGA Tours of Australasia,

CNBC first in business worldwide
CNBC Sports first in executive sports worldwide

Kosaku Shimada, Executive Director of the PGA Tour of Japan, and Finchem met with the world's media at Royal Birkdale. Schofield said: 'We are very pleased to make the commitment now in terms of the prize funds for the first three Championships in 1999, and to introduce our sponsors, Andersen Consulting, NEC and American Express. The purses for these three Championships will be set at five million dollars each.'

The programme was further enhanced with the confirmation that the year 2000 would see the introduction of the Federation's sanction of the International Golf Association's World Cup. It was announced that this event, first played in 1953, would take place in the United States, South Africa and Japan in the years 2000, 2001, 2002 respectively.

Finchem pointed out: 'We are delighted that from 1999 we will be adding Championships that allow us to structure competition at Tour level in a way that addresses the global market and the global nature of the game. We are delighted to be getting started. We are pleased to have come this far in the last three years in the planning, and we are now ready to go forward with the execution.'

That start has been penned into the world programme for La Costa Resort and Spa in Carlsbad, California, with the Andersen Consulting Match Play Championship on February 24-28 followed by the NEC Invitational at Firestone Country Club, Akron, Ohio on August 26-29 and the American Express Championship at Club de Golf Valderrama in southern Spain on November 4-7.

In essence the World Golf

Championships are a series of events featuring the game's top players competing against each other in a varity of competitive formats. The four events, including the World Cup, will rotate through a variety of outstanding venues world-wide, roughly half in the United States and half in the countries represented by International Federation of PGA Tours partners.

Paul McGinley and Padraig Harrington fly the flag for the World Cup after victory in 1997.

An extension to this progress was also announced at Royal Birkdale when the Federation welcomed the Asian PGA's Omega Tour as an associate member. Schofield explained: 'The Omega Tour has been based on consistency. The general feeling is that any Tour can join the Federation provided that they have demonstrated five years of consistent

operations and scheduling. We feel that the Omega Tour is well placed to become a full member of the Federation at the beginning of the Millennium.'

Ramlan Dato Harun, Executive Director of the Asian PGA, said: 'It was a truly historic day for Asian sport, and the greatest moment of my involvement with Asian professional golf. It is a question of credibility, and we now have a much increased standing in the eyes of the golfing world. Now that the Asian PGA's Membership has been approved, I am confident that Asia will be given the opportunity to stage a World Golf Championship event in the not too distant future.'

The European Tour has thrived under Schofield since 1975, operating a policy of 'opportunity and incentive', and so the arrival of the World Golf Championships fits well. 'These Championships will globalise the game,' Schofield said. 'The reality is that players representing the Tours can play their way into these elite Championships.' Finchem added: 'If we are successful in positioning our sport on a global basis it will create additional value down the road for all players.'

Padraig Harrington , who together with Paul McGinley won the World Cup for Ireland at Kiawah Island in 1997 before moving on to defend the crown at Golf Harbour in Auckland, New Zealand, in November 1998, supported the philosophy. Harrington, a Walker Cup player in 1991, 1993 and 1995, has now played on the European Tour for three full seasons. He said: 'It's up to us to improve to make sure we get ranked to play in the Championships.'

Mitchell Platts

ANDERSEN CONSULTING MATCH-PLAY CHAMPIONSHIP

Dates:

February 24-28, 1999	La Costa Resort and Spa Carlsbad, CA
February 23-27, 2000	La Costa Resort and Spa Carlsbad, CA
January 3-7, 2001	Australia
February 20-24, 2002	La Costa Resort and Spa Carlsbad, CA

Eligibility: Top 64 players on the Official World Golf Ranking

Format: 64-player Match-Play event

Wednesday	32 matches
Thursday	16 matches
Friday	8 matches
Saturday (am)	4 quarter-finals
Saturday (pm)	2 semi-finals
Sunday	Consolation match
	Final 36-hole match

Purse: $5,000,000

Television: ABC Sports and ESPN in the United States, More than 140 countries world-wide.

NEC INVITATIONAL

Dates:

August 26-29, 1999	Firestone Country Club Akron, OH
August 24-27, 2000	Firestone Country Club Akron, OH
August 23-26, 2001	U.S.A.
August 22-25, 2002	Firestone Country Club Akron, OH

Eligibility: All members of last-named Presidents Cup and Ryder Cup Teams

Format: 4-day, 72-hole stroke play competition, no cut
Minimum field: 36 players. Maximum field: 48 players:
12 U.S. players from the Ryder Cup
12 U.S. players from The Presidents Cup
12 European players from the Ryder Cup
12 International players from The Presidents Cup

Purse: $5,000,000

Television CBS Sports and USA Network in the United States. More than 140 countries world-wide.

AMERICAN EXPRESS CHAMPIONSHIP

Dates:

November 4-7, 1999	Club de Golf Valderrama, Spain
November 9-12, 2000	Club de Golf Valderrama, Spain
November 1-4, 2001	Chateau Elan
Oct 31-Nov 3, 2002	Europe

Eligibility:
1. Top 50 players on the Official World Golf Ranking.
2. Top 30 from the PGA Tour Money List, to a floor of 100 on the Official World Golf Ranking.
3. Top 20 from the European Tour Volvo Ranking, to a floor of 100 on the Official World Golf Ranking.
4. Top 3 from the Australasian Tour Order of Merit, to a floor of 100 on the Official World Golf Ranking.
5. Top 3 on the Japanese PGA Tour Money List, to a floor of 100 on the Official World Golf Ranking.
6. Top 3 from the Southern Africa PGA Tour Order of Merit, to a floor of 100 on the Official World Golf Ranking.
7. The No 1 player on the money list of each five Tours, without regard to the floor of 100 on the official World Golf Ranking.

Estimated field size: 60-65 players.

Format: 4-day, 72-hole competition, no cut.

Purse: $5,000,000

Television: ABC Sports and ESPN in the United States. More than 140 countries world-wide.

WORLD CUP TEAM

Dates:

December 7-10, 2000	U.S.A
November 15-18, 2001	South Africa
November 14-17, 2002	Japan

Eligibility: To be decided

Format: The existing World Cup of Golf, which started in 1953 and pioneered the staging of an annual two-man team competition comprising players from around the world, will become the team competition for the World Golf Championships in 2000, and will be known as the World Cup Team.

Purse: To be decided

Television: To be decided

La Costa Resort & Spa, Carlsbad, California

La Costa Resort and Spa was home for 30 years to the US PGA Tour's Tournament of Champions, known for the last five years as the Mercedes Championships. As with the Tournament of Champions, the Andersen Consulting Match Play Championship will be played over the resort's original 18 holes. The venue was enlarged to 27 holes in 1973, and another addition of nine holes was completed in 1985, for the present-day 36-hole layout.

The tournament course consists of holes 1,2,3, and 13-18 of the resort's North Course, while the entire back nine of the South Course will provide the challenging finishing holes.

La Costa's two championship golf courses were designed by master golf course architects Dick Wilson and Joe Lee. A classic pair of layouts by any measure and trademarks of Wilson design, the courses are fair and straightforward tests, but beware the many strategically placed bunkers and forbidding water hazards. The target is always in plain view before the golfer, but to score well you must plan your shots.

Open but hilly with plenty of sand, La Costa's North Course's front nine begins at the resort's heart and winds gently through foothills and canyons replete with wide fairways, big sky and open spaces. The greens can be treacherous.

Lee Trevino has said that La Costa's South Course has the longest playing back nine on the men's Tour. Prevailing winds off the Pacific Ocean and soft, lush fairways keep driving distances down and place a premium on mid-to-long-iron play. Once on the green, players can go right for the cup, as there is relatively little break on the South Course's mature greens. During Southern California's 'winter months' the rough grows at a healthy clip and woe to the golfer whose tee shot strays afield. The finishing four holes are known as 'the longest mile in golf.'

The Firestone Country Club, Akron, Ohio

The history of Firestone Country Club stretches back over half a century to August 10, 1929, when Harvey Firestone drove the first ball down the fairway to open the new South Course, designed by the late Bert Way. Throughout the years, the legends of the game have left their permanent footprints on the fairways of Firestone. The epic contests held on these grounds have become an important part of the game's history, and have made Firestone Country Club famous throughout the world.

The tournaments at Firestone Country Club began in 1954 with the Rubber City Open which continued through 1959. Firestone was chosen as the site of the 1960 US PGA Championship and during that memorable championship. Arnold Palmer triple-bogeyed the 625-yard, par-five hole, calling it a 'Monster'. The nickname proved popular, and in time, the entire course became known as 'The Monster'.

The American Golf Classic, inherited in 1961, began a new era of golf at Firestone. The World Series of Golf began under its old format in 1962, and in succeeding years the course played host to many other competitions, including the CBS Golf Classic and Big Three Golf, the

forerunner of The World Series of Golf.

In 1973, Firestone Country Club was the only course in the world on which three televised golf events – The American Golf Classic, the World Series of Golf and CBS Golf Classic – were conducted in one calendar year. In 1969, the North Course, designed by Robert Trent Jones was opened. This scenic challenge became the site of the 1976 American Golf Classic.

The US PGA Championship returned to the South Course in 1966, and again in 1975, making Firestone the first club to host this prestigious championship three times. In the fall of 1985 the South Course was again redesigned by Golforce, a Jack Nicklaus company, which started a new era of golf at the club.

VALDERRAMA GOLF CLUB, SOTOGRANDE, SPAIN

IN 1963 Robert Trent Jones, who has designed more than 600 courses around the world, built Sotogrande for Joseph McMicking, an entrepreneur and retired American colonel. It was a significant moment. In building Sotogrande, Trent Jones brought American golf and American grasses to Europe for the first time.

Then in 1975, in the hills above the old village of Sotogrande, Trent Jones finished a second 18-hole course – Los Aves which became The New – to go with The Old. Ten years later Jaime-Ortiz Patino, the Club President, formed a consortium which purchased the New Course, renamed it Valderrama and recalled Trent Jones to remodel the layout. In essence, the char-

acter of the course was not changed, but the shot-making values were enhanced. Valderrama was transformed into a challenging Championship examination and became host to the Volvo Masters from 1988 to 1996, to the Ryder Cup in 1997 and now in 1999 and 2000 the American Express Championship.

Trent Jones regards Valderrama, on Spain's Costa del Sol some 22 miles northeast of Gibraltar, spectacular for both its beauty and difficulty. It casts an imposing shadow similar to The Rock itself.

The American influence of this steeply undulating panoramic course is clearly visible: long, elevated, tree-framed tees, huge contoured greens, cavernous white sand traps that dazzle in the sun and, of course, water which is to be found not only in the form of a cascade at the fourth but also at the 17th which was remodelled in 1995 by Severiano Ballesteros, captain of Europe's winning 1997 Ryder Cup Team.

The 17th hole (top). The 12th hole (centre) and the 4th (bottom). Previous page, the 18th.

Pro-Golf – a perpetual winner for 28 years

One year to the next, little remains the same on the European Tour. Progress demands changes and world-class standards raise ambitions. But there is the one constant factor – after 28 years, **Pro-Golf**, the European Tour Media Guide, is still mastering the challenge of successfully chronicling the achievements and growth of the Tour as it approaches the new millennium.

The 1999 edition of **Pro-Golf** pays tribute to Colin Montgomerie for his remarkable record of winning the Volvo Ranking and Vardon Trophy six years in a row. In an arena crowded with some of the world's finest golf champions, Montgomerie looked to have taken on a 'Mission Impossible' task. But he did it.

And every personal tournament statistic of his route to remain Europe's No. 1 is detailed in **Pro-Golf**, the essential work of reference for all enthusiasts.

There are biographies of all the international stars who make the European Tour unique, more than 400 pages of illustrated records, statistics, facts, history – everything worth knowing from Montgomerie, Darren Clarke, Lee Westwood down to the newest rookie from the Qualifying School.

In 1999 the best of them will be going all out for places in the Ryder Cup team and the inaugural World Golf Championships. How, where, when? **Pro-Golf** tells all together with the richer-than-ever European Tour schedule based on incentive and opportunity.

It all makes for another fascinating edition, and ordering a copy of **Pro-Golf** 1999 is simple.

Send a cheque for £15 (which includes postage and packaging), made payable to the PGA European Tour, to Frances Jennings, Communications Division, European Tour, Wentworth Drive, Virginia Water, Surrey GU25 4LX, or telephone 01344 842881 with credit card details.

The 'Squire' circles the globe

Gene Sarazen's own tournament
emphasises that golf is truly global

Gene Sarazen was a global golfer long before it became fashionable to travel the planet with clubs in one hand and spikes in the other. As early as the 1920s, genial Gene thought nothing of tramping his way across Europe, Africa, Asia and South America by any form of transport readily available, spreading the golfing gospel and acquiring umpteen converts – and titles – along the way.

That pioneering spirit earned 'The Squire' his reputation as one of the game's greatest ambassadors, along with the honour of becoming the first player to capture the modern Grand Slam of the four majors – the Masters, US Open, Open Championship and US PGA.

So when the game's most famous nonagenarian sat down and devised the concept of a tournament at The Legends course at Chateau Elan in Georgia, which he co-designed, it was inevitable that the embryo event would embrace the four corners of the globe.

When the Sarazen World Open, later to be sponsored by Subaru, left the drawing board and became a reality in 1994, the eponymous hero, naturally, described the ambitious project as 'A Gathering of Champions'.

He didn't exaggerate. 'The Squire' decreed that national Open champions should be invited to play at the glorious setting near Atlanta. It didn't matter if it was a major championship like the US or British Open, or a less glamourous title such as the Vietnam or Fiji Open.

Any Open champion is an Open champion, insisted Sarazen, and so the World Open was born. On November 3, 1994, the inaugural tournament swung into action at the course which bears the Sarazen hallmark, and a life-sized bronze effigy of the original Legend, complete with trademark hat and shooting stick, overlooking the 18th green.

It was entirely appropriate that the first Sarazen World Open was won by a truly outstanding global competitor in Ernie Els. The powerful South African with the lazy, languid swing secured the $350,000 first prize with a wonderful closing round of 65.

New Zealander Frank Nobilo succeeded Els 12 months later, winning a rain-shortened tournament thanks to four birdies in five holes on the back nine for a round of 68 and three-round total of 208.

The European Tour was impressively represented by Miguel Angel Jiménez of Spain and Zimbabwe's Mark McNulty, who finished a stroke behind the Kiwi.

Nobilo returned the following year and proceeded to walk away with the trophy again. The New Zealander, who honed his game on the European Tour, turned a four-stroke deficit into a four-shot victory, out-scoring his nearest challenger, Scott Hoch, 66 to 74.

The prominence of the European Challenge Tour also rose to the fore with the performance of Gary Marks of England, who had won the Alianca UAP Challenge in 1996. Marks flew to America with Georgia on his mind and tied for 11th, winning $35,356.

It was in 1997 that the 'Sarazen' truly sprouted wings and took off as an internationally-acclaimed co-sanctioned event involving the PGA Tour and the European Tour.

Gene Sarazen (left) at the 1926 Open, and with Frank Nobilo, and Ernie Els. (Below) Ernie Els at Chateau Elan.

As the tournament grew in stature, with the total purse reaching $2 million in 1997 and Subaru's arrival on the scene, so the quality of the field improved.

World famous names of the calibre of Ian Woosnam, John Daly, Nick Price and Davis Love III were anxious to be involved in the end-of-season party at the magnificent Chateau Elan resort, which boasts 63 holes of golf, a winery, internationally acclaimed spa facilities and centres for tennis, equestrianism and conferences.

Sarazen summed it up eloquently: 'The game of golf has come a long way and it's going to go further. The supremacy of golf will no longer be in America; it will be in Australia, South Africa and Europe, because their players are hungry and determined to win.'

Former Open champion Mark Calcavecchia found himself in a formidable tussle with Europe's new rising star, Lee Westwood, in 1997. Eventually, Westwood, recent winner of the Volvo Masters in Europe, had to succumb to the American despite a courageous closing 68 to Calcavecchia's 71.

Calcavecchia won the Open at Royal Troon in 1989, 16 years after Sarazen's incredible hole-in-one at the 'Postage

Stamp' eighth using the five iron which now resides within the hallowed walls of the Royal & Ancient Golf Club of St.Andrews.

No one can doubt the razor sharp mind of the grand old man behind the Chateau Elan extravaganza. Asked for his recollections of Troon by a Scottish golf writer prior to the 1997 Open there, Sarazen fired back: 'Which one? Troon 1923 or 1973?' Of course, the remarkable Mr Sarazen HAD played in both, 50 years apart!

Calcavecchia was proud to be the Subaru Sarazen World Open champion and commented: 'I try to talk up the tournament as much as possible. It's got Gene Sarazen's name on it; it's a World Open and so it's got a lot of prestige to it.'

Mitchell Platts   287

Steeped in history

The Country Club at Brookline

is regarded as the cradle

of American golf

You are engulfed by history when you stand on the first tee at The Country Club, Brookline, Massachusetts, where on September 24-26, 1999, the 33rd Ryder Cup Matches will unfold.

It was here in 1913 that Francis Ouimet, a 20-year-old caddie who lived across the street from the Club, awakened American interest in the game by overcoming Harry Vardon, who won a record six Open Championships, and Ted Ray, winner of the 1912 Open, in a play-off for the US Open. Ouimet shot 72; Vardon and Ray 77 and 78 respectively. Bernard Darwin, golf correspondent of *The Times*, wrote: 'I felt like a war correspondent on some stricken field sending home news of the annihilation of the British Army. But the victory was so glorious that no grudging was possible.'

Historians of the game point to Ouimet's amazing achievement as a defining moment in American golf. Golf courses began to spring-up throughout the United States at a furious rate.

Fourteen years later at Worcester Country Club, little more than 40 minutes drive from Brookline, the history of the Ryder Cup began and so, with its first return since then to Massachusetts, nostalgia will once more be in the air at The Country Club with Europe seeking a record third successive victory.

Ben Crenshaw, the 21st individual to become captain of the United States, said:

The Country Club Roll of Honour (above). The Clubhouse (right).

'I get goose bumps just thinking about The Country Club. From a personal point of view it has special memories for me because it was there when I was 16 that I played in my first national competition. But The Country Club means much, much more than that. It is a very, very special venue; one that means so much to American golf. Francis Ouimet's victory provided a great boost for American golf and since then The Country Club has been a superb host to many important competitions. It's so distinctive. It's rugged. There are so many shots that you have to attempt during a round. It's the tilting fairways: the little cliffs are just in your brain. The greens are fascinating. You cannot know them enough. But it's also knowing how holes play off the tee with different wind angles. It's great to be going back.'

In fact, The Country Club is the only club to have hosted six different United States Golf Association competitions. It has been the site of three US Opens (1913, 1963, 1988), five US Amateurs (1910, 1922, 1934, 1957, 1982), three US Women's Amateurs (1902, 1941, 1995), two Walker Cup Matches (1932,

1973), the 1953 US Girls' Junior and the 1968 US Junior Amateur.

'The course will be essentially as it was in the 1988 US Open when Curtis Strange beat Nick Faldo in a play-off,' said Crenshaw. 'I've looked at fairway lines, and where actual contour cuts went, with Bill Spence, the extremely talented course superintendent, and there could be small slivers here and there that might change, but it won't change much at all.'

The Country Club lies in Brookline, where John F Kennedy grew-up, and only 15 minutes from the heart of Boston. It has been written that Boston is a colourful jigsaw of neighbourhoods with distinct personalities. Such a description is in many ways suitable for the course on which the Ryder Cup will be played with a selection of highly individual holes on

natural New England terrain. All of which should not be surprising. The Country Club was built in bits and pieces. It started with six holes, added three, and then two additional nines. Rees Jones, the architect who restored a number of holes in 1985, believes The Country Club: 'requires finesse, concentration and shot-making and is the perfect match-play venue'. Club members laid out the original holes in 1892. Those were modified several times until an additional nine were added by architect William Flynn in 1927. For the Ryder Cup, holes will be taken from each of the three nines which are known as the Clyde, the Squirral and the Primos.

That The Country Club has become, like Harvard, an institution, is due to J. Murray Forbes, a merchant in the China trade, who in April 1882, gathered

together in his town house in Commonwealth Avenue in Boston, 34 of his friends and laid before them the proposition of establishing, in Brookline, a club where there would be: 'a comfortable clubhouse for the use of members with their families, a simple restaurant, bedrooms, a bowling alley and lawn tennis grounds.' The prime reason for selecting the Stock Farm site on Clyde Street as the location of the Club was that it had a half-mile horse-race track which remained in place until 1969. When the first holes were constructed in 1892, at a cost of $50, the game was practically unknown in Massachusetts but 30,000 spectators will attend each day of the 1999 Ryder Cup Matches when, once again, history will be made.

Mitchell Platts   289

Hole by Hole Guide

The Country Club, Brookline, Mass.

35 - 36 = 71 • 7,033 Yards

HOLE No. 1 - PAR 4, 450 YARDS

A VERY LONG starting hole, which will require a long iron second shot to a medium-sized green which was redesigned for the US Open. Out-of-bounds on the left may come into play. Par will be a good score.

HOLE No. 2 - PAR 3, 190 YARDS

THIS HOLE will play longer than most 190-yard par threes because the green is elevated (and therefore partially blind), relatively small, and well-bunkered.

HOLE No. 3 - PAR 4, 451 YARDS

ONE OF THE MOST difficult holes on the course. If the tee shot is not hit to the left side of the fairway, the second shot to the small green will be over a high mound and this will be a blind shot. If the second shot is too long, it will wind up on the road behind the green or in the lateral water hazard just beyond the road.

HOLE No. 4 - PAR 4, 335 YARDS

MOST PLAYERS will hit an iron off the tee and a wedge to the newly-designed, small green. This may be a birdie hole, but players will be happy to escape with a par if either the fairway or the green is missed.

HOLE No. 5 - PAR 4, 432 YARDS

A GOOD, STRONG par four. The tee shot is blind because of a high mound between the tee and the fairway. A medium iron will be required for the second shot. Although the size of the green is generous, it will cause problems because of the tilt from right to left.

HOLE No. 6 - PAR 4, 310 YARDS

A FEW PLAYERS may try to drive this green, but most will lay up with an iron, then play a sand-wedge to the elevated green. One of the few good birdie prospects on the course.

The 3rd hole at The Country Club.

The 12th hole at The Country Club.

Hole No. 7 - Par 3, 197 Yards

A VERY DIFFICULT par three because of its length and because the green is elevated, very narrow, and well-contoured.

Hole No. 8 - Par 4, 378 Yards

ANOTHER BIRDIE POSSIBILITY, provided the tee shot does not go left into the trees. Most players will play a long iron or a fairway wood off the tee, leaving a short iron to the green. The drive should be kept on the right side of the fairway to avoid the trees which overhang on the left.

Hole No. 9 - Par 5, 513 Yards

THE PLAYER WHO hits a good tee shot to the left side of the fairway will have a chance to reach the green in two shots. However, a shot to that side is risky because deep woods border the left of the fairway. The green is elevated, relatively small, and surrounded by rough and bunkers, making a long shot to it extremely demanding.

Hole No. 10 - Par 4, 447 Yards

THIS IS THE FIRST of four very demanding par fours in a row. A good drive is essential because the player will not want to have a long iron to this green, which is very small.

Hole No. 11 - Par 4, 450 Yards

THE MOST DIFFICULT hole on the course. A good drive and a well struck long-iron are required to make par here. The green is not large and the pond in front of the green will catch any mishit second shot. Thus, double bogeys will be numerous. Arnold Palmer drove into a tree stump and made seven here in the play-off in the 1963 Open.

Hole No. 12 - Par 4, 486 Yards

ANOTHER LONG, hard par four to an elevated, blind green. The best angle of approach is from the right side of the fairway.

Hole No. 13 - Par 4, 436 Yards

THIS HOLE will play shorter than its measured length because it is downhill off the tee. If a player uses a driver off the tee, he runs the risk of having an extreme downhill lie for his second shot or, if he hits his drive to the right, it may wind up in a pond. Accordingly, most players will select a club for the tee shot which will put them on a plateau about 175 yards from the green.

HOLE NO. 14 - PAR 5, 534 YARDS

ANOTHER REACHABLE par five. Although it is a little longer than the ninth hole, the only other par five, it will probably play a little easier because the tee shot is not as demanding and the green, although elevated, is open in front.

HOLE NO. 15 - PAR 4, 432 YARDS

A GOOD STRAIGHT par four from an elevated tee. Although the green is larger than most, the hole is not a pushover because the green is well-bunkered, resulting in many tight pin locations.

HOLE NO. 16 - PAR 3, 186 YARDS

THIS IS THE EASIEST of the three par three holes, but it requires a well struck medium iron if a bogey is to be avoided. Overshooting the green can result in disaster because a ball carrying that far will likely come to rest against a boundary fence.

HOLE NO. 17 - PAR 4, 370 YARDS

THE ONLY PAR FOUR on the second nine under 400 yards in length. This slight dogleg to the left will yield a good many birdies. A long iron from the tee to the elbow will leave a nine iron or pitching wedge to the green, which has been redesigned.

HOLE NO. 18 - PAR 4, 436 YARDS

A GREAT FINISHING HOLE. The tee has been extended back about 15 yards. If the tee shot misses the fairway, it is not likely that the second shot will reach the green, which is elevated and features deep bunkers in front.

Hole	1	2	3	4	5	6	7	8	9	OUT	
Metres	411	174	412	306	395	283	180	346	469	2,976	
Yards	450	190	451	335	432	310	197	378	513	3,256	
Par	4	3	4	4	4	4	3	4	5	35	

Hole	10	11	12	13	14	15	16	17	18	OUT	TOTAL
Metres	409	411	444	399	488	395	170	338	399	3,453	6,429
Yards	447	450	486	436	534	432	186	370	436	3,777	7,033
Par	4	4	4	4	5	4	3	4	4	36	71

The 18th hole at The Country Club.

Ireland is host country for the 2005 Ryder Cup

K en Schofield, Executive Director of the European Tour, and Dr James McDaid, TD, Minister for Tourism, Sport and Recreation in Ireland, officially signed, during the BMW International Open in Munich in August, 1998, the agreement to locate the Ryder Cup Matches for the year 2005 in Ireland.

Dr James McDaid said: 'The package of promotions and benefits, extending over eight years will advance internationally Ireland's position as a golf tourism destination and promote ancillary benefits for the three Irish commercial companies who have joined with me in this agreement.

'The three Irish commercial companies are, in alphabetical order, Aer Lingus, Allied Irish Bank and Waterford Crystal. The agreement provides that IR£7.5m will be paid to the European Tour over the eight years in equal instalments in return for which, as well as locating the Ryder Cup matches in Ireland in 2005, an extensive range of promotion facilities and opportunities will be provided to Bord Failte an the three co-sponsoring companies.

'The three companies will contribute substantially and equally to the total sum of IR£7.5m and I wish to acknowledge and to thank them for this generous contribution. The Government, for its part, will contribute an amount approximating to the total contribution of the three com-

Dr James McDaid and Ken Schofield sign the agreement watched by, (left to right), Walter Coakley of Allied Irish Bank, James Flynn of Waterford Crystal, David Bunkworth of Aer Lingus, Richard Hills, Ryder Cup Director PGA European Tour and Sandy Jones, Executive Director Professional Golfers' Association.

panies. This is a splendid example of joint co-operation by Government and commercial Ireland in a project which will bring immense economic benefits to Ireland in increased tourism and prestige culminating in the holding in 2005 in Ireland of one of the great international sporting events of our time.

'The eight-year programme of promotion culminating in the Ryder Cup matches in 2005 will represent one of the most intensive and sustained tourist promotion programmes ever undertaken. Bord Failte and the co-sponsors will be given exhibition facilities at the major qualifying European events.

'Special arrangements will be made with the co-sponsors to link their products to European Tour activities. Bord Failte and the co-sponsors will be given special hospitality and ticket facilities at

the major qualifying events and the Ryder Cup Matches. There will be unique merchandising arrangements in connection with the 2005 Ryder Cup Matches which will be both promotional and lucrative for Bord Failte and their co-sponsors. Aer Lingus will be the official Ryder Cup carrier in 2005 and the official carrier for the junior Ryder Cup Matches in Boston in 1999 and 2003.

'I have no doubt that the sustained and intensive promotion programme we are now initiating for the next eight years will make Ireland the number one international golf destination. My prediction is that by 2005 we will have at least 500,000 golfers visiting annually, a doubling of present numbers. This increase will be experienced in all parts of the country and throughout the year – primary objectives of my policy for the tourist industry.'

293

Ireland

A Natural Home for the
RYDER CUP 2005

Making his Mark

Europe's new Ryder Cup

captain has all the

right credentials

Mark James, the 17th player to captain a team against the United States in the Ryder Cup, is well aware of the importance of the biennial match which, in 1999, will take place at The Country Club, Brookline, in Massachusetts.

He said: 'The Ryder Cup is the ultimate team event in our sport, and I believe I have the experience to get the best out of the team and cope with the pressures. I have reached the stage where I feel I can do the job.'

John Jacobs, the European Tour's first Tournament Director General and twice Ryder Cup captain, and Ken Schofield, the Executive Director of the PGA European Tour, both welcomed the appointment of James which was announced at the 1998 BMW International Open in Munich.

James is a popular choice. He does not suffer fools, but he is a genial character blessed with humour and patience. In response to the question as to which Tour player he would not invite to his own birthday party, James instantly replied: 'Colin Montgomerie.' Trouble at mill, you might think. Not a bit of it. James explained: 'Because Monty would eat all the cakes.'

There are many things to which James does not warm. Airports, queuing, ferries, rain and cats are among them. He is passionately in love with gardening. Golf, however, is his career and if on the fair-

Mark James in Ryder Cup line up (above), and reunited with a familiar friend (below).

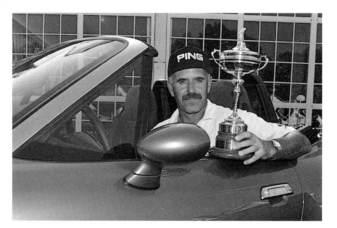

ways he does not visibly demonstrate the same passion that he might show in his garden then he is no less immersed in getting the job done right. What is true, as one experienced observer stated, is that James is a man who will stand up for his own principles, and for what he believes to be right, no matter what the personal cost.

He discussed the job with his wife, Jane, before accepting. 'I talked it over with Jane because the Lady Captain is an important member of the squad. We both felt that we would be able to get the best out of the team. I have played in seven teams so I know what is involved and the amount of work the captain has to do. I'm not going to be a bustling captain like Seve; I'll probably follow the Bernard Gallacher laid-back style.'

His attributes include tolerance and a fervour for fair play. James will want to captain a winning team at The Country Club, but in attempting to fulfil that aim he will listen to others in addition to ensuring that the competition is played in the best of spirits. He is similar in many ways to the United States captain Ben Crenshaw whose enormous respect for the game has been well demonstrated although Crenshaw, of course, would rather cast his rod to fish then grasp a fork to dig.

On the morning of his appointment, James answered the telephone in his hotel room at 6am. It was Crenshaw on the line from Texas; a courtesy call made to a friend as much as his soon-to-be-appointed opposite member. 'Ben and I think the same,' said James. 'Neither he nor I want to see people shouting and screaming too much as has happened at some times in the past. In fairness, I think the atmosphere at the match began to improve when Bernard Gallacher and Tom Watson encouraged a more balanced attitude in 1993 at The Belfry. The American crowds were absolutely fair to us at Oak Hill in 1995, and the Valderrama fans were well balanced in 1997. That's what you expect at a golf event, even if it is the biggest team event in the game. So with Ben and

297

I as captains I can't see anything controversial happening in Boston.'

So the ground rules of sportsmanship have been laid for the next exciting chapter of a match which, in the last two decades, has demonstrated beyond all doubt that the strength in depth of the European Tour has developed to the extent that the two teams are so evenly balanced that it comes down to who performs best on the week.

In fact the balance of power has, in recent times, rested with Europe. They enjoyed victories at The Belfry (1985), Muirfield Village (1987), Oak Hill (1995) and Valderrama (1997) as against the wins by the United States at Kiawah Island (1991) and The Belfry (1993) with one tie at The Belfry in 1989.

Now James is ready for the change of role from player to captain. 'I didn't have to be persuaded. I decided it was something I wanted to do. In fact I would say captaining is an easier job than playing. Yes, you have a responsibility as captain, but as a player you are responsible for bad shots. I may be a better captain than I was a player.'

In truth James has enjoyed an outstanding career. Initially he caddied for his father then struck his first shot with an old three iron and an eight iron which had dimples on the face and hollows instead of grooves. He was 12 when he was given his first full set of clubs since when he has progressed under the studious eye of coach, Gavin Christie.

His talent was slow to manifest itself more through lack of strength than skill. 'I had TB when I was ten, and I was never very big as a child. That didn't help. I wasn't really strong enough to swing a club until I was about 12. When I was

about 15 I could only just hit it far enough to reach par fours, and at that age in their lives the likes of Nick Faldo and Sandy Lyle were playing off scratch.' However, James struck a deal with his father. He could play all the golf he wanted as long as he studied diligently at school. That he did, achieving the distinction of passing

Mark James at Kiawah Island in 1991.

nine 'O' levels and two 'A' levels.

James did consider being an accountant but at the age of 18, and now off scratch, he went on the amateur circuit where he did not take long to make a reputation for himself. At 19, he captured the English Amateur at Woodhall Spa, reached the final of the Amateur Championship, losing to Vinny Giles at Hoylake, and won three out of four matches in the Walker Cup despite GB & Ireland losing.

With that James turned professional,

his father gave him £1,000 and packed him off to South Africa and the Safari Tour and the rest, as they say, is history. In his first year – 1976 – he finished joint fifth in the Open Championship at Royal Birkdale, where Johnny Miller overtook Ballesteros in the final round, and won the Sir Henry Cotton Rookie of the Year Award as he finished 15th in the Order of Merit. In the next 22 years he finished out of the top 32 of the then Order of Merit, more recently called the Volvo Ranking, on only one occasion.

His first victory came in the 1977 Lusaka Open. In all he has won 23 titles worldwide, including 18 on the European Tour, and earned more than £3,000,000. He played in the Ryder Cup in 1977-79-81-89-91-93 and 1995, and has represented England in no fewer than 30 international matches including those seven Ryder Cups, six Alfred Dunhill Cups, nine World Cups of Golf and five Hennessy Cognac Cups.

The Open Championship has eluded James despite a proud record which also includes finishing fourth in 1979, third in 1981, fourth in 1994 and eighth in 1995. Born in Lancashire and now based in Yorkshire, James was raised in the county of Lincolnshire not far from Boston where in 1630, ten years after the Mayflower, a group of Pilgrim Fathers set sail and founded the city of Boston, Massachusetts. The Concorde, of course, will carry Mark and Jane, and the European Team, to the other side of the Atlantic much quicker, but it will still be another great adventure in the life of a world class golfer for whom the uncertainty of the game remains the supreme challenge.

Mitchell Platts

Statistics reveal the true picture

Guardian Performance Data tell each European Tour player his strengths and weaknesses

Darren Clarke was rewarded for a season of consistency as he picked up the 1998 Guardian Performance Data Stroke Average Award at a special ceremony following day one of the Volvo Masters at Montecastillo.

Since the introduction of the Tour's official statistics service at the Johnnie Walker Classic in Thailand in January 1998, every player has had his game recorded in seven categories at every regular Tour event with the help of members of the European Tour Caddies' Association.

The season's final rankings were completed following the Belgacom Open, and while Colin Montgomerie, Lee Westwood, Ernie Els and José María Olazábal have all flirted with the top of the Stroke Average chart, Ulsterman Clarke eventually held them all off with his 1998 stroke average of 69.56.

The six remaining Guardian Performance Data categories tell the story of a fascinating season.

Only Severiano Ballesteros can claim to have the honour of leading two of the ranking tables. The former Ryder Cup captain was number one on both the Putts per Round and Putts per Greens Hit in Regulation charts, completing the scoring

Tony Johnstone, Darren Clarke, Alex Cejka and Pierre Fulke (above) receive their Guardian Awards. Seve Ballesteros (below(receives his putting awards

tournaments with an average of just 27.9 putts per round. And Guardian Performance Data really do tell the story of his season. He may be the master putter, but he finished down in joint 171st in terms of Greens Hit in Regulation, and 172nd when it came to Driving Accuracy having hit just 45.7 per cent of fairways from the tees.

Compare that with the accuracy of Sweden's Pierre Fulke who topped the Driving Accuracy rankings with 76.1 per cent, and the superb Greens Hit in Regulation display of Germany's Alex Cejka who is the head man with 78.5 per cent.

No one on the Tour can compare with the long driving of Italian Emanuele Canonica who finished the Guardian Performance Data season with an average drive of 295.8 yards – that's seven yards further than his nearest rival. And Zimbabwe's Tony Johnstone is the player least likely to worry if his shots land in the sand. He has topped the Sand Saves rankings with 81.6 per cent after visiting 76 bunkers.

Guardian Performance Data have been warmly welcomed to the Tour by players, spectators and the media during 1998, and further developments are already planned for 1999.

In 1999 up-to-date tournament and season statistics will be available within minutes of a player finishing his round, and a regular data service offering individual tournament analysis and personal progress charts will be instigated for the Tour professionals, allowing them to use the data to build on strengths and work on weaknesses.

Volvo Ranking 1998

				£
1	Colin MONTGOMERIE	(Scot)	(20)	993077
2	Darren CLARKE	(N.Ire)	(20)	902867
3	Lee WESTWOOD	(Eng)	(22)	814386
4	Miguel Angel JIMÉNEZ	(Sp)	(24)	518819
5	Patrik SJÖLAND	(Swe)	(24)	500136
6	Thomas BJÖRN	(Den)	(22)	470798
7	José Maria OLAZÁBAL	(Sp)	(23)	449132
8	Ernie ELS	(SA)	(12)	433884
9	Andrew COLTART	(Scot)	(23)	388816
10	Mathias GRÖNBERG	(Swe)	(25)	358779
* 11	Stephen LEANEY	(Aus)	(21)	310643
12	Peter BAKER	(Eng)	(23)	307163
13	Sven STRÜVER	(Ger)	(27)	293208
14	Sam TORRANCE	(Scot)	(22)	286807
15	Phillip PRICE	(Wal)	(24)	283885
16	Stephen ALLAN	(Aus)	(23)	267743
17	Robert KARLSSON	(Swe)	(21)	267285
18	Bernhard LANGER	(Ger)	(18)	262347
19	David CARTER	(Eng)	(23)	244424
20	Ian WOOSNAM	(Wal)	(19)	237570
21	Eduardo ROMERO	(Arg)	(19)	234148
22	Russell CLAYDON	(Eng)	(19)	233913
23	Jarmo SANDELIN	(Swe)	(27)	231375
24	Costantino ROCCA	(It)	(25)	220759
* 25	Greg CHALMERS	(Aus)	(25)	220672
26	Jean VAN DE VELDE	(Fr)	(27)	214163
27	Greg TURNER	(NZ)	(20)	210977
28	Gary ORR	(Scot)	(26)	209516
29	Padraig HARRINGTON	(Ire)	(25)	208013
30	Paul MCGINLEY	(Ire)	(25)	201970
31	Santiago LUNA	(Sp)	(22)	201624
32	David HOWELL	(Eng)	(27)	199040
33	Retief GOOSEN	(SA)	(24)	191249
34	Alex CEJKA	(Ger)	(24)	184673
35	Paul BROADHURST	(Eng)	(26)	181839
36	Peter O'MALLEY	(Aus)	(16)	172448
37	Steve WEBSTER	(Eng)	(24)	170871
38	Peter MITCHELL	(Eng)	(22)	167536
39	Gordon BRAND JNR.	(Scot)	(22)	167500
40	Ignacio GARRIDO	(Sp)	(27)	166866
* 41	Craig HAINLINE	(USA)	(20)	165792
42	Pierre FULKE	(Swe)	(21)	160418
43	Jamie SPENCE	(Eng)	(24)	158612
44	Robert ALLENBY	(Aus)	(16)	152413
45	Angel CABRERA	(Arg)	(20)	150792
46	Thomas GÖGELE	(Ger)	(26)	150041
47	Katsuyoshi TOMORI	(Jpn)	(22)	149789
48	David GILFORD	(Eng)	(20)	149569

49	Massimo FLORIOLI	(It)	(26)	137384
50	Van PHILLIPS	(Eng)	(29)	136768
51	Peter LONARD	(Aus)	(20)	136453
52	Ian GARBUTT	(Eng)	(24)	133991
53	Mark ROE	(Eng)	(23)	126149
54	Paolo QUIRICI	(Swi)	(22)	124731
55	Per-Ulrik JOHANSSON	(Swe)	(18)	123206
56	Olle KARLSSON	(Swe)	(22)	122501
57	Roger WESSELS	(SA)	(23)	121453
58	Mark JAMES	(Eng)	(21)	121351
59	Mats LANNER	(Swe)	(12)	113023
60	Tony JOHNSTONE	(Zim)	(21)	111268
61	Mats HALLBERG	(Swe)	(24)	111095
62	Paul LAWRIE	(Scot)	(22)	107099
63	Raymond RUSSELL	(Scot)	(24)	102276
64	Philip WALTON	(Ire)	(23)	101465
65	Jim PAYNE	(Eng)	(24)	100296
66	José COCERES	(Arg)	(19)	96957
67	Joakim HAEGGMAN	(Swe)	(19)	93989
68	Scott HENDERSON	(Scot)	(26)	93964
69	Thomas LEVET	(Fr)	(19)	93674
70	Dennis EDLUND	(Swe)	(24)	91803
71	Michael JONZON	(Swe)	(24)	91510
72	Bob MAY	(USA)	(19)	91342
73	Dean ROBERTSON	(Scot)	(26)	90062
74	José RIVERO	(Sp)	(20)	89526
75	Fredrik JACOBSON	(Swe)	(24)	88440
76	Peter SENIOR	(Aus)	(12)	87764
77	Derrick COOPER	(Eng)	(24)	87342
78	Andrew SHERBORNE	(Eng)	(23)	86548
79	Brian DAVIS	(Eng)	(28)	82654
80	Mark MOULAND	(Wal)	(25)	82214
# 81	Michael CAMPBELL	(NZ)	(20)	81797
82	Nick FALDO	(Eng)	(11)	78178
# 83	Andrew BEAL	(Eng)	(18)	77195
84	Michael LONG	(NZ)	(23)	77136
85	Andrew OLDCORN	(Scot)	(23)	75549
86	Jonathan LOMAS	(Eng)	(27)	75466
87	Marc FARRY	(Fr)	(24)	74845
* 88	Raphaël JACQUELIN	(Fr)	(26)	74844
# 89	Greg OWEN	(Eng)	(23)	73940
# 90	Anthony WALL	(Eng)	(21)	73494
* 91	Steen TINNING	(Den)	(22)	72153
92	Fabrice TARNAUD	(Fr)	(24)	70778
# 93	Olivier EDMOND	(Fr)	(15)	69269
94	Gary EVANS	(Eng)	(27)	67767
95	Paul EALES	(Eng)	(25)	65708
96	Daniel CHOPRA	(Swe)	(28)	65700

97	Per HAUGSRUD	(Nor)	(24)	64953
# 98	Mark DAVIS	(Eng)	(20)	63779
99	Rolf MUNTZ	(Hol)	(24)	63583
100	Roger CHAPMAN	(Eng)	(25)	63312
101	Rodger DAVIS	(Aus)	(17)	63158
102	Eamonn DARCY	(Ire)	(19)	62571
§ 103	John MCHENRY	(Ire)	(4)	61396
# 104	Jeev Milkha SINGH	(Ind)	(22)	59873
105	Stephen FIELD	(Eng)	(21)	58875
106	Paul AFFLECK	(Wal)	(22)	58809
107	Domingo HOSPITAL	(Sp)	(21)	58468
108	Seve BALLESTEROS	(Sp)	(21)	58068
# 109	Francisco CEA	(Sp)	(15)	56951
110	Barry LANE	(Eng)	(21)	56803
111	Silvio GRAPPASONNI	(It)	(21)	56705
112	Miles TUNNICLIFF	(Eng)	(26)	55257
113	Malcolm MACKENZIE	(Eng)	(27)	53572
114	Des SMYTH	(Ire)	(22)	53530
* 115	Søren KJELDSEN	(Den)	(23)	52847
# 116	Tom GILLIS	(USA)	(18)	52813
# 117	Mathew GOGGIN	(Aus)	(13)	52600
118	Iain PYMAN	(Eng)	(26)	52367
119	Klas ERIKSSON	(Swe)	(26)	51923
* 120	Michele REALE	(It)	(26)	51464
121	Richard BOXALL	(Eng)	(27)	49008
122	Clinton WHITELAW	(SA)	(18)	46631
123	Stephen SCAHILL	(NZ)	(7)	45889
124	Wayne RILEY	(Aus)	(27)	42904
* 125	David LYNN	(Eng)	(25)	42700
126	Carl SUNESON	(Sp)	(26)	42684
# 127	Gary NICKLAUS	(USA)	(19)	42064
# 128	John BICKERTON	(Eng)	(12)	40419
129	Steven RICHARDSON	(Eng)	(25)	38129
130	Ross DRUMMOND	(Scot)	(13)	36935
# 131	Jeff REMESY	(Fr)	(23)	36478
132	John WADE	(Aus)	(7)	36272
# 133	Andrew CLAPP	(Eng)	(20)	35674
134	Wayne WESTNER	(SA)	(15)	35180
135	Jay TOWNSEND	(USA)	(19)	34374
# 136	Pedro LINHART	(Sp)	(17)	33518
137	Anders FORSBRAND	(Swe)	(19)	33244
# 138	Steve ALKER	(NZ)	(20)	32693
139	Adam HUNTER	(Scot)	(26)	31583
140	Peter HEDBLOM	(Swe)	(25)	31571
* 141	Anssi KANKKONEN	(Fin)	(22)	31085
§ 142	Scott DUNLAP	(USA)	(4)	30724
143	Marco GORTANA	(It)	(5)	30221
* 144	Heinz Peter THÜL	(Ger)	(22)	27542
145	Nic HENNING	(SA)	(7)	27307
146	Carl WATTS	(Eng)	(27)	27174
147	Robert COLES	(Eng)	(23)	24434
# 148	Ivo GINER	(Sp)	(18)	24294
* 149	Knud STORGAARD	(Den)	(22)	23683
* 150	Kalle BRINK	(Swe)	(23)	23325

§ Denotes Affiliate Member

* Denotes 1997 Challenge Tour Graduate

# Denotes 1997 Qualifying School Graduate

• Figures in parentheses indicate number of tournaments played

Stroke Average

1	Darren CLARKE	(N.Ire)	(67)	69.45
2	Colin MONTGOMERIE	(Scot)	(62)	69.66
3	Lee WESTWOOD	(Eng)	(74)	69.85
4	Ernie ELS	(SA)	(36)	69.89
5	José Maria OLAZÁBAL	(Sp)	(75)	70.25
6	Bernhard LANGER	(Ger)	(54)	70.50
7	Miguel Angel JIMÉNEZ	(Sp)	(84)	70.57
8	Patrik SJÖLAND	(Swe)	(83)	70.59
9	Thomas BJÖRN	(Den)	(70)	70.64
10	Greg TURNER	(NZ)	(67)	70.67
11	Sam TORRANCE	(Scot)	(84)	70.80
12	Andrew COLTART	(Scot)	(77)	70.81
13	Peter O'MALLEY	(Aus)	(56)	70.86
14	Paul MCGINLEY	(Ire)	(84)	70.88
15	Robert KARLSSON	(Swe)	(63)	70.89
16	Nick FALDO	(Eng)	(30)	70.90
	Peter BAKER	(Eng)	(83)	70.90
18	Alex CEJKA	(Ger)	(81)	70.96
19	Eduardo ROMERO	(Arg)	(65)	71.00
	Ian WOOSNAM	(Wal)	(58)	71.00
	David GILFORD	(Eng)	(73)	71.00
22	Retief GOOSEN	(SA)	(66)	71.02
23	Jean VAN DE VELDE	(Fr)	(93)	71.04
24	Peter MITCHELL	(Eng)	(78)	71.05
25	Gordon BRAND JNR.	(Scot)	(71)	71.08
26	Padraig HARRINGTON	(Ire)	(83)	71.10
	Robert ALLENBY	(Aus)	(51)	71.10
28	Costantino ROCCA	(It)	(75)	71.12
29	Stephen LEANEY	(Aus)	(69)	71.20
30	Pierre FULKE	(Swe)	(68)	71.21
31	Phillip PRICE	(Wal)	(85)	71.22
32	Per-Ulrik JOHANSSON	(Swe)	(50)	71.24
33	Ian GARBUTT	(Eng)	(84)	71.25
34	Paul BROADHURST	(Eng)	(91)	71.29
35	Mathias GRÖNBERG	(Swe)	(81)	71.30
36	Joakim HAEGGMAN	(Swe)	(55)	71.31
37	Mark JAMES	(Eng)	(66)	71.35
38	Katsuyoshi TOMORI	(Jpn)	(76)	71.36
39	Jarmo SANDELIN	(Swe)	(93)	71.37
40	Santiago LUNA	(Sp)	(80)	71.40
41	Russell CLAYDON	(Eng)	(66)	71.42
42	Peter LONARD	(Aus)	(57)	71.44
43	Mats LANNER	(Swe)	(42)	71.45
44	Greg CHALMERS	(Aus)	(80)	71.49
45	Steve WEBSTER	(Eng)	(71)	71.51
	David HOWELL	(Eng)	(96)	71.51
47	Sven STRÜVER	(Ger)	(103)	71.55
48	Roger WESSELS	(SA)	(74)	71.58
49	Angel CABRERA	(Arg)	(69)	71.64
50	Mark ROE	(Eng)	(71)	71.66

Driving Accuracy %

1	Pierre FULKE	(Swe)	(68)	75.5
2	David GILFORD	(Eng)	(73)	74.5
3	Michele REALE	(It)	(78)	74.2
	Adam HUNTER	(Scot)	(71)	74.2
5	Stephen BENNETT	(Eng)	(40)	74.0
	Miguel Angel JIMÉNEZ	(Sp)	(84)	74.0
7	Colin MONTGOMERIE	(Scot)	(62)	72.6
	Van PHILLIPS	(Eng)	(92)	72.6
9	Paul EALES	(Eng)	(76)	72.4
10	Lee WESTWOOD	(Eng)	(74)	72.2
11	Pedro LINHART	(Sp)	(48)	71.9
	Andrew OLDCORN	(Scot)	(66)	71.9

Driving Distance (yards)

1	Emanuele CANONICA	(It)	(29)	295.8
2	Angel CABRERA	(Arg)	(69)	289.4
3	Ernie ELS	(SA)	(36)	285.2
4	Steve WEBSTER	(Eng)	(71)	283.1
5	Carl SUNESON	(Sp)	(67)	282.2
6	Darren CLARKE	(N.Ire)	(67)	280.8
7	Paolo QUIRICI	(Swi)	(67)	280.6
8	Colin MONTGOMERIE	(Scot)	(62)	279.2
9	Santiago LUNA	(Sp)	(80)	278.9
10	Ignacio GARRIDO	(Sp)	(76)	278.6
11	David THOMSON	(Scot)	(42)	278.5
12	Clinton WHITELAW	(SA)	(51)	278.4

Sand Saves %

1	Tony JOHNSTONE	(Zim)	(59)	79.1
2	Philip WALTON	(Ire)	(64)	77.5
3	Joakim HAEGGMAN	(Swe)	(55)	77.3
4	Olle KARLSSON	(Swe)	(68)	73.5
5	John BICKERTON	(Eng)	(42)	72.9
6	Ignacio GARRIDO	(Sp)	(76)	72.2
7	Stephen BENNETT	(Eng)	(40)	72.0
8	Stephen ALLAN	(Aus)	(73)	71.1
	Angel CABRERA	(Arg)	(69)	71.1
10	Bernhard LANGER	(Ger)	(54)	71.0
11	Sam TORRANCE	(Scot)	(84)	68.1
12	Per-Ulrik JOHANSSON	(Swe)	(50)	68.0

Figures in parentheses indicate number of rounds

Greens in Regulation %

1	Alex CEJKA	(Ger)	(81)	78.2
2	Colin MONTGOMERIE	(Scot)	(62)	76.6
3	Darren CLARKE	(N.Ire)	(67)	76.2
4	Peter BAKER	(Eng)	(83)	75.8
5	Miguel Angel JIMÉNEZ	(Sp)	(84)	75.4
6	Peter O'MALLEY	(Aus)	(56)	75.1
7	Andrew COLTART	(Scot)	(77)	74.8
8	Bob MAY	(USA)	(59)	74.5
9	Ian GARBUTT	(Eng)	(84)	74.3
10	Lee WESTWOOD	(Eng)	(74)	74.0
11	José Maria OLAZÁBAL	(Sp)	(75)	73.9
12	Ernie ELS	(SA)	(36)	73.6

Average Putts per Round

1	Seve BALLESTEROS	(Sp)	(60)	28.0
2	Jay TOWNSEND	(USA)	(50)	28.4
3	Padraig HARRINGTON	(Ire)	(83)	28.6
	Andrew BEAL	(Eng)	(54)	28.6
5	Russell CLAYDON	(Eng)	(66)	28.7
6	Paul LAWRIE	(Scot)	(68)	28.8
	Daniel CHOPRA	(Swe)	(81)	28.8
	Gordon BRAND JNR.	(Scot)	(71)	28.8
9	Paul BROADHURST	(Eng)	(91)	28.9
10	Robert KARLSSON	(Swe)	(63)	29.0
	Greg TURNER	(NZ)	(67)	29.0
12	John BICKERTON	(Eng)	(42)	29.1

Putts per Greens in Regulation

1	Seve BALLESTEROS	(Sp)	(60)	1.7358
2	Darren CLARKE	(N.Ire)	(67)	1.7363
3	Robert KARLSSON	(Swe)	(63)	1.7429
4	Gordon BRAND JNR.	(Scot)	(71)	1.7463
5	Padraig HARRINGTON	(Ire)	(83)	1.7484
6	Russell CLAYDON	(Eng)	(66)	1.7490
7	Jay TOWNSEND	(USA)	(50)	1.7495
8	Paul BROADHURST	(Eng)	(91)	1.7498
9	Bernhard LANGER	(Ger)	(54)	1.7500
10	Greg CHALMERS	(Aus)	(80)	1.7534
11	Andrew BEAL	(Eng)	(54)	1.7566
12	Patrik SJÖLAND	(Swe)	(83)	1.7567
13	Daniel CHOPRA	(Swe)	(81)	1.7585
14	Ernie ELS	(SA)	(36)	1.7604
15	Mark JAMES	(Eng)	(66)	1.7619

The PGA European Tour

(A COMPANY LIMITED BY GUARANTEE)

BOARDS OF DIRECTORS
N C Coles MBE – Group Chairman
D Cooper (Tour)
A Gallardo (Tour, Properties)
B Gallacher OBE (Tour, Properties)
T A Horton (Tour, Properties)
M James (Tour)
D Jones (Tour)
M G King (Properties)
J E O'Leary (Tour, Properties)
R Rafferty (Tour)
D J Russell (Tour)
P M P Townsend (Properties)
P A T Davidson (Non Executive Tour
    Group Director)
K S Owen (Non Executive Tour Group
    Director)
EXECUTIVE DIRECTOR
K D Schofield CBE
DEPUTY EXECUTIVE DIRECTOR
G C O'Grady
ASSISTANT EXECUTIVE DIRECTOR
R G Hills
GENERAL COUNSEL
M D Friend
GROUP COMPANY SECRETARY
M Bray
**PGA EUROPEAN TOUR
TOURNAMENT COMMITTEE**
M James – Chairman
M Lanner – Vice Chairman
A Binaghi
R Chapman
R Claydon
D Cooper
B Langer
C Montgomerie MBE
R Rafferty
D J Russell
O Sellberg
J Spence
S Torrance MBE
J Van de Velde

PGA EUROPEAN SENIORS TOUR
A Stubbs – Managing Director
K Waters – Deputy Managing Director
**PGA EUROPEAN CHALLENGE
TOUR**
A de Soultrait – Director
CHIEF REFEREE
J N Paramor
**SENIOR REFEREE / DIRECTOR OF
TOUR QUALIFYING SCHOOL**
A N McFee
DIRECTOR OF TOUR OPERATIONS
D Garland
**ASSISTANT DIRECTOR OF TOUR
OPERATIONS**
D Probyn
SENIOR TOURNAMENT DIRECTOR
M R Stewart
TOURNAMENT DIRECTORS
M Eriksson
M Vidaor
TOURNAMENT ADMINISTRATORS
M Haarer
J A Gray
G Hunt (Referee)
N Nesti
J M Zamora
TOURNAMENT OFFICIALS
P Talbot
D Williams

MARKETING DEPARTMENT
S Kelly – Marketing Director
G Oosterhuis – Corporate Sponsorship
    Director
I Barker – Account Director
M Haggstrom – Account Executive
STAGING DEPARTMENT
J Birkmyre – Director of Tournament
    Development
E Kitson – Director of Tournament Services
RYDER CUP LTD
R G Hills – Ryder Cup Director
PGA EUROPEAN TOUR (SOUTH)
A Gallardo – President
COMMUNICATIONS DIVISION
M Platts – Director of Communications
    and Public Relations
M Wilson – Consultant to
    Executive Director
G Simpson – Press Officer
GROUP FINANCIAL PLANNER
J Orr
GROUP FINANCE CONTROLLER
C Allamand
**CORPORATE RELATIONS
CONSULTANT**
H Wickham

Royal presence
at St Andrews:
The Duke of York
with Tiger Woods
during the Alfred
Dunhill Cup.

The Contributors

Mike Aitken *(The Scotsman)*
The Standard Life Loch Lomond

Jeremy Chapman
Alfred Dunhill Cup

Frank Clough
National Car Rental English Open

Norman Dabell
South African Open
Alfred Dunhill SA PGA Championship

Bill Elliott
Volvo Ranking Winner

Andrew Farrell *(The Independent)*
Italian Open

Mark Garrod *(Press Association)*
Dubai Desert Classic
Qatar Masters
Volvo Masters

Tim Glover
TNT Dutch Open

Martin Hardy *(Daily Express)*
Benson and Hedges International Open

David Hamilton
European Challenge Tour

Peter Higgs *(Mail on Sunday)*
Peugeot Open de España

John Hopkins *(The Times)*
127th Open Golf Championship

Renton Laidlaw *(The Golf Channel)*
Johnnie Walker Classic
Heineken Classic

Derek Lawrenson *(The Sunday Telegraph)*
Deutsche Bank – SAP Open TPC of Europe

Jock MacVicar *(Scottish Daily Express)*
Peugeot Open de France

Lewine Mair *(The Daily Telegraph)*
Canon European Masters

Michael McDonnell *(Daily Mail)*
The Year in Retrospect
Trophée Lancôme

Bernie McGuire
Turespaña Masters Open Baleares

Charlie Mulqueen *(Cork Examiner)*
Murphy's Irish Open

John Oakley
Open Novotel Perrier

Mitchell Platts *(PGA European Tour)*
Compaq European Grand Prix
The World Cup of Golf
World Golf Championships
The 1999 Ryder Cup Matches
Subaru Sarazen World Open

Chris Plumridge *(The Sunday Telegraph)*
Volvo PGA Championship

Byran Potter
European Seniors Tour

Gordon Richardson
Moroccan Open
Volvo Scandinavian Masters
BMW International Open

Gordon Simpson *(PGA European Tour)*
German Open
Belgacom Open
The Major Championships

Colm Smith *(Independent Newspapers)*
Smurfit European Open

Alex Spink
Madeira Island Open

Tony Stenson *(Daily Mirror)*
One 2 One British Masters

Mel Webb *(The Times)*
Portuguese Open
Cannes Open

John Whitbread *(Surrey Herald)*
Cisco World Match-Play Championship
Presented by Diners Club International

Roddy Williams *(PGA European Tour)*
Andersen World Championship of Golf
MacGregor Week
Linde German Masters

The Photographers

David Cannon /Allsport
1, 6, 7 top right, 22-26, 28, 31,
32 below, 46-50, 100-101, 104 top,
106, 158 below, 161 centre, 163 all,
198, 200-202, 228-230, 231 top, 234,
237 bottom, 238 bottom, 239 bottom,
255, 256, 257,261, 273 middle left and
lower left, 278 below, 282-284,
288-292, 298, 302

Michael Cooper /Allsport
266 right

John Gichigi /Allsport
120, 154 top left

Tom Able Green /Allsport
151, 152 below, 155, 199

Mike Hewitt /Allsport
13

Harry How /Allsport
259 centre, 300

Rusty Jarrett /Allsport
287 top left

Craig Jones /Allsport
9 bottom, 18-21, 161 top, 258 top left

Alex Livesy /Allsport
96, below, 97 top

Tim Matthews /Allsport
58-68, 76-86, 110, 132-136, 178-182,
210-214, 240-243, 265, 266 left,
268-269, 273 lower right, 303

Stephen Munday /Allsport
14, 37 top left, 122 top, 156, 158 top,
160, 222-226, 235, 236, 238 top, 245,
246 below, 249 below, 250, 252,
287 top right and below, 297 top, 299

Andrew Redington /Allsport
7 top and bottom left, 8 top, 9 above
centre, 10 top, 12, 16-17, 27, 29, 30,
32 top, 33, 50 bottom, 51, 52-57, 95,
96 top, 97 below, 98, 102-103,
104 centre and bottom, 107, 108-109,
118-119, 121, 122 bottom, 124-126,
159, 161 bottom, 162 top, 164,
184-190, 192, 196, 216-220, 231 centre
and bottom, 232, 237 top, 239 top,
244, 246 top row, 247, 248, 249 top
row, 251, 254, 258 below, 264, 273 top
row left and centre, middle and right
centre, 274-275, 280, 293, 304

Paul Severn /Allsport
4, 9 below centre, 10 below right,
34-39, 40-45, 70-74, 88-93, 112-116,
138-142, 144-148, 150, 152 top, 154 top
right and below, 166-176, 193, 194-195,
204-209, 260, 262, 270 left, 272,
273 lower centre, 296, 297 below

Allsport
278 top row

Allsport Historical
Collection © Hulton Getty
276-277, 286

Phil Inglis
270 centre and right

Alex Jackson
8 below, 9 top, 10 below left,
108 top left, 208 sequence top

Nick Walker
7 bottom right, 94, 157,
162 sequence below, 271

303